D1555223

PRACTICAL
KNOWLEDGE

PRACTICAL KNOWLEDGE

Applying the Social Sciences

Nico Stehr

H
61
˙S835x
1992
West

SAGE Publications
London · Newbury Park · New Delhi

© Nico Stehr, 1992

First published 1992

All rights reserved. No part of this publication may
be reproduced, stored in a retrieval system,
transmitted or utilized in any form or by any means,
electronic, mechanical, photocopying, recording or
otherwise, without permission in writing from the
Publishers.

SAGE Publications Ltd
6 Bonhili Street
London EC2A 4PU

SAGE Publications Inc
2455 Teller Road
Newbury Park, California 91320

SAGE Publications India Pvt Ltd
32, M-Block Market
Greater Kailash – I
New Delhi 110 048

British Library Cataloguing in Publication data

Stehr, Nico
    Practical Knowledge: Applying the Social Sciences
    I. Title
    330. 15

    ISBN 0–8039–8699–8

Library of Congress catalog card number 92–050194

Typeset by Photoprint, Torquay
Printed in Great Britain by Biddles Ltd, Guildford, Surrey

Contents

Preface

This book presents a sociological analysis of social science knowledge and its practical consequences. It also makes a case for a **pragmatic social science**. I approach both goals by inquiring into the conditions necessary to make a social science with a pragmatic focus a possibility. In view of the severe deficiencies I will show in the now dominant understanding of the theory/practice relationship, a radical shift in perspective is suggested. A social science based on a pragmatic orientation and with practical intent attempts to avoid, however – to borrow Karl Mannheim's (1932:43) formulation – not only the mere scholasticism to which any 'pure' theory is bound to be reduced but also a theoretical social science knowledge unconcerned with empirical matters. A pragmatic social science, in this sense, is not a practical social science (for example in an Aristotelian sense), nor an applied scientific-theoretical science (especially in a mere instrumental-technocratic sense), nor a politically and ethically naive, merely technical, social science. Nor is it, finally, based on evident illusion that social science will produce theoretical knowledge capable of intervention into human conduct which somehow holds out ambivalent 'hope' for, or the threat of 'mass behavioral changes'.[1] Under most circumstances, the payoff will be small. Modesty is the key. The central concern of this book is therefore with those conditions for the construction of scientific knowledge which might translate into practical knowledge. It is not concerned with the interaction between occupants of different positions in functionally differentiated systems such as science and politics (cf. Tichy, 1974; van de Vall and Bolas, 1981; Giesen and Schneider, 1984), with the relative permeability of the cognitive and social boundaries between different societal institutions in modern society, or with the influence of external ideas and institutions on the development of social science discourse (cf. Brownlee, 1990; Furner and Supple, 1990a; Wagner, 1990).

My observations are addressed mainly to and reflect the intellectual conditions of academic social science discourse that is ostensibly devoted to the advancement of knowledge and anchored organizationally in universities and other institutions of learning and research. Social research located in other contexts is often subject to a very different and locally specific knowledge that guides interests and constraints. In some countries, for example in the Netherlands and in the Scandinavian countries, the cognitive differentiation between research based in universities and non-academic organizations has been blurred as the result of political decisions or other factors about the social function of social science.

The expectation (or hope) that academic social science knowledge will be in demand as useful is frequently reduced to a correspondence between social institutions, as is the case, for example, in economics and the economy (see Giersch, 1961:24). In the case of some of the other social sciences, such correspondence is of course absent. Sociology and anthropology, to mention the obvious cases, lack, in contrast to law and economics, a direct societal basis (cf. Claessens, 1963:265; Luhmann, 1977), and therefore are without a political-bureaucratic 'partner' or social power-base.

The manuscript has benefited from a constructive reading by Günter Büschges and Christoph Lau. Volker Meja's competent editorial advice has been most useful. I am grateful to Robert Skidelsky for directing my attention to certain relevant Keynes materials. Paul Booth has been helpful with the analysis of the macro-economic data used in this study. I have had the opportunity to discuss my thesis about the features of social science knowledge which may make such knowledge useful in practice in a series of lectures at various universities in 1990/91, including the universities of Bamberg, Essex, Nürnberg, Munich and Pavia as well as the CSFR Academy of Science. I am grateful to students and staff at these institutions for their interest and critical response.

Notes

1   As Moynihan (1969:191) in his study of the 'war on poverty' programs puts it.

Introduction

Laments about a disjointed relationship between science – and here social science in particular – and politics are by no means new. By the same token, however, claims about extraordinary successes achieved by social science and even dire warnings about the emergence of a powerful, priest-like caste of intellectuals inspired and guided by social science, can still be occasionally heard even today. Yet, in general, a pessimistic, rather resigned view dominates which maintains that social science has fallen behind in the kinds of practical accomplishments, especially the social, economic and cultural influence in modern society that is almost taken for granted in the case of the natural sciences and technology, and that social science may even be condemned to political, economic and social irrelevancy.[1]

Is it possible to reduce the tension between science and politics to the difference between Weber's ideal types of an ethic of responsibility (*Verantwortungsethik*) and an ethic of ultimate ends (*Gesinnungsethik*)? Is it even meaningful to argue for efforts to rationalize the sphere of the irrational or decisionism? What social scientific knowledge is in fact translated into practice, and how? And does this process differ from the case of the practical application of natural scientific knowledge? Is the apparent magic of scientific knowledge claims sufficient to assure its use in practical circumstances?

The immediate point of departure of my observations and the subsequent analysis is the relatively sober, perhaps even skeptical image, among social scientists as well as practitioners, of the extent of the practical usefulness of social science knowledge today. This image contrasts sharply of course with the almost euphoric conception of a social technology based on social science held by generations of positivists, Marxists and pragmatists, from Comte to Marx and Lundberg (e.g. Neurath, [1931] 1973; Lundberg [1947] 1967; Dewey, 1970) or even with the somewhat more ambivalent hopes and fears of other generations of social scientists who saw their discipline as a science of the twentieth century (cf. Marcuse, 1964; Schelsky, 1976). By distancing my own analysis from these predecessors, however, I do not want to commit the opposite fallacy of suggesting that social science ought to aspire to be largely self-sufficient and self-referential and therefore leave the questions of its possible usefulness aside in order to concentrate on developing adequate social science knowledge. Despite the deliberate polemic contained in Helmut Schelsky's portrait of the impact of social science on the consciousness of modern individuals, he is by no means mistaken when he regards social science knowledge as a potential form of 'ideological knowledge' which may well provide one of the central sources of meaning of contemporary generations. In other words, the potential practical importance of social science is enormous and requires critical and careful attention, as does the impact of natural science and technology on society. At the same time, such images of the practical impact of social science and the process by which this occurs is at odds with the dominant understanding of social scientists about the nature and limits of the effect of social science knowledge on social relations. Thus, the disparity between the possible impact of social science on society's 'superstructure', the intellectual transformation of common-sense understanding, the prevailing skepticism among social scientists and, last but not least, persistent and growing public and private troubles underline the urgency of an inquiry into the conditions of the use of social science.

My main aim here is to present a comprehensive and critical theoretical as well as empirical analysis of the preconditions for constructing practical social science knowledge. What is at issue are the characteristics of social science knowledge which affect its chances of being employed in practice and therefore contribute to practical changes of some sort. The **specific** modalities of the inter-relation between science and politics in a society, or the distancing between the political system and the scientific community, which varies from society to society, require a comparative, socio-historical analysis which cannot be provided in this particular inquiry (cf. Skocpol, 1987). Nor am I interested in missed opportunities or past inopportune involvements of social scientists in political affairs. My concern is with future prospects in the relationship between social scientific and political practice.

However, I cannot avoid mentioning, in no particular order of significance, some of those questions which, while pertinent for the relationship between the production and the use of social science knowledge, cannot be considered here in any detail:

1. A critical and comprehensive review of the history of theories of the social role of social science knowledge. As a matter of fact, in most social science disciplines such a history would be

fairly brief (cf. Coleman, 1978:678–87) because social scientists have expended little effort to analyze the factors and processes which assure that social science knowledge will have a social role. The result is that I am able to summarize the prevailing views in the form of a brief theoretical model of application which has dominated the discussion in social science.

2. What are the implications of different data **collection** procedures and data **analysis** techniques widely practiced by social researchers on the potential usefulness of the information generated in this manner? For example, what is the significance or cost of specific 'sophisticated' statistical techniques (cf. Berk, 1987) in generating knowledge claims for practice?

3. Nor will the history of efforts to generate and attempt to apply social science knowledge designed for practical purposes be a central concern of my inquiry. However, claims that social science knowledge is useful coincide with the emergence of modern social science. Attempts to live up to this promise and efforts to judge its practical realization have of course resulted in innumerable reports either celebrating successes or identifying shortcomings. I refrain from analyzing in any detail the changing fortune of optimism and pessimism to live up to the calling of social science in different national social science communities (but see Abrams, 1985; Bulmer, 1985; Coleman, 1987; Bryant and Becker, 1990).

4. An analysis of obstacles and resistance to social science knowledge in so far as such resistance is a result of the peculiar situations faced by different groups and organizations in society, for example, the context of policy-makers (cf. Hammond et al., 1983), the spirit of the age (cf. Dahrendorf, 1989) or other societal developments which may in some way account for a diminished or even exhausted audience for social science knowledge. Among 'obstacles' of this kind could even be the possibility that sociological discourse already has achieved intellectual domination in society, as some critics of sociology in fact have concluded.

5. Thus, the broader question of the possible 'scientization' of social conduct in modern society cannot be an immediate focus of this study. In particular, the scientification of social relations and orientations brought about by a penetration and replacement of everyday knowledge by social science knowledge generally and the possible 'need' of the administrative apparatus increasingly to rely on social science knowledge in particular (cf. Lau and Beck, 1989), is not at issue in this inquiry. None the less, the possibility that such a process is in fact under way

must be examined. After all, the impact of social science knowledge implied by the thesis of the scientification of modern social relations could well be one of the most significant ways in which social science knowledge has become practical knowledge. However, the broader issue of the scientification of society and of the conditions for a growing demand for scientific knowledge are best reserved for discussion in the context of a theory of modern society which addresses such matters more directly (cf. Stehr, 1992).

Notes

1   Compare, for example, Schelsky's (1976) warnings about the immeasurable practical success of sociology and the lament issued by Myrdal (1972), at about the same time, about still rapidly expanding social problems and the relative scientific backwardness of contemporary sociology (for the discipline of economics compare for instance Leontief [1971] 1985; Adams, 1978; Meehan, 1982:117–73; Kuttner, 1985). In a more positive vein, Janowitz (1972:133) defends sociological inquiry, at the beginning of the same decade, as an important pillar of a democratic society. The practical impact of sociology has not impaired reason but reduced 'the mistrust and revolt against reason', thus, vigorous sociological discourse serves to strengthen 'the essentials' of a free society.

1

Knowledge as a Capacity to Act

Science remains without effect, but only as long as it encases itself into a tower of ivory and refrains from all contact with the outside world. As soon as it attempts the slightest application, the ivory tower must be left.

Henri Poincaré[1]

John Maynard Keynes's extraordinarily influential *General Theory of Employment, Interest and Money* was first published in 1936. The work remains controversial, in regard to an assessment of its practical impact on the course of economic development of capitalist societies. This of course also makes the work attractive. Keynes's book closes with the following, now almost classic, observations:

> the ideas of economists and political philosophers, both when they are right and when they are wrong, are more powerful than is commonly understood. Indeed the world is ruled by little else. Practical men, who believe themselves to be quite exempt from any intellectual influences, are usually the slaves of some defunct economist. Madmen in authority, who hear voices in the air, are distilling their frenzy from some academic scribbler of a few years back. I am sure that the power of vested interests is vastly exaggerated compared with the gradual encroachment of ideas. Not, indeed, immediately, but after a certain interval; for in the field of economic and political philosophy there are not many who are influenced by new theories after they are twenty-five or thirty years of age, so that the ideas which civil servants and politicians and even agitators apply to current events are not likely to be the newest. But, soon or late, it is ideas, not vested interests, which are dangerous for good or evil. (1936:383–3)

These sentences contain a prophetic anticipation of the practical fate of the ideas of Keynes's own *General Theory* but also a biting rhetorical attack against classical economic theory which is the central critical subject of his work. For Keynes, Karl Marx is one of the major representatives of classical theory. But Keynes also argues, and this bears directly on the topic at hand, that the potential **practical influence** of social science knowledge is propelled by the 'ideas' produced by social science. The ambivalent term 'ideas' was probably chosen quite deliberately by Keynes and signifies that the practical consequences (or their lack) depend not so much, as many social scientists are convinced, on contributing to the discussion and informed decision about the **means** of social action, assuming that such a differentiation is sensible at all. The intriguing question raised by Keynes's closing remarks in the *General Theory* is whether he was trying to generate, in this manner, a measure of self-encouragement. Furthermore, is Keynes generally correct when it comes to emphasizing the political and practical influence of economic ideas, including his own?

The central question this inquiry therefore attempts to discuss concerns the conditions and attributes which either facilitate or limit the effectiveness of social science **knowledge**. In conventional terms, I will re-examine the venerable theory/praxis debate.

But how do we conceptualize knowledge and its role in social action? In the context of a general theory of social action, **knowledge** can best be defined as a faculty or **capacity for action**, or may be described as the ability to indicate, in the case of a particular thing or process, how that thing is generated or **set in motion**. A description of the conditions of action, for example, the distribution of the unemployment rate among regions and groups faced by a policy-maker, constitute not knowledge but information. But an account of the differences in the rate of employment or how these conditions may be changed represents a **capacity** for action. Given such a conceptualization of knowledge, one is of course immediately reminded of Francis Bacon's famous proposition about the power of knowledge about nature, or implicitly about the **power of knowledge**. Bacon uses the phrase 'scientia est potentia', whereby the term potentia, that is, **capacity**, is employed to describe the power of knowing. More specifically, he asserts at the outset of his *Novum Organum* that 'human knowledge and human power meet in one; for where the cause is not known the effect cannot be produced. Nature to be commanded must be obeyed; and that which in contemplation is the cause is in operation the rule' (Francis Bacon, *Novum Organum* I, Aph. 3). Knowledge and power join forces if human knowledge is knowledge about the causes of events in nature. If human action follows rules, the rules which bring about a thing or event, it follows that human knowledge represents the capacity to act, to set a particular process in motion or to produce something. The success of human action can be gaged from changes which have taken place in reality or from the reproduction of society (W. Krohn, 1981; 1987:87–9). In short, how individuals act varies with what they know.[2]

It is, of course, possible to employ knowledge in different concrete capacities of action, for example, as a means of power, as a justification for a decision, as a means of orientation, or as a means of rationalization. In the tradition of philosophical anthropology (e.g. Gehlen, [1950] 1988; Plessner, [1928] 1981) knowledge becomes an anthropological constant which has the general function of reducing the plasticity of human nature, as the result of man's openness toward the world, in specific situations. Humans need to act and action becomes possible as the result of knowledge. More precisely, knowledge acquires an 'active' role in the course of social action only under circumstances where such action does not follow purely stereotypical patterns (Max Weber) or is strictly regulated in some other fashion. Knowledge assumes significance under conditions where social action is, for whatever reasons, based on a certain degree of freedom in the courses of action which can be chosen. Karl Mannheim ([1929] 1936:102) defines, in much the same sense, the range of social conduct, in which knowledge plays a role, as restricted to spheres of social life which have not been routinized and regulated completely. For, as he observes, 'conduct, in the sense in which we use it, does not begin until we reach the area where rationalization has not yet penetrated, and where we are forced to make decisions in situations which have as yet not been subjected to regulation'. The question of the relation of theory to practice then is restricted, for Mannheim, precisely to situations which offer a measure of discretion in social conduct and have not therefore been reduced to a corset of strictly ordered and predictable patterns of social action, although it cannot be ruled out that even under these circumstances, in situations which are repeated with routine regularity, elements of 'irrationality' remain.

The definition of knowledge as a capacity of action indicates simultaneously that knowledge also is the result of social action; that is, it both leads to and follows from action. But knowledge is not identical with action. Knowledge is a capacity for action. This is by no means a trivial matter but happens to be, certainly in this age, a kind of moral imperative. As Joseph Needham (1986:22), for example, has forcefully stressed, 'the Taoists saw already in the early Middle Ages, that ultimately mankind must be prepared to know, yet not to do. If mankind is not able to learn this lesson, then the utter destruction of all life on earth is inevitable'. The sobering thesis that knowledge must at times remain a capacity for action indicates that there is a particular linkage between ethics and knowledge, a connection which has frequently been denied (cf. also Meja and Stehr, 1988).

Knowledge is therefore, from a social action perspective, underdetermined.[3] Even in the case of the production of knowledge it functions as a capacity for action, for knowledge initially represents the capacity for the production of novel knowledge. The notion of knowledge as a capacity for social action has the advantage, it seems to me, that it permits one to stress not merely one-sided but multifaceted consequences of knowledge for action. In particular, this definition of knowledge allows for the recognition of a '**duality of knowledge**',[4] the fact that knowledge is both a medium of social action and the result of human conduct.

The definition of knowledge as a capacity for action has, in addition, the distinct advantage that it allows the formulation of a 'dialectical' theory of knowledge use. The notion of knowledge as faculty of action indicates that knowledge may remain unused or dormant, that it is by no means assured that knowledge is employed in any optimum sense, and that knowledge can also find application in the pursuit of highly irrational ends. Knowledge as a capacity for action does not prejudice its use nor does it determine the ways and the circumstances in which it may find application. Knowledge is not a *deus ex machina*.

Moreover, the conception of knowledge advanced opposes any kind of universal scientific or technological determinism. As Katz, for example, remarks in the context of an analysis of the impact on the private sphere of the rapid development of computers and telecommunication devices:

> there is no inherent necessity that either a certain step in technology must be taken or that there can only be one human response to the situation imposed by the machinery in our environment. In particular, it is fallacious to think that because a technology can be created, it will. It is equally fallacious to think that if a technology is created, it will be used . . . the museum of unwanted inventions is full. (1987:83)

Knowledge use and impact depends on local conditions and contexts.

Moreover, though it is highly significant, (social) scientific knowledge represents only one faculty for action. As Fiske (1986:79) observes, 'social phenomena have always been perceived and known in diverse ways. To such bodies of knowledge, social scientists have added many others, each with a perspective and with one or more methods for observing'. The competition among forms of knowledge thus becomes an important aspect of any attempt to understand the translation of knowledge into action (cf. Lammers, 1974). All knowledge represents a capacity for action. But in contrast to a mere faculty for action, I will call knowledge which has in fact been translated into action, **action knowledge** (*Handlungswissen*), and I will call knowledge which is, from the beginning, designed to serve as a capacity for action, **practical knowledge**. Whether scientific and social scientific knowledge is more likely to be translated into action than other forms of knowledge is not primarily at issue. What is at issue, however, are, first, the necessary conditions to make possible the production of practical knowledge and, second, the translating of social science knowledge into action. I assume of course that such attributes can be specified and therefore are neither elusive nor possess a kind of situational ad hoc character. Any discussion of the practical efficacy of social science knowledge incorporates, at the same time, reflections about chances of the realization of social science knowledge (cf. Albert, [1971] 1972:37) and an examination of knowledge in action.

Notes

1 Quoted in Hutchison, 1937.

2 Compare Barry Barnes's discussion (1988:44–6) of the society as a distribution of knowledge.

3 As indicated already, this assertion denies the general and undifferentiated claim that knowledge always leads to its realization. The capacity for action is not identical with action. However, the separation between knowledge and action runs counter to certain linguistic theories, for example the theory of verbal behavior developed by John Searle (1969), which implies that one already acts as one enunciates a certain idea.

4 Giddens (e.g. 1990:106) conceptualizes 'social structure' in an analogous manner when he stresses social structure as both a medium and a product of social action.

2

Social Science and Practice

During the interwar period, many now classical works in social science were completed. The *General Theory of Employment, Interest and Money* by John Maynard Keynes and *Ideology and Utopia* by Karl Mannheim were both published in English in 1936. At the time, and in numerous retroactive evaluations, assessments of the state of social science thought in general and economic thinking in particular conclude that it was in a state of crisis. Though such assessments varied considerably from country to country and discipline to discipline, the sense of crisis was frequently associated with the strong perception that social science lacked public credibility and hence self-confidence. These two aspects of the state of social science were interrelated because workable remedies and solutions to practical issues, for instance, in the face of persistent mass unemployment, appeared to be absent (or ineffective) while the failure to advance such advice reinforced the sense of failure and the perception that the authority of social science was severely undermined. Yet, the sense of crisis did not always contribute to a malaise of fatalism. Both Keynes and Mannheim represent such different responses. The sense of crisis strengthened their conviction that it was time to experiment with a new beginning.

By the same token, there have been periods during the short history of the social sciences in which social scientists have attended with particular vigor and great conviction to practical matters (cf. Howard, 1981; Stanfield, 1985). Not surprisingly, phases in which practical concerns were foremost on the agenda of social science were accompanied, perhaps even made possible, by optimistic expectations that social problems, for example social divisions and injustices linked to various forms of inequality, poverty and prejudice, would be conquered and arrested in short order and with decisive results. But such upbeat, optimistic periods have given way to calls for a concentration of intellectual efforts in the social sciences on the extension and improvement of social **scientific** knowledge and a consolidation of the role of the scientist in the social sciences (e.g. Parsons, 1959:548). One therefore can easily surmise that social scientists respond, more or less directly, to changing societal and political conditions and expectations, though the state of the social science community itself is also a factor. Once the social sciences reached a critical mass during the years of their extensive expansion during the 1950s and 1960s, it became even easier for many social scientists to attend to internal disciplinary intellectual concerns first. But what is the present thinking of social scientists about the practical role and efficacy of social science knowledge? The prevailing self-conception of social scientists is rather skeptical. Once again social scientists appear to lack self-confidence and public credibility. And in the wake of such lack of self-assurance, the assessment of the ability of social scientists to respond effectively to urgent and growing public problems is therefore far from confident; at best, it is muted and ambivalent. I would like to sketch and characterize the prevailing skepticism, while also highlighting some of its apparent contradictions.

The self-conception of social scientists

Judged against the background of widespread methodological and theoretical dissensus in the social sciences today, the broad agreement among social scientists that their disciplines cannot point with any pride to a strong and positive record of practical successes appears to be somewhat of an anomaly, though some might view the very absence of any perceived practical success itself as a result of the all pervasive cognitive dissensus in the social sciences. Claus Offe (1981:99), for example, sums up and characterizes this consensus when he refers to the likelihood that we are faced with a 'complete disjuncture of political will, on the one hand, and social scientific knowledge, on the other hand'. Again and again, we find reference in recent years to the fact that demography, economics, political science and sociology have, for the most part, failed to anticipate decisive and consequential social, economic and political developments (for instance Leontief, [1971] 1985; Boulding, 1973; Katona, 1978; Lipset, [1979] 1985; Converse, 1986) or contributed to viable social policy formulations (e.g. Harris, 1990) and workable solutions for pressing social problems (cf. Inciardi, 1987). Marxists cannot, as is glaringly evident now, exculpate themselves from this 'indictment'. Their predictions about socio-historical changes are, as Alvin Gouldner has already documented (1970), very far off the mark. Actually, Gouldner believes that the failure of Marxist predictions is particularly blatant, while efforts to build modern societies on the basis of Marxist ideologies have been equally beset by failure and now are widely dismissed, have fallen into disrepute and are being abandoned. None the less, it is hardly productive to limit oneself to reciprocal, and soon hostile, efforts to balance the books of evident failures, nor is it immediately clear what the exact nature of the calculus one might be able to employ in this instance ought to be. The conclusions by no means lead to robust inferences about the reasons for the practical failures of the social sciences. This can already be seen if one compares judgements about the practical efficacy of (essentially the same) social science knowledge at different periods of time and in different socio-political contexts. In West Germany, to take one recent example, only a decade ago, observations (and, as the case may be, warnings) about the increasing (and undue) influence of the social sciences, which affect, as 'meaning'-producers, everyday life and the political culture of modern society, led to confident (and dire) predictions about the rule of the social sciences. Today, by contrast, there is a considerable degree of self-doubt among virtually all social scientists about the practical consequences of their work.

The consensus about the failures of social science is by no means complete. Not surprisingly, there are dissenters, even today (see Lipset, 1979; Bulmer, 1990:129–36).[1] Nonetheless, even such dissent does not alter the fact that the widely shared optimism about the practical role and potential accomplishments of social science knowledge which dominated the self-conception of social scientists after the Second World War and continued to do so well into the late 1960s, has been replaced by a radically different assessment of the efficacy of social science. The dramatic change has already had its repercussions on the development of social science itself and on the growing mood of doubt and even defeat among social scientists. As a result, the lowered self-appreciation of social scientists has become a salient factor in social science knowledge, and in the diminished attractiveness of social science disciplines to students and others. If, with Raymond Aron ([1960] 1985:199), for example, one distinguishes between an indifferent and a hostile reaction to the social sciences among the public, one must ask whether the previous image of social science may not soon be converted into a hostile one. The social sciences, to be sure, are not altogether innocent victims of these developments, having participated in the creation of both the prevailing public image and changes in public beliefs concerning social science.

The widespread self-doubt among social scientists raises questions about the reasons for the continued, even growing demand for social science knowledge by public and private institutions in advanced societies (e.g. Weiss and Weiss, 1981:839). The social sciences are, of course, capable of triggering and fulfilling a fair range of intellectual and political functions including, for example, the *ex post facto* justification of corporate or personal interventions (cf. Sieber, 1981). Even if the ability of the social sciences to offer 'objective' information and knowledge is considered by its clientele to be (still) limited or judged to be invariably restricted, the demand for social science knowledge need not be affected much, because the social sciences may be capable of adequately fulfilling certain other functions or offering expertise and intelligence considered prudent to invoke by both public and private enterprises. Offe (1981:105), for example, describes the potential versatility of social science for modern administrative-political organizations as based on certain relatively trivial side effects of social science knowledge. Indeed, if social scientists perform such functions well, it could explain the demand for social science knowledge even during what appear to be otherwise adverse times for the social science community. Social science research projects can be launched, for example, for the purpose of gaining time by delaying decisions, or the results of projects may be used to legitimize political programs which have long been agreed upon (e.g. Horowitz, 1970; Weiss, 1983:208; Ross, 1987).[2] Research initiated by government and other corporate actors can also be employed in a kind of impression management to portray the political system or business as a responsible entity, anticipating problems of all sorts in due time and attempting to deal with them in a rational fashion. In any event, these comments at least indicate that any adequate conception of the use of social science cannot be reduced to a simple formula or conception of the 'use' of 'objective' knowledge generated in social science.

However, more important than enumerating different diagnoses of the efficacy of social science, it is necessary to refer to a number of apparently common epistemological, methodological and discipline-bound reasons given both for successful applications of social science knowledge or perceived failures to do so. These communalities, which transcend existing deep cognitive divisions within social science, provide a first hint of the **orthodox image** of the kinds of conditions and attributes which would facilitate the use of social science knowledge and, conversely, tend to obscure, limit or minimize its usefulness.

These common convictions among social scientists begin, in most instances, with the widely shared assumption, independent of the cycle of doubt and promise expressed by social scientists about their own disciplines, of a considerable **deficit** of knowledge in many institutions and organizations outside of social science itself. The deficit in capacities for action is seen as endemic to all modern social institutions. Therefore, there is no shortage in potential clients for social science knowledge 'out there'. Such a view, one could surmise, is little but the reflection of a 'normal' professional ethos, namely the conviction that the product or the service offered corresponds somehow to a genuine need and therefore enjoys a meaningful demand. In part, this may indeed be the case; from a crude functionalist perspective, the very existence of social science in modern society may already explain the need for its knowledge. But the assertion by social scientists about an external deficit in knowledge often involves much more than a mere pointing to a diffuse general need for social science knowledge.

The deficit postulated by most social scientists cannot easily be served by other forms of knowledge; it cannot without considerable costs and serious negative consequences be replaced by alternative means as capacities for action. On the contrary, the social sciences (at least potentially) produce a form of knowledge which corresponds quite closely in its major attributes to the kind of knowledge which is (or ought to be) in demand to cope with the peculiar contingencies of modern social institutions. The social sciences offer, it is argued, a scientific form of knowledge. capable of reducing the external deficit in a rational and much more effective sense than alternative forms of knowledge. That is to say, closely aligned with the postulate about a deficit and therefore a potential demand for social science knowledge is the thesis about a steep **gradient in the rationality** of scientific and other forms of knowledge (cf. Beck and Bonss, 1984:382–3) and therefore between science and other institutions in modern society. Individual, administrative or political decision-making processes for example are viewed as governed by a 'logic' which is (still) in need of a 'higher' rationality and which implies that an improvement in the quality of the knowledge which informs these decisions can, for the most part, only be offered by social science knowledge. The process of rationalizing the irrational can only be served, in other words, by knowledge which itself is rational. Individuals and institutions are not suited to generate such knowledge for themselves. They must rely on what science offers.

In light of the prevailing doubt and skepticism among social scientists, it is not surprising to find also a widespread perception of an **internal deficit** in social science knowledge, a deficit for which the social science community may not even be responsible. The social sciences have always been faced with the challenge of having to account for the relative 'backwardness' of their development when compared to the natural sciences. Even if one does not accept such a standard as the basis for self-appraisal of the status of social science knowledge, the social science disciplines have rarely had the luxury of being able to argue that the development of their knowledge did not, in its practical impact, lag behind the evident practical successes of natural science knowledge. But in addition, social scientists now perceive a persistent and perhaps even growing gap between the urgent demand for useful social science knowledge and the ability of social science to respond effectively. Part of the common diagnosis of the current dilemma faced by the social sciences is therefore the feeling that there is a particularly glaring gap today between the need to provide useful knowledge and the ability of the social science disciplines to deliver such knowledge reliably. The gap between urgent public problems and solutions offered by social science knowledge appears to grow. It is virtually impossible, perhaps even unnecessary, to cleanly separate the question of the relative backwardness of the social sciences from the question of the growing deficit of useful social science knowledge. As the discussion of the prevailing responses in the social sciences to these questions will indicate, the reasons for both gaps are often seen to lie in similar, if not identical conditions. Moreover, a lack of scientific knowledge already constitutes, for most observers in this area, a lack of practical knowledge. Thus, King and Melanson (1972:86) remark in the context of an overall assessment of the practical success of the social sciences in the 1960s in the United States that 'social scientists failed to appreciate the actual paucity of their knowledge and the complexity and unintended consequences of manipulating social change' (cf. also Moynihan, 1969). This observation implies, of course, that adequate social science knowledge will be capable of 'coping' even with complex social developments.

As long as one is prepared to attribute the primary reason for the present widespread doubt among social scientists about the practical efficacy of social science knowledge to conditions **external** to social science, it almost becomes a certainty that the cycle of optimism followed by skepticism in assessments of the social importance and impact of social science knowledge will be repeated with regularity. Yet, these varied assessments will continue to be rather impotent because they fail to carry any lessons for the future intellectual development of any of the social science disciplines. If one assumes that a decline in the perception of the usefulness of social science is, for example, somehow linked to a noticeable reduction in a naive belief in social progress, then a reversal in the fortunes of social science is wedded to a change in the climate of public opinion about social progress as manageable progress in general and the role of science in this process in particular. But such a diagnosis, interesting and telling as it may be, relies first and foremost on factors over which the social science community has little control. The question of why social science knowledge appears to be both in considerable demand and somehow even effective merely becomes a matter of waiting for opportune, fortuitous historical moments. This is clearly not a very satisfactory state of affairs.

A more meaningful and less fatalistic analysis of these cycles in the social fortune of social science may be possible with the help of an inquiry into the preconditions that would make possible any practical success of scientific knowledge and social science knowledge specifically. Such an approach might well lead to the conclusion that any practical success does not come about more or less automatically; for example, as the result of knowledge claims which, as long as they conform to criteria that certify such claims as 'scientific' knowledge, already will or must constitute eminently practical knowledge. The expectation that knowledge claims automatically regulate their own practical success is probably as naive as the belief that the use of social science knowledge is solely driven by factors external to the community of social scientists or that sufficient 'age' of social science practice and hard-won experience, now lacking, represents the answer to a disjuncture between urgent public problems and the state of social science knowledge.

The deficit of social science knowledge

The reasons typically given for the widely perceived internal deficit of practical social science knowledge directly affect the basic issue of my analysis. As a matter of fact, the predominant answer to the question of the 'causes' for the existing inability of social scientists to respond adequately, efficiently and concurrently to the changing nature of social problems and presumably to the changing, even growing need for social science knowledge, can be reduced to a single core response. Moreover, the answer is virtually taken for granted among social scientists, perhaps even a boringly familiar lament. And given this state of affairs, enthusiasm for a critical analysis of the habitual response is lacking. However, I hope to show that such an analysis need not deteriorate to a mere reiteration of what appears only to be too obvious to many at this point.

The specific reason for the deficit of both general and applied social science knowledge may be found in the **extraordinary complexity** of the subject matter of social science, namely the perplexing and intricate nature of social phenomena. To put the matter somewhat crudely, physics is for the most part concerned with relatively simple phenomena while the social disciplines, sociology and economics, must analyze inherently complex phenomena. The great complexity of social, in contrast to natural processes, by some orders of magnitude, as many social scientists would maintain, is reflected in the peculiar difficulties arising at all stages of the manufacture of social science knowledge. Against the background of the consensus about the impact of the complexity of social processes and structure, other factors which might be invoked as reasons for the slow progress in the development of social science knowledge – for example, the acceleration of urgent social problems as part of the process of modernization or, the lack of adequate research resources and manpower in social science – clearly become insignificant.

Let us take but two instances in which this argument figures prominently. One of the consequences of the complexity of social life is that social science knowledge can at best, at least for the foreseeable future, produce middle-range theories – using a term first explicated by Robert K. Merton ([1949] 1957:5–10), though not precisely for these purposes and not in quite the sense used here, indicating that sociological theory ought to confine itself to the advancement of modest accounts which have as their empirical referent, in terms of size, time and space, a limited range of applicability. Seymour M. Lipset ([1979] 1985:340) makes more explicit what is implied: the social sciences are generally capable of best handling 'interrelationships between two or more variables within specific delimited structures. As social science moves out to deal with macroscopic systematic trends and tendencies, it accounts for smaller and smaller parts of the variance.' And in order to underline the conditions which are responsible for the present inability of the social sciences to produce knowledge with a greater range and explanatory power, Lipset ([1979] 1985:340), only cited here as a representative voice, adds that all social science disciplines suffer from the difficulty of coping adequately with 'total system behavior', that is, of dealing effectively with the full complexity of social phenomena.

The distinction between sciences which deal with simple or complex phenomena implies, to take a second instance, that it is extremely difficult if not impossible, for the observer mentally to reproduce complex phenomena in a manageable and precise form. This means, as an economist for example formulates it: 'The **number of conditions** which have to be invoked either retrospectively or for the purpose of a genuine prediction of economic developments or individual economic measures, is legion' [emphasis added] (Giersch, 1961:28). The organized complexity of economic or political relations can only be grasped adequately if one aims to deal 'simultaneously with a sizeable number of factors which are interrelated into an organic whole' (Weaver, 1948:539).

While it is quite common to introduce the notions of 'total system', 'complexity' or 'intricate context', as terms designed to capture the peculiar and difficult conditions faced by social scientists when confronting their subject matter, it also is very noticeable that this often is done in an unexplicated fashion or in a manner in which these concepts are introduced in a highly ambivalent way. It is possible that the usual treatment of the concepts is intended to signal that these are very complex themselves, that they are linguistic examples of a complex social reality. This would appear to be a somewhat unsatisfactory state of affairs. Thus, a somewhat more elaborate discussion and explication of the notion of complexity, which follows, may shed some light on the phenomenon and therefore clarify the extent to which it is justified to speak of the complexity of social processes as the main hurdle to a more rapid deployment of practical knowledge, if not to the progress of knowledge in the social sciences generally.

The characterization of social processes and social action as complex, however, appears to have at least the function of deflecting attention from, if not outright delegitimating, any appraisal of social phenomena in terms of a deliberately limited range of attributes. In fact, many social science explanations, past and present, have been based on very few, often simple, dimensions. Despite their relative prominence, such accounts simultaneously are often assessed as weak, perhaps preliminary and therefore as a deficient form of social science knowledge. In any event, the question of the range of attributes of phenomena required to be taken into consideration in the research process for the purposes of producing practical knowledge will play an important role in the subsequent analysis.

Notes

1   A notable exception is, for instance, the report of the Committee on Basic Research in the Behavioral and Social Sciences of the National Academy of Sciences, Washington, DC: Adams et al., 1982. Of course, one cannot ignore the occasion for and the timing of the report as well as the recipient of the generally favorable balance sheet of accomplishments attributed to social science. (cf. also Lazarsfeld et al., 1967; Abt, n.d.).

2   Following the lead of C. Wright Mills ([1959] 1970:91–6) who already stressed the historically much greater ideological rather than bureaucratic 'use' of social science, Horowitz (1970:340) emphatically underlines the ideological service of social scientists as the 'Great Legitimizers' in an age that announced the end of ideology: 'social scientists engaged in government work are committed to an advocacy model defined by politicians. For the most part, they do not **establish** or even verify policy – only **legitimize** policy. They are, in effect, the great mandarins of the present era.' [emphasis added]

Excursus

The Authority of Complexity

The social realm is a natural realm which differs from the others only by a far greater complexity.

Emile Durkheim[1]

The assertion about the unique 'complexity' or the peculiarly intricate character of social phenomena has, at least within sociology, a long, venerable and virtually uncontested tradition. The classical theorists, Georg Simmel (1890) and Emile Durkheim ([1955] 1983),[2] for example, make prominent and repeated reference to this attribute of the subject matter of sociological discourse and the degree to which it complicates the development of sociological knowledge. During the past 100 years, this observation has been repeated, with great regularity, with little further differentiation. No serious social scientist, one might say, is prepared to deny the proposition that economic, political and social systems are complex. The assertion that social phenomena are complex and intricate affects all aspects of the search for robust social scientific knowledge and its application. However, there is much less agreement about the precise nature of the complexity of social life; nor is there consensus about the extent and the duration to which the intricate nature of social phenomena will affect the manufacture of social science knowledge. Finally, a closer examination of the repeated observation about the perplexing nature of social processes shows that social scientists have yet to find an epistemological calculus or a methodological recipe, let alone uncontested measures, to combat the limits this imposes on the reliability and validity of our reflections. Nor have the social sciences, it appears, precise ways of generating useful social science knowledge, in spite of the complicated nature of social phenomena. What remains beyond doubt, and is taken for granted, is that social reality is complex. The complexity of social reality moreover has a most inhibiting effect on the production of social science knowledge.

At the beginning of this century, Emile Durkheim ([1955] 1983:90) argued with conviction, in an attempt to distance himself from observations and promises by Auguste Comte about the power of scientific knowledge, that Comte's expectations about the practical efficacy of the sciences are quite excessive. In particular, Durkheim is convinced that Comte's firm conviction that sociology will soon be in a position to issue 'guidelines for public consciousness', is not only too optimistic but a **premature** prognosis about the intellectual capabilities of the discipline. Such a 'promise' is rejected by Durkheim as premature because 'sociology, as [Comte] himself recognized, has a more complex object than other sciences. It can only express fragmentary hypotheses, and so far these have had scarcely any effect on popular consciousness.' But in line with the emerging consensus of sociologists and other social scientists about the inhibiting effects of the complexity of their subject matter, Durkheim does not expect that this attribute of social phenomena constitutes a more permanent and impenetrable barrier against obtaining an 'intricate' and therefore adequate understanding of society. None the less, Durkheim's observations establish quite clearly that there is a connection between the attribute 'complexity' and inadequate knowledge about social life. Objective social science knowledge must, in a mirror-like fashion, reflect the complex nature of social reality. As long as the social sciences are incapable of fully reflecting the nature of their subject matter, social science remains handicapped. The challenge posed to social scientists by the complexity of social phenomena is one which can be met, at least in the long run. But what precisely happens in the long run must remain uncertain.

In contrast to the insecurity, in a variety of senses, which accompanies the epistemological and methodological status of the complexity of social phenomena, there can be little doubt about the reason for the intellectual origin – the widespread acceptance and persistence of the notion of the complexity of social life among sociologists.

As long as one is not satisfied with a psychological explanation, for example, with Lundberg's ([1947] 1967) suggestion that the lack of familiarity with any object produces the response of attributing complexity to the unknown object, one has to consider the institutional, cognitive and political struggles which have accompanied efforts to establish the legitimacy of the social sciences. These struggles often take place with reference to the alleged superior theoretical and practical accomplishments of the natural sciences and of technology. The comparison, contrast and even confrontation with the natural sciences, which began at the end of the last century, has formed one of the most salient and perplexing points of reference for proponents and opponents of social science alike. The notion of the complexity of social phenomena serves as a symbolic and rhetorical weapon in this struggle.

On the one hand, a reference to the inordinate complexity of social phenomena can serve to excuse the absence of practical knowledge here and now. But on the other hand, in the hands of non-social scientists, the same device is turned into a reminder of apparently glaring deficiencies. The mathematician Henri Poincaré (1914:19–20), for example, observes that social scientists find themselves in an embarrassingly difficult position, since the observable and measurable elements of human behavior, 'the elements, which for him are men',

> are too dissimilar, too variable, too capricious, in a word, too complex themselves. Furthermore, history does not repeat itself; how, then, is he to select the interesting fact, the fact which is repeated? Method is precisely the selection of facts, and accordingly our first care must be to devise a method. Many have been devised because none holds the field undisputed. Nearly every sociological thesis proposes a new method, which, however, its author is very careful not to apply, so that sociology is the science with the greatest number of methods and the least results.

While Poincaré's pessimistic observations are shared by many sociologists today, the embarrassment they trigger is not diminished as a result.

The discovery of the complexity of social life does not simply coincide with the origin of the social sciences. Only after the first extravagant promises had failed and the social sciences began to face resistance, did social scientists seriously discuss the cognitive handicaps associated with the complexity of their subject matter.

Paradoxically perhaps, even though most social scientists subscribe to the thesis of the intricate nature of social life, among them scholars belonging to the early founders of specialized social science disciplines (e.g. Mill, 1950:308–9; Spencer, 1961:66; Comte, 1975:75–7), many also treat another trait of social life as a kind of anthropological constant, namely the human tendency to simplify the complexity of processes and things. Most classical social theories present relatively straightforward, even simple, uncomplicated or decomposed accounts of social life and its development. Similarly, classical theorists employ, on the whole, fairly uncomplicated methods of empirical observation. In short, the theoretical and empirical reflection of complex social phenomena appears to be reduced, in most instances at least, to a few dimensions of social action which are assumed to be strategic attributes of social conduct and its evolution. A limited number of attributes, in many instances a single factor, acquires central significance in 'explaining' and foretelling the nature and/or the course of societal developments. Examples of such core concepts include such notions as economic needs, relations of production, social division of labour, psychological drives such the readiness to fight, innerworldly asceticism, the division of material and ideal culture, etc.

A persistent restriction to but a few variables in present day theories of society, critics maintain, is the result of the use of either obsolete statistical techniques which are not designed to grasp the organized complexity of social phenomena or extremely simple concepts (cf. Weaver, 1948:540; Luhmann, 1970:70).

From the point of view of practically useful knowledge, single factor theories or theories which rely on a concise bundle of factors may, paradoxically, be themselves highly complex or ambivalent. A single concept or a handful of central concepts, critics argue, do not alone assure clarity, far less empirical validity. But, what might be even more crucial, theoretical simplicity does affect the ability to influence the same attribute(s) under specific social contingencies. It is dubious to assume, the same critics therefore maintain, that the enumeration of a few factors as such increases the probability that social science knowledge as a capacity for action improves its own chances of being translated into action. Most contemporary social theorists therefore would agree with Niklas Luhmann's assessment of 'factor-theories' (1970:70). Such theories, he observes, have failed in all respects because they employ a **simplistic** conceptual apparatus.

The assertion that social phenomena happen to be complex phenomena is designed to sensitize the social sciences, from an epistemological perspective, for example, to the kind of explanatory and methodological devices that are equal to the task. Thus, complexity means that a particular social process, for instance, exchange rates, is set in motion, reproduced or changed by a multiplicity of interdependent factors and that it is most difficult to make a detailed and precise forecast about price changes. Since social systems exhibit properties of organized complexity, their structure contains, as Brewer indicates (1973:75), 'overlapping interaction among elements, positive and negative feedback control loops, and nonlinear relationships, and they are of high temporal order'. Any empirically valid representation, and therefore any effective and manageable control of such a complex process, requires, according to this conception, a faithful and complete understanding of all the intricate factors involved and of their interconnections. Anything less amounts to a sterile and, above all, defective reflection of social reality.[3] In short, as Harold D. Lasswell (cited in Brewer, 1973:3) maintains, reflecting the views of much of the social science community, 'the most promising answer to the challenge of complexity is not to ignore the challenge but to devise ways of meeting it'.

But what is one to make of the typical social science knowledge generated under these difficult circumstances? Since exact knowledge cannot be produced directly and immediately, the apparent detour, or deficient knowledge, becomes a hesitant but necessary step in the right direction and such knowledge is therefore not without 'scientific' merit. Knowledge which fails to capture adequately the complexity of social phenomena is a precursor of the kind of knowledge which social science aspires to generate one day, but is necessary none the less (e.g. Simmel, 1890:7–8). Immediate relevance, one might say, is sacrificed for ultimate relevance (cf. Lynd, 1940:2).

Despite these conclusions, it also can be suggested that the **methods** of data collection practiced in mainstream social science fail to recognize and capture adequately the historicity, the lack of recalcitrance or the fragility of social relations as well as the possibility that the magnitude of these very attributes has become more prominent in advanced society. The methods of data collection and analysis prevailing in the social sciences today are, for the most part, preoccupied with the opposite task, namely with undertakings designed to arrest and to minimize the fluid nature of social phenomena ('Kompliziertheit der Objekte'; cf. Simmel, 1890:8), that is, the 'complex' nature of social existence.

However, the idea that modern social relations may be subject to a peculiar and increasing fragility or plasticity, which limits the ability of social scientists to offer rigid or reliable predictions about future conduct, is not, in most instances, part of the more conventional discussion about the unique complexity of social phenomena. When Almond and Genco (1977:494) observe that social action is 'the outcome of processes that exhibit plastic rather than cast-iron control' which is embedded in history and involves 'recurrent "passings-through" of large numbers of human memories, learning processes, human goal-seeking impulses, and choices among alternatives', the authors want to stress that 'the regularities we discover appear to have a short half-life. They decay quickly because of the memory, creative searching, and learning that underlie them. Indeed, social science itself may contribute to this decay, since learning increasingly includes not only learning from experience, but from scientific research itself.' A lack of recalcitrance, the possible increase in the fragility of social conduct, the historicity of social phenomena etc. all speak against the kind of image usually associated with pleas to capture the full and intricate complexity of social life since such an assault, under these circumstances, appears to be a futile undertaking.

In short, the claim that it is complexity of the domain which has limited the production of practical knowledge in social science, and the corollary claim that such a deficiency is not a permanent affliction, may yet turn out to represent both a defensive claim and be much more permanent than is now assumed by social scientists. The peculiar combination of resignation and hope in this account is, moreover, consistent with other extravagant promises by social science. If the subject matter of social science indeed changes in ways which will make it more 'complex' and, therefore, diminish the ability of social science to capture its domain in fixed accounts, the debate about complexity will continue for a long time. The alternative is to radically reconsider the notion of complexity as an obstacle to practical knowledge.

That is to say, it may be suggested that the taken-for-granted supposition about the temporary deficiencies of social science knowledge which can be repaired through gradual improvements and approximations to the 'real' complexity of social phenomena, itself suffers from deficiencies which originate, moreover, not with attributes of the domain of social science but which are subject to the control of the community of social science – at least in so far as they involve deficits in the understanding of practical knowledge because these flow from peculiar misconceptions found in social science.

A science which maintains that it is restricted, as a result of the complexity of its domain, to what is possible at the time (but how does one determine what is possible at any given time?), constitutes, at first sight, a responsible form of science. The epistemological and methodological obstacles to adequate, objective knowledge are openly acknowledged. But we should not underestimate therefore the political, psychological or even apologetic function of the orthodox account of the current limits to social science knowledge because, in the final analysis, this account contains an optimistic message. The upbeat message is that the extent to which social science is capable of producing practical knowledge increases in direct proportion to its ability to manufacture scientific knowledge claims.

Max Weber and Karl R. Popper are among the few but notable philosophers of (social) science who appear to be quite unimpressed with the familiar assertion about the intricate complexity of social phenomena. Popper ([1957] 1972:140) is convinced that the thesis actually constitutes a subtle form of prejudice which has two origins. First, the judgement is a result of a meaningless and inaccurate comparison of circumstances; for example, of a comparison of limited and controlled conditions found in a laboratory and real social situations. Secondly, the thesis is the result of the orthodox methodological conception which demands that any adequate description of social phenomena requires a complete account of psychological and material circumstances of all actors. Since humans behave in most situations in a rational fashion, Popper maintains, it is possible to reconstruct social interaction with the aid of relatively simple models which assume such rational conduct among the participants. Max Weber ([1904] 1949:72) emphasizes in his seminal essay on 'Objectivity in social science and social policy' that social science as a science of concrete reality (*Wirklichkeitswissenschaft*) is not capable of capturing social reality in all its complexity and therefore does not fully reproduce the multiplicity of social configurations faithfully:

> All the analysis of infinite reality which the finite human mind can conduct rests on the tacit assumption that only a finite portion of this reality constitutes the object of scientific investigation, and that only it is 'important' in the sense of being 'worthy of being known'.

A serious proponent of the thesis that the social sciences must capture the full and complete richness of social reality cannot really respond, without compromising the very principle at issue, that Weber's plea for a reasonable limitation of social science knowledge involves, at any given time, merely the demand to reproduce social life in a manner possible and manageable under the circumstances. It is evident that Weber (cf. [1904] 1949:88) is skeptical that such a limitation can be temporary and strategic. This becomes clear, for example, in his opposition to the conviction and the pretension of some economists to be able to formulate 'laws' which are capable of capturing the 'totality of existing historical reality'. In addition, Weber even questions the possible value of such insights.

Whether or not one is prepared to accept Popper's conclusions and remedy, it is a quite questionable position to remain content with the ambivalent conclusion that a mirror-like reproduction of complex social reality is a necessary and sufficient precondition for maximizing practical knowledge, its social relevance and acceptance. As a matter of fact, the fallacy of this conclusion is the subject of my entire inquiry. For this reason, I will, at this point, only refer to two difficulties associated with the orthodox thesis about the desirability of matching social complexity and social science accounts of this complexity as the only effective solution to the construction of practical social science knowledge. First, effective 'control' and change of social conditions is not always and under all circumstances identical with and possible based on the complete intellectual control of the complex origins and process of social situations. Secondly, efforts to raise the theoretical complexity of social science knowledge may, on the contrary, have the unanticipated effect of propelling such knowledge into an even greater distance from social action (cf. Luhmann, 1970).

Keynes's theory as an exemplary case

Undoubtedly, the Keynesian theory of economic action is one of the most influential and important theoretical designs in economics generally and in the economy of developed market economies in particular. Peter Drucker ([1980] 1981a:1) does not exaggerate when he observes that 'economics today is very largely "The House that Keynes Built"' (see also Kaldor, 1983:27). In comparison with other prominent examples of social science theories, Keynes's theory is of the same status as Freud's or Marx's. One measure of the status of his theory is the fact that his economic ideas and policy recommendations continue to be discussed with critical intensity and in controversial debates. Keynes may have contributed to, or even provoked, the intensity of the discussions, given his own polemical style. But intellectual debates carried out with great emotional intensity are the salt of scientific discourse. One can fairly assume that Keynes knew this and attempted to turn it to his advantage. Polemical rhetoric improves upon the visibility of ideas, especially in an otherwise gray context filled with responsible contributions.

The now orthodox status of the Keynesian theory, especially so-called 'Keynesianism', that is, the specific economic policies associated with Keynes's doctrines which emerged and were widely accepted after the war, and the critical reactions it spawned, are today viewed with the suspicion that both Keynes's theoretical underpinnings and policy tools are in a state of crisis, at least since the beginning of the 1970s, in most advanced countries. A growing number of economists express skepticism about the practical efficacy of Keynes's theory. However, there are also voices which observe that a Keynesian understanding of market economies continues to be pertinent and continues to produce effective practical knowledge. As a matter of fact, the continuing political influence of Keynesian ideas on policy is seen by some economists as the very cause for the economic crisis of the 1970s (cf. Davidson, 1981). Even more generally, the crisis of Keynesian economic knowledge in this sense has become the crisis of economic theory (see Hicks, 1974; Pilling, 1986).

It is precisely the contradictory evaluation of the intellectual and especially practical status of Keynesian economic theory and the kind of economic policies connected with it, though this is not the only reason, which elevate these ideas to an exemplary case for a sociological analysis of social scientific knowledge and its practical impact. If one also assumes with Drucker ([1980] 1981a:3) that 'the next economics will be "post-Keynesian"', then it is evident that Keynes's theory has to be recognized, as even his more severe critics acknowledge (e.g. Pigou, 1950:65), as representing one of the outstanding examples of modern social science theory.[4] In short, there are good reasons to suppose that the analysis of the conditions for the possibility of practical social science knowledge and the probability of translating social science knowledge as a capacity of action into real action, can be fruitfully analyzed on the basis of the history of the varied efforts to utilize Keynesian economic ideas in different political and socio-economic contexts. What makes Keynesian economic theory of interest as an exemplar for an analysis of social science knowledge is,[5] furthermore, the possibility of testing the efficacy of his knowledge, which Keynes himself did not doubt, or its lack of practical usefulness, empirically. At least, I will try to achieve such a test. It can already be said that such an empirical test should be easier to accomplish than, for example, a test of the practical efficacy of Freudian psychoanalysis or Marxian political economy. Any empirical test of Keynesian ideas should be less complicated and less controversial than those one might design for the purposes of testing Freud's or Marx's theories, if such a test is considered possible at all. None the less, such 'simplicity' need not imply that the results do not speak to comparable cases in social science, that is, it is hoped that one can devise some general principles from the test which shed light on those properties of social science knowledge which make it effective or, for that matter, irrelevant to praxis.

It is not unusual to encounter the view that Keynes is not only responsible for the very survival of capitalism but also for the intellectual demise and the loss of credibility of Marxism in Western societies (e.g Galbraith, 1971:43–4). Keynes discovered a system of control of economic forces by the state which relies on market processes and thus he 'promised to make it possible for rules to achieve politically necessary economic results without sacrificing market and political liberties' (Skidelsky, 1979:55). The wide appeal of Keynesian ideas in economically developed countries, especially after the Second World War, certainly has one of its significant sources precisely in a promise to join economic success and political ideals. Indeed, Keynes (e.g. [1932] 1982b:53) himself leaves no doubt that he considers his theoretical efforts, consciously designed as an alternative to both *laissez-faire* and Marxism (cf. Fitzgibbons, 1988), and the economic policies he favors as means, as intended to stabilize, in the final analysis, a particular type of socio-economic system. As a result, it is hardly meaningful to assume that he tried to sidestep the question of the value neutrality of theoretical work in the social sciences. As a matter of fact, for Keynes economics is ultimately a moral and not a natural science.[6] Keynes (1936:381) therefore does not hesitate to recommend his theory and its implied economic policies as measures which serve multiple political and moral aims in a harmonious manner:

> The authoritarian state systems of to-day seem to solve the problem of unemployment at the expense of efficiency and of freedom. It is certain that the world will no longer tolerate the unemployment which, apart from brief intervals of excitement, is associated – and, in my opinion, inevitably associated – with present-day capitalistic individualism. But it may be possible by a right analysis to cure the disease whilst preserving efficiency and freedom.

None the less, vigorous and passionate objections to his theory are often based on the argument that Keynes's ideas are totally useless or counterproductive when it comes to deriving policy lessons from them. Keynes certainly envisioned that his ideas one day would find their way into heated political debates. In a letter to George Bernard Shaw, written in 1935, he predicts, 'when my new theory has been duly assimilated and mixed with politics and feeling and passions, I can't predict what the final upshot will be in its effect on action and affairs. But there will be a great change' (Keynes, [1973] 1987:492–3). His predictions were indeed fulfilled. And, one can surmise that the polemical style of Keynes's writings may have fueled the public attention they found in many countries. The passionate debate, both within economics and among the public, about Keynes's work continues to this day.[7] But tragically its initial penetration and acceptance among economists and practitioners occurred too late to prevent the 'political disintegration in Central Europe, let alone permit the Western world to arm itself betimes, on the basis of its abundant superfluity of material resources, against the Nazi assault' (Balogh, 1982:39).

A critical discussion and analysis of the divergent assessments of the practical efficacy of Keynesian economic theories requires a more general understanding, both of successes and failed attempts to translate economic knowledge into action, that is, of the attributes of social science knowledge which assist its utilization or increase the probability that it will become a form of knowledge in action and not merely for action. The rhetorical style in which social scientific knowledge claims come to be formulated and communicated in all likelihood plays only a minor role though it does affect the visibility such claims should find among the public.

However, before an attempt is made to spell out the crucial attributes of economic knowledge in particular and social science knowledge in general which assure that this knowledge is practical knowledge, it is necessary to describe in some detail the dominant understanding of these issues in social science. As was the case in the prevailing self-conception of social scientists, I maintain that one can discover, despite the profound cognitive dissensus in all social science disciplines, a kind of orthodox and relatively coherent conception of what makes for and constitutes useful social science knowledge. There are nuances, even significant differences in the accounts offered by different social scientists. These will be noted. However, a dominant conception can none the less be discerned. I will sketch this model next.

Notes

1   Durkheim, [1912] 1965:31.

2   The reference refers to lectures by Durkheim published in French for the first time in 1955.

3   Friedrich Hayek (1952) is, in contrast, more inclined to live with the complexity of social life and is reconciled that economics deals with different phenomena than physics. Economics will not, as a result, one day achieve the kind of technical competence physics has in some fields.

4   Joseph A. Schumpeter (1954:1181), for example, describes the status of Keynes within economics as follows: 'It was the intellectual performance spiced by the – real or putative – relevance to burning questions of the time which achieved what, in our field (of economics), neither could have achieved by itself.'

5   In addition, one can legitimize an inquiry into the usefulness of knowledge produced by economics by pointing to the apparent success with which economists have taken up advisory positions, for example with government. Niskanen (1986:237), a former member and acting director of the US Council of Economic Advisors, estimates that the federal government of the United States now employs about 6000 economists. On the basis of such numbers, it seems, Niskanen suggests that, over the past several decades, economists have become the most influential and pervasive group of policy advisors in the United States.

6   cf. Keynes (1980:43).

7   An interesting summary of the multiple and contradictory images of Keynes and the central message of his work among economists has recently been compiled by Fitzgibbons (1988:2): 'There is Joan Robinson's Keynes, who delivered the funeral oration for *laissez-faire*, and T.W. Hutchinson's Keynes, who defended *laissez-faire*. There is R.F. Harrod's Keynes, whose goals were truth, unworldliness and other absolute values, and Robert Skidelsky's Keynes, who was on his way to a party via Marx and Freud. There is Don Patinkin's Keynes, who admired mathematical economics, and Paul Davidson's Keynes, who overthrew general equilibrium theory. The Keynes the public knows stands for big government, whereas F. von Hayek's Keynes wanted government to be small.'

3

The Science of Application

There is nothing as practical as a good theory.

Kurt Lewin[1]

Reference to a science of the application of scientific knowledge is contradictory because, if one accepts the orthodox understanding of the use of scientific knowledge, any attempt to turn the question of the application into an independent and researchable issue becomes redundant or meaningless. Kurt Lewin's motto that there is nothing as practical as a good theory underlines, from his point of view, the redundancy and futility of a separate search for the conditions for the application of theoretical knowledge, once formulated properly. For adequate scientific knowledge itself solves the question of its application and provides the reasons for its success as practical knowledge. The distinction between basic and applied research is, at the same time, at best one of convenience or suitable perhaps to justify 'basic' research. Applied research is the outcome of, and requires, basic research (e.g. Rossi et al., 1978). The investment of society in basic research, it is argued, will be repaid by augmenting the practical usefulness of science at some future time. However, the exact time and place when this will occur cannot be determined in advance. But if scientific knowledge should be in little or no demand then the cause has to be found in almost accidental, even mysterious circumstances, and any salient attributes we might ascribe to it therefore cannot really offer any hints as to why it finds no interest among potential users. The case becomes even more complicated if one observes that apparently 'inadequate' scientific knowledge is somehow applied. Keynesian economic theory might be just such an example since many economists consider it to be highly suspect from a 'scientific' point of view, though many political measures taken by governments today are somehow driven and/or justified by ideas Keynes inaugurated. In any event, the use of competing forms of social scientific knowledge or the disinterest among practitioners for other knowledge claims by social scientists remains, given the confines of the orthodox account of why knowledge is translated into action, somewhat of a mystery.

The reluctance of social scientists to assign to the issue of the application of knowledge a status similar to that of other questions confronted by social science, for example data analysis or theory construction, means that the prevalent solution is merely derivative and superficial. In addition, it has the paradoxical consequence that such an intellectual disinterest is consistent with both excessive claims for successful application of social science knowledge and its exact opposite, namely a grievous lament of societal ignorance about the value of social science knowledge and the lack of any influence such knowledge appears to have in society.

But a social scientific analysis of the application of scientific knowledge is only meaningful as long as one is prepared to dispense with or challenge the dominant view, that is, is willing to consider the issue **not** already resolved by virtue of ritual reference to the attribute of the **scientificity** of knowledge claims. It is, of course, true that there is nothing approaching a meaningful consensus among social scientists about what makes for a 'good' theory. None the less, if one subscribes to the thesis that it is the 'adequacy' of a theory which drives and determines the successful application of theoretical knowledge, then there are no serious intellectual grounds for inquiring into the question of the conditions which may affect the use of social science knowledge. It would instead be necessary to concentrate on efforts, however difficult, to achieve increasing adequacy of theoretical knowledge and assure that knowledge becomes increasingly assimilated to those methodological ideals which rule the characteristics of what a 'good' theory looks like. As a matter of fact, it probably is a fair description of much of the philosophy underlying training in the social sciences, particularly instruction designed to teach the methods of data collection and analysis of the social sciences, that such cognitive labor is aimed at realizing 'good' theory. However I assume that the question of the reasons either for the use of social science knowledge or for its failure to somehow make a difference in practical circumstances is not resolved by virtue of mere deference to essentially contentious methodological criteria.

The model of instrumentality

The standard account of the application of social science knowledge, however, is not exhausted with the claim that adequate knowledge is eminently practical knowledge. Further attributes of this orthodox model are noteworthy. But if one follows initially only the broad and general outlines of the orthodox account of the reasons why social science knowledge is applied, it becomes particularly evident that the model is ruled by the assumption that the transformation of knowledge into action or – what I have called the translation of a capacity for action into action – occurs in a most straightforward and uninhibited manner. Niklas Luhmann (1977:16) has suggested calling these and related expectations the 'model of instrumentality'. That is to say, the model of instrumentality conceives of theory as a kind of intellectual tool which may be employed in practical situations. Theory, as long as it is 'true' or 'adequate', is also reliable and useful. Theoretical knowledge alone does not guarantee a successful execution of social action nor does it assure the value of the means chosen to reach a specific goal. But theoretical knowledge, the model asserts, secures a kind of technical relief for the actors. In addition, actors are not required to manufacture the knowledge for themselves, nor is it necessary to comprehend the scientific context in which the theoretical knowledge was generated (cf. Luhmann, 1977:16; also Giddens, 1987: 45–6).

Upon closer inspection, the model of instrumentality – or the handmaiden functions performed by social science – contains a variety of further assumptions. The model finds its strongest support among social scientists who would uphold a strictly technical or even technocratic conception of the use of social science knowledge. The model of instrumentality has not been spelled out anywhere in the literature as a fully differentiated and elaborated idea. On the contrary, the various attributes and stipulations enumerated below are taken from different sources. In most instances, these attributes are discussed in an *ad hoc* fashion. None the less, they do belong together and constitute a part of the ideal typical model of instrumentality. This means also that the description which follows is, moreover, not necessarily complete. For the purpose at hand it should suffice, however.

Among the attributes to which the model of instrumentality fails to speak, is the need to develop a position *vis-à-vis* the actual existence of and competition of different forms of knowledge originating with different scientific disciplines. One needs to examine, from the point of view of the model of instrumentality, for example, the question of possible differences between social and natural scientific knowledge, the issue of the cognitive division of labor in science, and the effect of the growing differentiation and specialization in science on the usefulness of theoretical knowledge produced in such communities. At the same time, the kinds of issues need to be raised which figure more prominently in the next part of my discussion, namely the special virtues of social science knowledge under changing socio-historical conditions. For example, is there a kind of convergence between the characteristics and benefits of social science knowledge and the peculiar demands of the day, that is, the requirements for knowledge brought about by specific historical circumstances? Will it be possible to achieve a kind of meshing between the knowledge manufactured by social science and the knowledge that secular conditions and trends appear to demand? What have been the effects of the growing rationalization of society, as described by Max Weber, upon the kind of social science knowledge which is suitable under these conditions? Max Weber in fact did address this question, although this is perhaps not widely known. His ideas on this subject will be discussed in the next section (cf. also Bauman, 1978).

Aside from these limitations of the standard account, the characteristic attributes of the model of instrumentality made explicit in the literature can best be summarized in the form of **positive** stipulations, intended by their proponents to underline the special accomplishments of social science knowledge. The outstanding features of the model of instrumentality, which I would like to discuss first, concern the virtue of a strict separation of the distinct (intellectual and social) spheres of the production and use of social science as well as the assumption that neither the social and intellectual context of production nor the context of application affects the ways in which useful social science knowledge is generated and then employed. In short, objective knowledge is seen as independent of individual assent, conviction and willingness to apply it.

1 Prevailing societal conditions, in which the production of social science knowledge are embedded, demand recognition of the fundamental fact that the social **spheres of the manufacture and the use of social science knowledge are strictly separate contexts**. One of the most distinguished academic American sociologists, and one most experienced with research with a practical intent, therefore draws what accordingly are the institutional boundaries of 'sociological rationality' without difficulty:

> Thus at some point, the researcher must hand over his results to the policy maker and more generally to the public. The more interpretable and intellectually digestible he can make them, the better. The task of political digestion itself, however, is not the task of the researcher, but of the whole political process. The research informs that process but it does no more. It cannot, even if its information is perfect, take the place of that process. (Coleman, 1972a)

Although the culinary concession to the context of use appears to be slight deviation from strict adherence to the model of instrumentality, it is more important to stress that the intellectual and social differentiation of the production of social science knowledge does not constitute, as one might perhaps imagine, a disadvantage. On the contrary, the organizational and cognitive separation of the milieu charged with the generation of social science knowledge, the social science community with its various disciplines and specialties, and the social context in which such knowledge may be applied actually has to be seen as a **precondition** for the possibility of adequate practical knowledge. In fact, the distance achieved and dispensation from urgent demands of the day, including the emergence of a particular ethos of the scientific community – for example, the requirements and consequences for knowledge of organized skepticism within science – form crucial features of the required special organizational and intellectual conditions that would permit the formation of knowledge claims that – aspire or need to – transcend the local contingent features of specific situations.

The thesis about the functional separation between manufacture and use of scientific knowledge is basic to the model of instrumentality. But it requires some elaboration. In what way, for example, does this stipulation of the model of instrumentality govern our understanding of the use of social science knowledge?

But first a brief comment may be helpful about the likely intellectual genesis of this thesis about the inalienable and indispensable separation of spheres: Karl Mannheim ([1929] 1936:122–4) regards the strict separation of 'theory and praxis' as a prerequisite of modern bourgeois intellectual life. The defense of the strict distinction among spheres of life suppresses, however, the question whether emotional (irrational) considerations are linked under certain circumstances to rational reflections in a much more direct and intimate way, for example, may even affect the categorical apparatus. As a matter of fact, Mannheim is puzzled whether such a separation and isolation of thought and action and therefore of the evaluative from the 'rational' elements of thought can *de facto* be achieved.

Be that as it may, the model of instrumentality too adheres to the optimistic view that the manufacture and use, to the advantage of both, of social science knowledge must take place within distinct social organizations and that social science knowledge strives to conquer a sphere of action radically purged of irrationalism. On a more psychological plane, the initial basic thesis of the model of instrumentality resonates strongly with the widely held idea that the hard and frugal work of invention and discovery comes with the original development of an idea, and that the subsequent work of transmitting the idea to others is negligible by comparison . . . all the information is seen as packed into the initial conception, with transmission regarded as mere reproduction, whereby the initial conception is either preserved or lost, depending on the receptive-ness of the targeted customers (cf. Fuller, 1992).

2   The second basic stipulation sheds further light on the import-ance of the assumption about the isolation of 'theory and practice' for both theory and practice: both the translation of social science knowledge as a capacity for action into action as well as the production of such knowledge is not affected, in any meaningful way, by the local attributes of the **context of application**, for example in the sense in which the term **indexicality**, developed and employed by ethnomethodologists, signals such an effect.

The model of instrumentality therefore stipulates not only, in accordance with prevailing 'positive' epistemologies, that the de-velopment of social science should not be driven and contaminated by considerations peculiar to the time and place of the situation under which knowledge originates in the first place, but also that knowledge should not be 'polluted' by the potential context of application. Knowledge, at the point of manufacture, is not sup-posed to be limited by the time and place of its ultimate use. The model of instrumentality of course recommends selectivity. The selection of attributes considered researchable and relevant to the problem at hand, however, is determined by existing theoretical perspectives and not by local circumstances of the context of application. Selectivity in data collection and analysis is strictly propelled by disciplinary-bound criteria, and these criteria in turn aim at generating knowledge claims which transcend narrow and specific situations and therefore aspire to transcend time and place. The application of such knowledge claims then also transcends time and place. The question of whether other strategies of data collection and analysis are possible will be discussed in some detail later on. The model of instrumentality clearly maintains that the historically specific and contingent attributes of social situations should be of limited or even no significance in the production of knowledge claims.

3   As already indicated, consideration of the peculiar social and cognitive context of the **production** of knowledge also can be set aside in any discussion of the application of social science know-ledge. To put it somewhat crudely perhaps, knowledge is not primarily determined by the structure of human groups but by the 'logic' of reasoning in conjunction with the 'objects' of conscious-ness (cf. Elias, 1971). A further instance of the same striking position is a dictum by Karl Popper (1972a:109) that 'knowledge in the objective sense is **knowledge without a knower: it is knowledge without a knowing subject**' [emphasis added]. Whether or not one accepts the possibility of knowledge as a phenomenon which knows

no subject, time and place, the view, especially in conjunction with the second stipulation of the model of instrumentality, implies that the **transfer and translation** of knowledge occurs independently of local features. Luhmann (1977:29) suggests designating the extent to which knowledge can be transferred in such a decontextualized fashion the degree of technicity knowledge may have achieved. The technicity of knowledge is high once the application of knowledge does not require any comprehension of the context of production of such knowledge claims (cf. also Cicourel's distinction between 'procedural' and 'declarative' knowledge [1986:92–4]).

Some observers doubt that social science knowledge claims are capable of achieving any degree of technicity. Collingridge and Reeve (1986:5), for example, emphasize that there appears to exist a basic discontinuity in the kinds of demands which practical knowledge, in contrast to scientific knowledge, judged by the contingencies of the context of political decision-making for instance, must satisfy:

> The conditions for effective scientific research, including the analysis of already existing evidence, cannot be met when the results of science are supposed relevant to policy. Contrary to the myth of the power of science, there is a fundamental and profound mismatch between the needs of policy and the requirements for efficient research within science which forbids science any real influence on decision-making.

If these observations indeed are correct, it would follow that selection criteria for data collection and analysis which are solely governed by the context of the production of knowledge are a liability for practical knowledge. With Elias (1971), one might therefore want to distinguish knowledge claims according to their object- or subject-centredness. In this instance, the model of instrumentality only recognizes barriers to the application of social science knowledge which originate and tend to increase with the subject-centredness of knowledge claims. In short, according to the model of instrumentality, the cognitive and social context of the manufacture of social science knowledge, aside from the desired correspondence between the quality of the knowledge and central epistemological 'standards', does not measurably affect the use of knowledge.

The remaining stipulations of the standard account to be enumerated are, for the most part, derivative of the basic attributes of the orthodox model, though it is not always self-evident that these conditions and alleged achievements of social science knowledge are characteristics of the dominant model. I will summarize the more or less connected and, in a logical sense, not necessarily mutually exclusive attributes of the model briefly:

4   Social science knowledge itself is the author of its success (or failure). This implies that the attribute of 'rationality' acquired by social science knowledge in the context of its production, or the extent to which it is certified as 'rational' by the social science community, is evaluated to a kind of 'natural', in the sense of fixed attribute of social science knowledge. The use of such knowledge in other situations does not mean therefore that it loses this attribute or that these features have to be reconstituted in a different context. And in this sense, social science knowledge is the author of its own practical accomplishments.

5   The ability of successfully translating social science knowledge into action increases, it is maintained, with the number of variables a theoretical system manages to manipulate simultaneously.

6   The degree to which knowledge adequately reflects the nature of its objects determines the usefulness of knowledge. The criteria which govern 'adequacy' or 'good theory' are attributes internal to the discipline in question or even to science in general. The calculus which generates and sanctions such adequacy uniquely originates and is maintained within social science discourse itself. Even more narrowly, the proper locus for a discussion and for legitimizing criteria of this kind is the philosophy of (social) science.

7   Experimental, not speculative, knowledge is practical knowledge.

8   Social science knowledge is made available to its users primarily in the form of instrumental knowledge and is primarily in demand as a form of technical rationality. The model of instrumentality relies, in this instance, to a great extent on the possibility of distinguishing in a manageable manner between the means and ends of social action.

9   Everyday knowledge is capable of repairing or correcting (cf. Giddens, 1984:336) and, as a result, the openness of the life-world to manipulation (or, as many would maintain, improvement) with the aid of social science is taken for granted by the model of instrumentality (e.g. Dahrendorf, 1963).

10   Social science knowledge and advice, as it is employed in practical situations, improves the transparency of the situation for the actors and ultimately their success in gaining desired ends (factual efficacy, cf. Biddle, 1987).

11   The practical success of social science knowledge in fact can be more or less directly attributed to social science knowledge, that is, the 'work' social science knowledge accomplishes in practical contents is visible and, in most instances, can successfully be traced back to expert social science knowledge claims.

12   Theoretical knowledge functions, on the whole, not unlike

good medicine: to the point, prompt and beneficial (cf. Bulmer, 1990).

13   Completing this enumeration of stipulations of the standard account, the model of instrumentality asserts, finally, that the translation of social science knowledge into action implies that such knowledge does not lose its identity by, for example, becoming trivialized. This stipulation also implies that social science knowledge as such cannot be misused in another context. It should not be possible to translate a social scientific concept into a kind of mythical notion in a social context external to the social science community (but Elias, 1989:502).

The model of instrumentality assumes, to summarize the central message of the various stipulations, that the practice of social science becomes the prevailing social practice in modern society. Every suggestion about the undiluted unity of theory and praxis asserted by the model of instrumentality is forced to build on such a premise. Although the agreement among social scientists about the standard account is considerable, especially when judged against widespread disagreements on many other matters of social science discourse, such consensus is one matter and the (empirical) reliability of its assumptions and observations on which it is founded, is another thing.

My view and assessment of the model of instrumentality as well as each of its basic and derived attributes, designed to account for the conditions of possibility of the use and the practical success of social science knowledge today, at least in the definitive sense with which each thesis has been stated here, can be summarized by saying that the orthodox model is neither based on sound philosophical reasoning nor on reliable sociological observation. In fact, the standard model is naively mistaken about the reasons for or the lack of 'power' of social science knowledge in modern society. The model of instrumentality not only underestimates the importance of the social and intellectual division of labor within and among social institutions in modern society, but it fails to take into consideration that knowledge does not travel unimpeded across these cognitive and social boundaries and closures.

None the less, it is not my intention to devise a detailed critique of the various stipulations of the model of instrumentality by engaging in a comprehensive effort to discredit each. Such a detailed critique is not even necessary, not only for reasons of space, but because the different attributes of the model of instrumentality are of unequal importance; they can be collapsed into a bundle of attributes from which the rest derive and to which a general critique of the former applies as well. My initial distinction of basic and derivative stipulations of the model of instrumentality already suggests such a differentiation in cognitive importance of attributes of the standard account. I will elaborate on some of the assumptions of the standard model and question the soundness of its central stipulations.

Although there are frequent complaints about the growing isolation and division between applied and 'basic' social science research (e.g. Bulmer, 1978; Payne et al., 1980), the various stipulations of the model of instrumentality make it evident that there has to be a fundamental discontinuity between basic and applied social science and social science knowledge and practice. It follows that the complex distribution of knowledge in modern society does not significantly affect the practical efficacy of even highly 'specialized forms of knowledge' manufactured by social science discourse. The issue of the use of such knowledge claims becomes merely a distributive matter. In contrast to Luckmann's (1981) concern that the increasing cognitive and social differentiation of 'advanced' or 'higher' forms of knowledge is invariably accompanied by 'de-pragmatization' and 'theorytization' of such forms of knowledge, the standard model suggests that social and intellectual differentiation, in the final analysis, advances the practical efficacy of scientific knowledge.

The dominant account of the ways in which practically useful social science knowledge is generated and employed also has the result that the specific knowledge claims are treated as a black box in a number of empirical studies designed to examine issues of their utilization. Attention focuses, in contrast, on a large and often varied number of dimensions linked to the context of application. These social or intellectual dimensions are investigated and identified as either barriers or hindrances for the use of social science knowledge (e.g. van de Vall and Bolas, 1982). The actual knowledge offered for use is not, however, linked to the same set of extraneous factors.

Using the language of a systems-theoretical perspective, the positive features of the dominant model of the application of social science knowledge can be summarized as follows. Despite the differentiation of the production and the implementation of capacities for action (knowledge), the distance between social systems does affect the ultimate application of this knowledge in other subsystems. This relationship holds with particular force as long as it is assured that disciplinary knowledge is based on methodologically adequate and objective procedures.

Constitutive for differentiated social systems are, according to Luhmann (1981:119), communicative systems. Such communicative systems determine what constitutes adequate knowledge claims.

This interpretative accomplishment is internally driven, that is, independent of the cultural accomplishment of other social systems and 'de-coupled' from its external consequences. But it appears that Luhmann, in outlining these features of differentiated social systems, is referring above all to the responsibilities of the scientific community and to the application of scientific and technical knowledge and is much less concerned with the preconditions for applicable knowledge in the first place. None the less, Luhmann's systems-theoretical perspective underlines the problems of employing social science knowledge generated in increasingly differentiated social contexts and propelled by internally sanctioned norms.

According to the model of instrumentality, the practical usefulness associated with knowledge claims generated under the indigenous auspices of the scientific community is linked solely to the internally conceived 'scientific character' of such knowledge. As a result, the model subscribes to what might be called a naive notion of rationality. It assumes that knowledge which conforms closely to existing scientific norms will always be superior in practice and literally do away with the need for competing forms of knowledge, should such competition occur at all. One really does not need to attend too closely and in any comprehensive manner to the various barriers, at times enumerated with great vigor, that impede the use of social science knowledge, especially those which are governed by social conditions under which social science knowledge is applied. In the final analysis, these external barriers, be they problems of communication (cf. Nowotny and Lambiri-Dimaki, 1985) or the resistance generated by vested interests, are minor hindrances; in fact, they can be disregarded for most purposes. The model of instrumentality asserts that these barriers to utilization tend to be accidental matters and historically specific problems but not systematic impediments. From the perspective of the standard model, there is ample justification for the conclusion that one can, without serious cost, ignore situationally specific conditions in the **construction** of social science knowledge. Such certainty is made possible given the denial of any meaningful linkage between knowledge guiding interests governing the production, and interests determining its eventual application. In fact, the connection is thought to be much more direct since the adequacy of scientific knowledge itself rules successful application (cf. Kaufmann, 1977:46).

John Maynard Keynes observed (and complained about) in the early 1930s, in work leading up to his *General Theory*, the lack of social recognition given to one species of social scientists, namely economists. The low social prestige of economists is the result, in Keynes's view, of the dubious practical value of the knowledge economists have to offer. In other words, he evidently assumed a kind of linear relation between social prestige and the scientific quality of the knowledge economists made available: 'For it now seems to me that the economists, in their devotion to a theory of self-adjusting equilibrium, have been, on the whole, wrong in their practical advice and that the instincts of practical men have been, on the whole, the sounder' ([1973] 1987:406). The same inability to generate adequate theoretical knowledge therefore explains, as Keynes comments in the same context, 'the low standing of economists as practical experts and the unwillingness of statesmen and business men to accept their advice'. Nothing is as practical, this appears to be Keynes's conclusion as well, as is a good and scientifically valid theory.

The assumption of the model of instrumentality that the use of social science knowledge invariably generates meaningful consequences and that its benefits, moreover, increase almost in a linear fashion with the quantity of knowledge employed, rarely has been made the subject of explicit critical reflection. For instance, it is assumed that the 'quality' and 'rationality' of decisions taken with the aid of social science knowledge 'improve' measurably. In addition, social and political action becomes, now subject to fewer uncertainties and risks, a much more manageable, predictable and reliable form of social and political action. Representative for these views is, for example, the optimism of Harold Orlans (1976:6) when he suggests that the empirical social sciences, despite certain recognized shortcomings, 'supply the most reliable knowledge obtainable about man and society and the soundest basis for public policy'. The optimistic message justifies the call for greater resources for the social sciences since additional financial support will enable the social sciences to become even 'more scientific and to make the information and analysis they can offer more reliable scientifically'.[2]

More recently, however, it has become plain that the possible practical consequences of social science knowledge are by no means restricted to instrumental or technical uses. Research concerned with applications issues has, at least in some countries, changed its traditional focus.

If one, for example, reads Helmut Schelsky's *Die Arbeit tun die anderen: Klassenkampf und Priesterherrschaft der Intellektuellen* ('The others do the work: Class struggle and the priest-like rule of the intellectuals') not so much as intended by its author and confirmed by the reception among social scientists, as a polemic directed against the social sciences, but as an attempt to analyze the use of social science knowledge in modern societies, it becomes evident that Schelsky's treatise represents a profound critique of the conventional idea that knowledge generated by social science serves primarily, perhaps even exclusively, as a form of **instrumental** enlightenment. That is, whatever one may say about the virtue and validity of Schelsky's polemic, he presents plausible arguments that one of the most salient practical consequences of social science knowledge consists in the impact it has on social and individual **interpretations** of reality. Along with the model of instrumentality, Schelsky's analysis also contains an 'optimistic' message about the general practical efficacy of social science knowledge in modern society. For Schelsky, social science discourse has radically transformed the identity of modern individuals. Whether one is prepared to describe the specific utilization process as a 'social scientification' of collective and individual patterns of meaning can be left open, for the time being. But later in this study, in the context of an excursus on 'sociology as enlightenment', I shall return to the thesis Schelsky argues.

But, as a result of these observations, one is able to suggest with Beck and Bonss (1984:392) that many of the current problems faced by social science in practice are related to the fact that the self-understanding of many groups and actors is affected, if only indirectly, by elements of social science knowledge. The empirical analysis of social problems by social science research then evolves into a kind of self-reflection or doubling of social scientific conceptions. But if one formulates the matter in such a trenchant or radical manner and asserts with Schelsky that the self-understanding of modern actors is determined by social scientific conceptions, or with Beck and Bonss that the key to any proper understanding of the theory/practice relationship for the social sciences is constituted by the social scientification of everyday beliefs, one surely runs the risk of conceptualizing the range of issues pertinent to the question of the use of social science knowledge somewhat restrictively. For example, only victims, it would appear then, populate modern society. Contemporary social science is victimized by its own success while modern individual and corporate actors are the pawns of the social science community. Who is able to extradite herself or himself from these cognitive chains? And, who can be content with discovering that social science knowledge operates in an invisible fashion?

None the less, these considerations are quite important. After all, they refer to significant effects social science knowledge has in society. The conventional model either underestimates or completely ignores such an impact. There is no room for 'ideological' consequences in the orthodox understanding of the use of social science knowledge. Beck and Bonss (1984:392–5) refer with justification therefore to the 'trivialization' of social science knowledge in society and the immense difficulty in tracing empirically how social science knowledge 'travels' in practice and what impact it in fact has on social action. Social science knowledge penetrates but also vanishes into patterns of meaning and is most difficult to track.[3] Whether attribution of responsibility is still possible under these circumstances is dubious.

The difficulty of tracing the possible ideological effects of social science knowledge, is, at the same time, a critique of Schelsky's specific complaint about the power of identifiable social science conceptions in modern society, namely critical theory. Under the circumstances, is it indeed reasonable to assert with confidence that the origins and therefore responsibility for certain meaning patterns and prevailing self-interpretations can be tracked with some assurance and by assigning blame to certain theoretical traditions? Whether all forms of social science knowledge or only some traditions are destined to vanish with few and uncertain traces into socio-cultural contexts outside of the social science community and are invariably subject to trivialization is not certain. In any event, the actual practical consequences of social science knowledge may occur in a much more unintended, indirect and less immediate fashion than one would expect following the conventional model.

However important and neglected the assertion about the ideological impact of social science knowledge on everyday life still may be, the virtually unintended consequences of social science knowledge are not the central issue of this inquiry. I assume that ideological effects are among the most important practical outcomes of social science knowledge. At the same time, I maintain that the range and the process of possible practical outcomes of social science are not limited to those covered by the observation about the ideological power of social science. For example, it is not necessary to envision, in a radical reversal of the orthodox model, that the use of social science is solely propelled by the needs and the attributes of specific publics and that one therefore can readily dispense with issues pertaining to the construction of social science knowledge. Considerations of the problem of what constitutes useful social science knowledge should not shift attention exclusively from the context of production to the context of application and maintain that use is exclusively driven by the 'logic of practice'. An examination of the relationship which obtains between the two contexts is most likely the more important focus for a meaningful as well as useful answer to questions about the conditions for the possibility of constructing practical social science knowledge.

It is noteworthy also that the thesis about the trivialization of social science knowledge in everyday contexts, inadvertently perhaps, affirms the conception of the model of instrumentality that a basic divide in terms of rationality exists as one moves from the context of science to everyday life. The notion of a trivialization can only mean that social scientific knowledge is stripped of certain of its 'rational' and 'objective' attributes as it finds its way into the social contexts of everyday life. Trivialization cannot mean, therefore, that social practice is somehow 'repaired' as the result of its encounter with and use of social science knowledge. But practical contexts turn out to be more influential in determining the fate of social science knowledge. The encounters of these two types of knowledge are viewed as somewhat one-sided affairs. In other words, the trivialization thesis raises the danger that the analysis of the use of social science knowledge itself becomes trivialized. The convergences between approaches is, in short, remarkable and requires further comment.

The logic of justification and the logic of practice

In his well-known treatise *Knowledge for What?*, devoted to an appraisal of the practical accomplishments of social science at the time, Robert S. Lynd (1940) distinguishes between two types of orientation separating the group of 'scholars' from 'technicians' in social science. While scholars become remote and even tend to disregard immediate relevancies in their work, technicians often are willing to accept the definition of the emphases of the institutional environment of the day. Lynd warns that the scholarly group among social scientists is in some danger precisely because of its 'leisurely urbanity' and self-sufficiency.

In analogy to Lynd's observations, one is able to distinguish two apparently opposing views of the use of social science knowledge. On the one hand, the model of instrumentality is animated by an image of the use of social science knowledge, unimpeded by the constraints and contingencies of local contexts but driven by the 'logic of justification'. On the other hand, the conception of the application of knowledge which stresses a largely context-dependent implementation, ruled by the 'context of practice', would seem to represent the most radically opposing view.

The reversal of the perspective is evident: from a realization of knowledge primarily propelled by the scientificity of knowledge to a utilization of knowledge dependent on the peculiar circumstances of the context of use. The logic of practice, one is able to conclude, replaces the logic of justification as the decisive moment in estimating the likelihood that a capacity for action becomes knowledge in action. All assertions which run counter to this argument are then seen as manifestations of an obsolete 'scientistic' or science-centered conception of application. For, as Beck and Bonss (1989a:24) sum up recent research findings into the application of social science knowledge: 'The application of findings has nothing to do with the findings which are used' (cf. also Beck and Lau, 1982).

The emphasis on the logic of practice as governing knowledge use is strengthened by viewing social action as essentially open toward the future or as characterized by a lack of determination of many social and political situations. A correlate of the openness of future social action implies, as Karin Knorr-Cetina (1981:156) stresses, 'the local **convertibility** and **essential contestability** of structures presumed to rule action (like laws and regulations, knowledge or plans)' [emphasis added]. In this sense, the use of social science knowledge may be conceived, in direct opposition to the model of instrumentality, as determined by the circumstances of the context in which it finds employment. The implementation of social science knowledge is open and not predetermined by the logic of justification.

The orthodox understanding of knowledge application views the distance and the differentiation of spheres of social action, especially the autonomy of knowledge generation in social science, as assuring that the production of knowledge is unaffected by external conditions and approximates, in the end, to a truthful description of reality. Subjective interests and irrational purposes are immaterial. The contrasting image of the use of knowledge views the differentiation of knowledge production and application more as a matter of evolved differences in structure of action and different modes of a more or less spontaneous recourse to social science knowledge, depending on the nature of the situation.

However, in stressing the logic of practice as determining the use of knowledge, the counter model fails, in ways similar to the model of instrumentality, to consider the varied and multiple **interrelations** of knowledge production and application as relevant to the question of why some knowledge claims come to be used and others are perceived as largely irrelevant. These interrelations need to be tackled in order to assure an adequate understanding. Neither knowledge use nor knowledge production takes place in splendid isolation from the other, though the degree of separation can at times be extreme. Without attention to the relations, however close or remote, of knowledge generation and application, perhaps in the form of a kind of process model (cf. Havelock and Benne, [1966]

1969), any comprehension of the successful use of social science knowledge will remain a mystery.[4]

The convergence of intellectual traditions

Evidence for the breadth and depth of the support in social science for the model of instrumentality can easily be adduced (cf. Bulmer, 1990). What is more surprising perhaps, is the fact that social scientists who strongly support rather divergent theoretical traditions and find themselves in opposing epistemological and ideological camps – for example, critical theorists and conservative sociologists – can be found among the avid and, in some instances perhaps, inadvertent proponents of the model of instrumentality. A brief illustration of this peculiar convergence of traditions follows.

The conviction that social science is capable of producing a form of knowledge which *a priori* constitutes a kind of 'social technology' is at the center of the convergence I would like to discuss. The thesis in question often is argued in strict analogy to 'material technology' produced on the basis of natural science knowledge. Although the scholars who formulate these views do not consider themselves proponents of such knowledge, their observations none the less require a strong affirmation of the model of instrumentality.

The notion that social sciences can be governed by a knowledge guiding interest which is technical in nature (e.g Adorno et al., 1969; Habermas, [1964] 1974; Giddens, 1987:45–6) is, despite the philosophical and political intentions of critical theory, also a faithful assent for the possibility of social science knowledge as reconstructed and recommended by the model of instrumentality. The critique that social science is in danger of becoming a form of social technology indiscriminately serving repression and domination affirms, at least on the surface, the special power and usefulness of 'positive' social science. But in warning about a crude form of instrumental rationality, critical theory cannot but be impressed by the potential power of such knowledge in practice; otherwise, it would make hardly sense to advocate and develop an alternative theoretical program based on an alternative knowledge guiding interest. Paradoxically, critical theory finds itself arguing, without critical consciousness, for the practical efficacy of social science knowledge portrayed by the model of instrumentality.

The qualities of social science knowledge described by the model of instrumentality are best and most efficiently translated into practice if one assumes a convergence in the rationalities of social science knowledge and social action. The persistent and successful transformation of contexts of action of individual and corporate

actors in modern society by science gradually heightens the rationality of social action as well. Social contexts which have already been
successfully transformed by, and made responsive to, instrumental
knowledge assure the kind of receptivity taken for granted by the
standard model of the use of knowledge. It is only under these
circumstances that it will be possible for technical knowledge to
mesh closely with a corresponding existential reality. The transformation of social phenomena into 'rational' contexts represents a
kind of neutralization of 'irrational' attributes of practical situations. It is only then that society can in fact serve as a laboratory in
which 'scientifically' constructed effects can be reconstructed with
ease. At least the model of instrumentality already assumes that
such a constellation of forces exists in reality or that there is strong
predisposition for such a transformation.

In the case of the theory of society formulated in the early 1960s
by the conservative German sociologist Helmut Schelsky, such a
relational constellation becomes a rather explicit basis of his
reflections as well as urgent concerns about science and society in
advanced society. Schelsky's theory of the 'scientification of our
world and its life' (1961:9) or of the emergence of a 'scientific
civilization' in modern society argues that we are increasingly
subjected to a calculability of social action in virtually all spheres of
life. As a result, we are faced with the likelihood that more and
more social, political and economic decisions become matters of
mere deduction from technical data. Schelsky expects that the
dualism between science and the humanities as well as the social
sciences will rapidly become, as a consequence of the increasing
technical nature of the knowledge produced in all scientific disciplines, a matter of the past. The social sciences will be as effective
in practice as are the natural sciences. And, correspondingly, the
schism between culture and civilization (or, the two cultures) in
society will gradually vanish. Schelsky is, by no means, an apologist
for the developments he describes. But in the context of Schelsky's
critical and distancing attempt to assess the practical accomplishments of the social sciences, he cannot escape the then prevailing
optimism about the usefulness of social science for society and the
prevailing conviction that social science knowledge can in fact be
most powerful in practice.

Schelsky asks, for example, what does it mean that we have been
able to develop 'human technologies' (*Humantechniken*) which
allow us to probe the consciousness of individuals, their immaterial
inner and most private longings and convictions? What does it mean
that we are able to dissect and reduce previously inaccessible
phenomena to mere technical information and, in the end, will be

able to manipulate and control them? What does it mean that we today encounter in almost all organizations 'moral divisions' and 'human-relations departments', that is, units which inquire into and attempt to control in the desired direction, with the means of scientific research, the willingness to work, leadership qualities or marital attitudes? Finally, what does it mean that the institutions which evolved in a quasi-natural fashion are now subject to deliberate design (cf. Schelsky, 1961:9)?

To ask these critical and alarming questions of social science can only be tantamount to an affirmation of its potency in controlling and generating social relation and processes. The development of social science into a purely productive science is possible, according to Schelsky, because society became a scientific civilization. And this in turn means that

> every technical problem and every technical success . . . invariably and immediately also becomes a social, psychological problem. It becomes a social problem in the form of a technical solution which though created by humans now confronts them as a socio-psychical demand which in turn allows for no other solution than a technical one . . . Man transcends the limits imposed on him by nature only to subject himself to the constraints of his own creations. (Schelsky, 1961:16–17)

The close correspondence, if not the compulsion of a tight coupling between the logic of science and society, especially in the field of the social sciences, implies that the human technologies produced by social science are extraordinarily efficient in practice and take on a life of their own while they produce inescapable constraints for social action.

Michel Foucault's conception of the power of knowledge represents, finally, another version of essentially the same type of argument. He too asserts that there is a strong **parallelism** between social science knowledge and the execution and legitimation of power in society. However, for Foucault, the impetus for the parallelism between knowledge and power is reserved. Knowledge finds itself being pressured to be pre-structured in a fashion which then assures its instrumental effectiveness. Social science increasingly produces knowledge which conforms and is employed to hide the social distribution and the basis of power. Such knowledge operates in the form of political technologies throughout societal institutions, for example, in schools, prisons and hospitals. Instead of gaining power by fertilizing power, social science is emasculated by power.

In short, the varied but highly critical reproach suggesting that the social sciences have become producers of mere social technology and that social scientists are advocates, whether intended or not, of a form of decisionism and therefore lack any critical consciousness toward these and any other social and political developments or, finally, the warning about the growth of human technologies and the extent to which society becomes its victim, all share, despite opposing world views, a strong adherence to the model of instrumentality and the conviction that positive social science can in fact be exchanged into effective practical reason. It goes without saying that the same critics of positive social science, inadvertently, affirm the vitality of positivism and the possibility of the scientificity of social science knowledge as a key to its practical power. The predominant vision of social praxis becomes the practice of social science in society (cf. Kaufmann, 1969), that is, social praxis is seen as increasingly identical with the practice of social science (and science) and therefore the power of scientific knowledge. In other words, Schelsky as well as the representatives of critical theory or Foucault fail to critically inquire into the claims of positivism for itself. Critical theorists or conservative sociologists simply accept the premises and promises of the model of instrumentality. They fail to ask whether social science in fact is capable of producing these effective capacities of action in the form of social technologies. As a result, it seems to me, they become proponents of the very model they reject and add to its widespread acceptance in the social science community.

Even more significant perhaps, the belief in the efficacy of the model of instrumentality is the basis for the very identity of alternative models; for example, the need for knowledge guiding interests which lead to the production of emancipatory knowledge which ought to be able, among other purposes, to combat and keep the power of instrumental reason in check. The support for the model of instrumentality is, summing up, widespread and comes at times from unexpected intellectual quarters. In any event, the epistemological and political affirmation of the model of instrumentality certainly transcends many other and often trenchant intellectual divisions in social science.

The widespread support for the model of instrumentality constitutes one of the keys for an explanation of the dominance as well as of the longevity of the model in social science. For decades, among proponents and critics alike, there has been a kind of basic consensus on the nature and the potential social power of scientific knowledge. The basic consensus maintained that scientific knowledge will displace, before long, other forms of knowledge in society. The decisive advantage scientific knowledge enjoys in its struggle and competition with non-scientific forms of knowledge, according to this conception, is the conviction that it does not know any institutional boundaries. This view is very much affirmed by the model of instrumentality. While political knowledge, for example, is only effective within the boundaries of the political system, everyday knowledge in everyday social contexts or religious knowledge within the confines of religious activities, scientific knowledge is unaffected by institutional boundaries. Scientific knowledge is assumed to be able to travel freely across such boundaries and is, therefore, **not limited** by such divisions. Finally, typical for the view that scientific knowledge ultimately will conquer other forms of knowledge, is the conviction that only it is capable of growing and progressing while other forms of knowledge, which in fact are islands of ignorance, cannot but contract in their sway over social action in modern society. Only scientific knowledge is dynamic, other forms of knowledge are static. Science does not produce ignorance, it eliminates it. Scientific knowledge is much more efficient, last but not least, as the result of its ability to transcend institutional boundaries. Non-scientific forms of knowledge are doomed, in the final analysis. The close linkage to local social and cognitive conditions proves to be the undoing of such forms of knowledge. Scientific knowledge cannot but displace non-scientific knowledge. And, the more scientific knowledge is able to rationalize the irrationality of everyday life, the easier it will be to link theory and practice. The scientification of everyday life is both the motor and the end product of this inescapable development.

What is perhaps less well known is that Max Weber's advocacy of the usefulness as well as the peculiar virtues of social science knowledge in modern social and political contexts also is based on the conviction that we are facing a relevant, though not the same, dramatic convergence postulated in more recent theories of society in the rationalities of the spheres of science and society. I will discuss the origins and the nature of Weber's views in some detail in the following Excursus.

Notes

1   Lippitt (1968) cites Kurt Lewin.

2   Collingridge and Reeve (1986:2) characterize these and related convictions among social scientists as the 'myth of rationality'. It is based on the belief that the first step 'in making any decision is to reduce the uncertainties with which it is surrounded by gathering in as much relevant information as possible'.

3   As Carol Weiss (1978:23) suggests, referring to the 'utilization' of social science by policy-makers for example, government officials 'use research to help them in thinking about issues and defining the problematic of the situation, to new ideas and new perspectives . . . But the process is so indirect, it is not easily traceable' (cf. also Knorr, 1977).

4   The conception of knowledge use as propelled by the logic of practice raises a number of interesting methodological and epistemological issues as well which, however, cannot be discussed in this context. For example, to what extent does a scientific knowledge claim retain its identity as it is employed spontaneously in practical situations? How important is any characteristic of social science knowledge and to what extent, and why do they impinge upon the demand for such knowledge? How does the selection and diffusion of social science knowledge take place?

Excursus

Max Weber and the Political Virtues of Social Science Knowledge[1]

We are the epigoni of a great age, and are unable to reawaken, by way of precocious reflections, the impetuous yearning of idealism, which needs the illusions that have now been shattered for us in consequence of a more lucid understanding of the sober laws of social life.

Max Weber[2]

Introduction

At the age of 23, Max Weber joined a circle of equally young political economists in Berlin attracted to 'Manchester liberalism' but opposed to *Kathedersozialismus* which favored state intervention, to reduce class divisions and tensions. Weber thereby openly manifested his radical departure from the increasingly pessimistic and indifferent political views of the generation of his parents. Eventually, this association led Weber to become one of the most active members of the *Verein für Sozialpolitik*, initially founded in 1873. Weber became a member of the *Verein* as it shifted its activities from addressing mainly the political realm to scholarly discourse. As Marianne Weber (1926 [1975]:128) puts it, the association for the most part ceased to engage in 'activities of agitation and replaced propagandistic with academic discussion'. Obsolete economic doctrines, Weber and his fellow members believed, were to blame for the demise of a traditional liberalism which had become impotent in the face of contemporary economic and political challenges and which appeared to be too self-serving and restricted in its appeal, and unable to meet the challenge of the socialist critique of industrial society. The newly and, in Germany, belatedly emerging industrial society demanded and required instead an active social policy by the state and for the state.

In a letter dated 30 April 1888, addressed to the historian Hermann Baumgarten, who was quite influential in the development of Weber's political views but also a representative of the generation of his parents, Weber justifies his decision to join this circle and characterizes some of the desirable salient personal traits, political concerns and approaches to politics the members of the group have in common (Max Weber, 1936:298). At about the same time, Weber began to plan a further significant switch, namely to shift from his studies of law to political economy (cf. Mommsen, [1959] 1984:18–19).

Weber's growing concern with the social consequences of industrial society and the political responses it generated also brought him into close contact and intense collaboration with the Lutheran Christian social reform movement which, inspired by a Christian world view and led by Lutheran ministers, voiced its decidedly political support for social reforms. But the Christian social reform movement and the creation of the *Evangelisch-sozialer Kongress* in May of 1890 in Berlin,[3] among whose central activities were exchanges of ideas between theologians and social scientists, also signaled a crisis of the Protestant Church. This crisis involved an increasing disaffection among leading members with its inability to effectively respond to modern socio-economic conditions, as well as its subservience to the state and its aloofness from the newly formed proletariat (see Fischer, 1951; Bigler, 1972; Groh, 1982).

The initial invitation issued for the Congress read in part: 'The impending danger that lies in the increase of social democracy and its growing alienation from the Church must fill all friends of the Lutheran Church with concern. The undersigned address themselves to men of all political and Christian parties which stand firm in their support of the state and their friendly relation to the churches.' The meetings of the first Congress were lead by the economist Adolf Wagner, one of the prominent *Katheder-sozialisten*.

Thus, some fifteen years prior to starting his work on Protestantism and capitalism in 1903,[4] Weber was very active – along with prominent social scientists and individuals who like Weber later attained considerable scholarly repute – as part of a lobby of Protestant theologians and clergymen.

The activities in which Weber engaged on behalf of various groupings and functions of the Lutheran social movement ranged from correspondence on its behalf, the assessment of manuscripts for a journal, *Evangelisch-soziale Zeitfragen*, and the promotion among friends of a newspaper, which his cousin Otto Baumgarten, a Lutheran minister, had started (cf. letter to Hermann Baumgarten of 3 January 1891 in Weber, 1936:324–30) for the purposes of acquainting Lutheran theologians with the social issues of the day and of enhancing support for the Christian social movement. He became a frequent contributor to the periodical *Die christliche Welt*:

Evangelisch-Lutherisches Gemeindeblatt für Gebildete aller Stände, edited by his friend Paul Göhre, another Lutheran pastor. And, from the beginning of the formation of the Lutheran Social Congress, Weber was an active participant in its annual meetings. He became an officer of the Congress in 1892, offering various courses on its behalf in Berlin and, finally, directed the inquiry of the Congress into the conditions of farm workers in Germany in 1892–3.

The questions which might be raised, therefore, are not merely whether Weber at this time, through his active involvement in the Congress, established and articulated some of the main themes of his later work, but also, importantly, did Max Weber and the other social scientists then display in their actions and beliefs, for example, in the virtues he defended as those of modern social science discourse, an ethos, inspired by Protestant convictions, which is in some way self-exemplifying?[5] That is to say, was the nature of these activities itself a manifestation of the very ethic Weber described years later as inspirational for the emergence of capitalism and other equally consequential secular activities, especially modern science and technology? In particular, what roles did these social scientists attempt to play within the Lutheran Social Congress? Did they see the activity and the expertise they lent to the Congress as those of social scientists and in the interest of social science? What kind of legitimacy did they assign to their roles, and in what way did they attempt to further the acceptance of social science discourse? Finally, is it possible that a substantial basis for the legitimacy they assigned to their scholarly efforts on behalf of the Congress was religious in nature?

Such questions may of course be raised with the help of different sources, methods and purposes in mind. What I do not have in mind is a psycho-biographical approach. I do not want to search for hidden motives in the work and the activities of the social scientists that are in concordance with definite presumptions about the presence and the nature of a struggle and entanglement with hidden motives; and in which much of what needs to be examined in the first place rests, for example, 'ultimately in the suppressed hostilities of sons against fathers' (Mitzman, [1969] 1985:7). Nor do I propose to examine the entire career, work, activities and academic context[6] of those social scientists who chose to become part of the Christian social movement in the 1890s.

I restrict this brief excursus, in the first place, to the decade prior to the turn of the century – an era of profound social transition and crisis, an era between worlds, of the dissolution of German agrarian society and the establishment of Germany as an industrial society.

As Wilhelm Hennis ([1987] 1988:64) argues, Weber is very much bound to and torn between the society in decline and its emerging counterpart (between *Agrarstaat* and *Industriestaat*, cf. Weber, 1897:111). He turns the struggle between these two forms of social order into the major empirical problematic of his work, which is, to use contemporary terminology, the relation between social structure and personality:

> Max Weber was firmly placed in a modern 'disenchanted' world, whose lack of commitment left nothing to men and women except recourse to their own resources. For him there was no way back. Nevertheless, his scale of values and his entire system of categories derived from the waning *ständisch* agrarian old-European world. The methodological intention of his conceptual formation can be summarized in the following terms: a break with the preoccupations implicit in the values of the past world, without at the same time falling under the influence of the contemporary belief in progress.

I also restrict the excursus, in the second place, to the immediately relevant public record of these few years rather than attempting to cover the entire opus of the main actors. As indicated, in the case of Max Weber, the period under consideration precedes his work on the *Protestant Ethic and the Spirit of Capitalism* by another decade. In short, the aims of this essay are modest indeed: I shall examine the public and historically specific record of a limited period in time and not attempt to search for transcendental drives and aspirations hidden from all but the 'knowing' observer.[7]

Society, culture and science

The question which must be addressed first is what constitutes (or, for that matter, might fail to exemplify) sources of legitimacy for social science which are in some way religious in nature and also show an elective affinity to the Protestant ethic?

Robert K. Merton's work on the origins of modern science in seventeenth century England, inspired last but not least by Weber's essay on the Protestant ethic, is perhaps of some assistance in finding a meaningful answer to this question. Merton ([1970] 1973:175) describes one of the principal themes of his inquiry into *Science, Technology and Society in Seventeenth Century England* as 'the modes of interplay between society, culture and science'.[8] Indeed, the issue of the multiple relations between society, culture and science it outlines is also the framework within which my much more specific case and restricted issue can be located.[9] While each of the elements takes on a much more limited value, the general thesis which asserts modes of interdependence among spheres of social activity remains in force. Aside from the intrinsic interest which the specific actors may arouse, the era being considered holds fascination for its being characterized by a struggle for ever greater autonomy and increasing differentiation of societal institutions. Although the state, the economy, religion and science and the various social classes all acquire greater independence during this period, they also enter into new forms of reciprocal dependence.

The formation and the activities of the Congress are part of these cultural and socio-political developments. But the social and cultural differentiation of institutions also means that their legitimacy is increasingly 'home-made'; that is, both internal conceptions and external assent or opposition to the legitimacy draw more and more on a single source, namely the purposes explicated and defended by the institution on its own behalf. In the case of science, this means that knowledge itself becomes the primary source of the legitimacy of the scientific community (see Merton [1970] 1973:182). And this means, in turn, that the culture of rational discourse in science – a set of rules concerned with the justification of its assertions which does not proceed by invoking authorities but prefers voluntary assent instead – also begins to assert itself at the turn of the century for the **social** sciences. The authority of discourse takes the place of the discourse of authorities. It is a culture of discourse which, in the case of the social sciences as well, now increasingly rests on the premise that the 'coercive power and the public credit of societal authorities has been undermined, restricted, or declared irrelevant, and that the use of manipulative rhetoric is limited by institutional and moral restraints' (Gouldner, 1976:39).

In the case of Merton's study ([1970] 1973:183), the model he develops for seventeenth century science 'does provide for the mutual support and independent contribution to the legitimizing of science of both the value orientation supplied by Puritanism and the pervasive belief in, perhaps more than the occasional fact of, scientific solutions to pressing, economic, military, and technological problems'.[10]

Religion and scientific activity

But what does Weber have to say about the link between religion and science? Aside from the brief and better known comment which Weber offers toward the end of the *Protestant Ethic* about the desirability of examining the significance of ascetic rationalism for the development of empiricism, as one of the tasks ahead, he also commented on this issue in the critical exchange with Rachfehl, although it seems this is widely unknown. Weber ([1910] 1978c:1129) begins these observations with a dual note of caution: 'The development of the **practical**-rationalistic regulation of the conduct of life is obviously something quite different from the development of **scientific** rationalism and is not necessarily associated with it. The first foundations of modern natural science emanated from **Catholic** regions and Catholic minds' [emphasis added]. This represents both a qualification and an important modifying addition to the terse comment in the *Protestant Ethic*. But Weber continues the historical specification and adds 'it is only the **systematic** attempt to apply science to **practical** objectives which is primarily Protestant. Likewise, it seems that certain conceptual principles which are important for the regulation of conduct have a kind of affinity to the Protestant way of thought'.[11] However, Weber leaves the statement in ambivalent suspense since 'a more extensive comment is beyond the scope of this essay'.[12]

In the case of the social sciences, however, we must assume that its representatives at the end of the nineteenth century were still engaged in the initial struggle to assert an intellectual and social independence and identity for its activities. Indeed, Weber's activities within the Congress were aimed, to a considerable degree, at persuading his audience that social science discourse was not merely a legitimate scientific activity, but, as I will show, an endeavor consonant with socio-historical developments and an appropriate as well as realistic political response.

To sum up, I am trying to locate rationales – although other motives, for example personal[13] and political considerations,[14] undoubtedly played a role as well – in which social scientists, and Max Weber in particular, legitimized their active support as social scientists for the aims of the Lutheran Social Congress in Wilhelmine Germany and tried to further the acceptance of rational social science discourse. What are the distinctive **virtues** of social scientific discourse concerned with **practical problems** of the day for the possible political solution of these problems?

The legitimacy of social scientific activity

The creation of the Lutheran Social Congress coincided with a reorientation of both Church and state toward 'the social question'. In a reversal of political strategy, changes of social policy directed toward improvements in the welfare of the growing working class now became the order of the day, instead of concerted efforts to merely suppress or ignore the aspirations of the Social Democratic Party and its followers. The Congress attracted both conservative and liberal Lutheran theologians and clergymen[15] as well as civil servants,[16] students, soldiers, a few workers, teachers, businessmen and a larger number of university professors.

In a statement of purpose, the Congress described as its aims and activities in 1891 'to investigate impartially the social conditions of our people, to measure them against the moral and religious demands of the Gospels, and to attempt to implement these commandments in contemporary economic life to make them more fruitful and effective than they have hitherto been' (*Verhandlungen* 1891:126). In turn, Max Weber (1893a:col.767) emphasizes that it was not possible to ignore any longer, and the Protestant Church could not afford to overlook, the extent to which conflicts of interests in the material sphere of life affect moral commitments in society. The way to accomplish the aim of the Congress, at least for the more liberal wing of the theologians, was to rely primarily on 'unprejudiced investigation' or expert information (Harnack, 1890:567). In defending the activities and the purposes of the Congress against the criticism that clergymen should or might be turned into amateurish social workers, Weber (1893a:col.767) formulates the matter as follows:

> It cannot, after all, be doubted that, if, in the present situation of social tensions a cleric 'dabbles' in politics he does not do so out of any preference for the dilettante but because necessity demands it, since it is already, and increasingly so, becoming impossible to ignore the influence of the material conflict of interests on the moral foundations of people's lives.

Socio-economic conditions as well as self-interest ought to force the Church to pay careful attention to social science and formulate questions for it. Neither Church nor social science can accept the dictum *ne sutor supra crepidam*. In addition to the annual meetings centered on presentations by theologians and social scientists on a range of themes,[17] the activities of the Congress also extended to course offerings (compare Naumann, 1893; Weber, 1893a) for the public in general and for the clergy in particular which would familiarize them with the principles of political economy. Finally, the activities of the Congress included the initiation of social research. In the period covered here, the major effort in this regard consisted of a follow-up study of the socio-political conditions of agricultural laborers, a study first undertaken by Max Weber (e.g. 1893b and 1893c) on behalf of the *Verein für Sozialpolitik* (Weber, [1892b] 1984).

The *Verein für Sozialpolitik* study (see in particular, Riesebrodt, 1984b) was based on a questionnaire sent to more than 3000 employers of agricultural laborers in all of Germany; some two-thirds of the questionnaires were returned (cf. Boese, 1939). Weber (1893c:col.535–6) admits to the shortcomings of the research design but indicates that the farmworkers themselves would have been unable to respond to a questionnaire. The follow-up inquiry relied on local clergymen (initially approximately 15,000 copies of the questionnaire were mailed out to all Protestant clergymen in Germany) who carried out interviews with farmworkers. Weber (1893c:col.559) reports that approximately 1000 questionnaires were returned and that the quality of the data is superior to the results obtained by the *Verein für Sozialpolitik* study. The primary purpose of the follow-up study was to probe into the **psychological** preconditions and consequences of the structural transformations brought about by the dissolution of traditional rural labour relations.[18]

As it happens, this series of studies proved to be crucial for Weber's academic reputation. It evolved into a sophisticated early example of social research concerned with the transformation of agriculture under capitalism and the dissolution of authority relations based on personal ties between subordinates and superiors (cf. Weber, 1894d:col.476). But only recently has Weber's empirical work of the early 1890s on the confrontation between patriarchism and capitalism in Eastern Prussia been the subject of a number of essays which attempt to shed light on the importance, relevance and relation of this work to his later writings (e.g. Tribe, 1983; Scaff, 1984; Riesebrodt, 1985).

The authority of discourse

Throughout this period, in launching and then defending the importance of the study for the Lutheran Social Congress, Weber repeatedly stresses with force the authority of a certain mode of discourse rather than the authority of an individual delivering an inspired speech or pronouncement but not a factual lecture, the importance of written rather than oral communication in settings akin to academic contexts but not gatherings where applause signifies assent and common commitments, where persuasion toward a specific range of socio-political goals is attempted or ideological views are celebrated and political enemies are chastised. In the lecture courses, the attitude of self-conscious skepticism on the part of the teacher is emphasized repeatedly, and this attitude is seen as both unavoidable and desirable for a scientific discussion of practical social problems. In short, in many of his public utterances during this period, Weber tries to educate his audiences about the existence and the necessity of a succinct intellectual and social differentiation of spheres of scientific and political discourse and about the dangers of mixing its distinct features.

Weber (1892a:col.1104) reacts, for example, with noticeable irritation, in a published rebuttal to the review of a study, based on what would be described much later as participant observation, of 'worker's life situations' written by his friend Göhre (1892), to what he considers a case of illegitimate mixing of standards and points of reference of judgement by the original reviewer of the book. Weber accuses the reviewer of judging the merits of the author rather than the qualities of the treatise under review. The same reasons later led to Weber's dissatisfaction with the *Verein für Sozialpolitik* (cf. Lindenlaub, 1967) and his support for the creation of the German Sociological Society in 1909.

These convictions clearly anticipate Weber's more explicit and insistent justification of different modes of discourse, for example in his 'Objectivity' essay (Weber, [1904] 1949) or in his lecture on 'Science as a Vocation' (Weber, [1919] 1922). They are also reminiscent of Weber's even earlier emphatic rejection of the defense and practice of a fusion between scholarship and politics by the historian Treitschke.[19]

A crucial part of the work designed to persuade his audiences about the benefits and virtues of social science research, then, is quite explicitly devoted to a detailed justification of the merits of such efforts for practical purposes generally and the contingencies faced by the clergy specifically. At this point in time, social science discourse is by no means a self-justifying activity.

The virtues of social scientific discourse advocated by Weber, and some of his colleagues, resemble or even represent, so it seems, **ascetic rationalism**. Notably, the benefits of ascetic rationalism are by no means restricted to the academic community. On the contrary, Weber offers an array of extrinsic justifications which are intended to demonstrate the value of social scientific discourse for the political realm: the emphasis is always on needs, which the realm of politics itself demands, and the corresponding capacity of the social sciences to provide knowledge consonant with these very needs.

Later, in *Economy and Society*, Weber ([1922] 1968:600) describes the kind of (rational) orientation modern politicians are sometimes forced to adopt in the following terms: 'today, however, the *homo politicus*, as well as the *homo oeconomicus*, performs his duty best when he acts without regard to the person in question, *sine ira et studio*, without hate and without love, without personal predilection and therefore without grace, but sheerly in accordance with the impersonal duty imposed by his calling, and not as a result of any personal relationship.' Weber suggests, it seems, that there is a convergence of sorts between the demands of public (or, political) and scientific discourse, that the virtues of scientific discourse correspond to secular developments and demands in the political arena and that scientific discourse therefore has the potential to represent a form of 'political' knowledge. However, correspondence should not be mistaken for identity. None the less, Weber asserts that the usefulness of social research derives from cognitive attributes which it happens to share, given underlying historical forces, with those forms of thought which now increasingly govern political discourse and practice.

What are the major features and qualities of social science discourse which Weber and his colleagues discern?

1   Above all, it seems to me, Weber alerts his audience to and favors a particular quality of judgements produced only by social science discourse, namely **sober**, realistic and matter-of-fact judgements ('die *Nüchternheit* des Urteils' [Weber, 1893a:col.767]).[20] Arguing in detail for the value of an extensive survey of the agrarian workers, to be carried out by the Lutheran Congress, Weber (1892b:5) concludes his plea, for example, by saying that 'the more factual the answers that are given in the course of such a survey, the fewer generalizations or complaints and the more **facts** they convey, the more clearly the voice of the worker whose opinions are being stated is heard over that of the observer in these reports, the more **useful** they are from our point of view' (emphasis added). And elsewhere, in reporting on the findings of the survey, Weber (1894a:73) emphasizes that the Church simply cannot ignore profound social changes, in particular, the change from personal to class authority, since that would mean to proceed with judgements on social policy questions based on totally **unrealistic** assumptions: 'to turn a blind eye on these facts is a futile effort. Any position taken by the Church regarding social issues which does just that and continues in the tradition of personal responsibility alone, relies on **unrealistic** assumptions. Class struggle exists and is an integral part of the present social order.' Social science discourse as rational discourse is therefore free of any form of manipulative rhetoric and does not defer to authorities in any way.

2   Social science discourse encourages the use, in this case by the clergy, of **methodical**, that is, systematic, detailed and concrete observational techniques of social conditions (e.g. Weber, 1893c: col.537). Methodical observation increases the chances of novel insights into significant rather than accidental societal developments. Weber (1894a:63) refers to the questionnaire as such a methodical device: 'We have, above all, devised the questionnaire

also with the intention to train the social policy thinking of the observers, to assist them in familiarizing themselves with discerning in the multitude of phenomena they experience daily between those with lasting significance for social development and those which are accidental and insignificant.'

3   Social science discourse offers both enlightenment and demystification with regard to the (economic) causes of social affairs. More specifically, social science discourse helps us to discern general patterns in contrast to the confusion engendered by a multitude of bewildering empirical information about social developments. As Weber (1894a:63) notes, the scholar's achievements are particularly valuable in that he is capable of providing 'an overview about the relative importance of concrete objects for the general pattern of development'.

4   Social science discourse also encourages asking the proper practical questions about the reasons for the very possibility of certain social problems. It assists us in discerning likely barriers and difficulties in implementing policy.

5   Among the distinctive cognitive virtues of social science discourse is, finally, the likelihood that any encounter with its characteristic sobriety of judgement and methodical observation of social life produces a persistent change in the kinds of methods employed by non-academics in arriving at future insights about social conditions and policy recommendations.

6   Last, but hardly least, Weber (e.g. 1892a:col.1106) stresses that social sciences discourse can significantly lower the social and intellectual distance between observed groups and their observers. In that sense it can alter and therefore undermine traditional (in this particular case, patriarchal) conceptions of political and social life. Social science discourse therefore effectively provides for emancipatory possibilities, that is, in analogy to the manner in which critical theorists many years later would describe their version of the purposes of empirical social research (e.g. Adorno, [1957] 1972) as a form of emancipatory research.[21]

The calmness, matter of factness and realism of social science discourse (cf. also Wagner, 1892:90, 94) is also in demand and peculiarly suited for a nation and historical era largely void of strong emotional causes. This is, of course, meant in contrast to the prevailing political climate just a few decades earlier in Wilhelmine Germany where national unification was at the forefront of the political agenda and struggle. As Weber ([1895] 1921) therefore emphasized in his inaugural lecture at the University of Freiburg, 'we cannot appeal to great emotions shared by the whole nation, as was the case when it was a question of creating a unified nation and a free constitution'. Weber points emphatically, it would be fair to underline – as is the case for the *Protestant Ethic* – to the historically specific constellation and appeal of a certain mode of social science discourse. It is the case that Weber asserted, as von Schelting (1934:9; translated in Beetham, 1985:23) claims, that the attainment of responsible political action 'stands and falls with the possibility of achieving objectively valid knowledge of the empirical relationships pertaining in those areas of social and economic life which are relevant for the standpoint of the actor' as an almost universal proposition which Weber would want to defend. While Weber in 1896 emphasizes the extent to which social and political relations themselves have become 'rationalized' (1896:123), we should recall that he also argues strongly for and supports the expansion of the political and economic sphere of influence of Imperial Germany as a solution to various ills. Included is the need for employment of a growing population: 'For us it is a vital question . . . that the territorial extension of Germany alone can guarantee them [the general population] continued employment in the country and the opportunity of advancement. The fate of the rising generation in particular is inseparably linked to Germany's rise to an economic and political world power, to the fatherland's position of influence and power.' In a contribution to the discussion of the meeting of the Congress in the following year, Weber (1897:113), although he later saw his own position of the day as a kind of *Jugendsünde*, underlines strongly the identical theme and even speaks of the necessity 'to declare as gospel a nation's duty to fight' ('Evangelium des Kampfes als einer Pflicht der Nation') if a nation is to survive in a struggle for existence among nations. In other words, for Weber, responsible political action derives from values and not from the possibility of achieving objective knowledge.

Conclusion

Judged from a contemporary perspective, the roles played by Max Weber and his fellow social scientists within the Lutheran Social Congress are remarkable in a number of ways. In the final instance, it is hardly imaginable that professional social scientists would turn today to a Church organization in order to promote social science discourse as an exemplary and urgently required form of judgement. Social scientists would find it most difficult to claim to generate and sustain the same degree of contagious optimism and even passion; they would have difficulty finding an audience equally patient to listen, willing to learn, and ready to be persuaded. Last, but not least, social scientists today have, in many cultures, withdrawn from public discourse. Paradoxically, Weber's call for sober and methodical judgements on public affairs was more political in practice than most of our contemporary social science discourse which has taken to heart his demand for a separation between science and politics as a vocation.

However, the arguments shared by Weber and his fellow social scientists were clearly not based on theological or religious conceptions. Instead, they offered an ascetic rationalism as appropriate to the demands of the day. Nevertheless, the pursuit of rationalism occurs within the confines of an organization devoted to an 'irrational' conception of the world. It thus exemplifies and represents an instance of the same paradox dissected in the *Protestant Ethic*, namely the crucial role that irrational forces play in ushering in modern rational economic relations.

As a matter of fact, in the eyes of some of its members, the linkage between theology and economic activities is however much more direct. For example, Paul Göhre (1892:1), the general secretary of the Congress in its early days, issues the following plea to the membership, enjoining them to work diligently toward the realization of the organization's goal: 'to make, in a systematic and rational way, the moral values and forces of the gospel more and more applicable to the field of current economics and, consequently, to show their significance for economic policy'. They will then 'contribute to the realization of the password which rings through all of today's moral life: to realize step-by-step the idea of God's Kingdom on earth by tackling social ethics problems!' The realization of the Kingdom of God in this world is to be advanced through systematic and sober application to economic matters of ethical demands derived from religious beliefs. And, as Weber ([1910] 1978c:1129) himself put it just a few years later, 'the **practical** and not merely incidental but, rather, **systematic** inclusion of natural science in the service of the economy is one of the keystones in the development of regulation of life **in general**. Certain specific influences from the Renaissance as well as the Reformation . . . have contributed decisively to this development.'[22]

The academic efforts of Weber and some of his colleagues, and the advocacy of an increased role for the social sciences in practical political affairs are, in some ways at least, self-exemplifying. At the same time, the intellectual nature of the social sciences by no means remained unaffected, for, to quote Weber ([1895] 1921:21) this one last time, not only is public interest in social science issues on the rise, 'we find the economic mode of thought advancing in all spheres: social policy in place of politics, economic power relations

in place of legal relations, cultural and economic history in place of
political history.'

Notes

1   An earlier version of this *Excursus* was presented at an International Work-
shop, 'Fifty Years of the Merton Thesis', Institute for the Philosophy and History of
Science and Ideas, Tel-Aviv University, Israel, May 1988. Rita Aldenhoff and Karl-
Ludwig Ay from the Max Weber Forschungsstelle of the Bayerische Akademie der
Wissenschaften in Munich were kind enough to provide me with much of the Max
Weber materials I needed for this essay. For their helpful comments on a previous
version of the essay I would like to express my thanks to Steve Kalberg, Volker
Meja, Robert K. Merton, Guenther Roth, Gerd Schroeter and Edward Tiryakian.
An essay in German based on the same material was published in *Sociologica
Internationalis* 27 (1989):129–47.

2   Weber (1892a:col.1109).

3   The translation of *Evangelisch-sozialer Kongress* used here, namely 'Lutheran
Social Congress' is the third version I have come across. Lieberson (1986) uses
'Protestant Social Congress' and the translators of Aldenhoff's (1987) essay render it
rather misleadingly 'Evangelical Social Congress' (which can also be found in the
translation of Marianne Weber's *Lebensbild*, e.g. M. Weber ([1926] 1975:131, 219).
The translation I have opted for comes closest, I believe, to the self-conception of the
participants at the time, namely as representatives of the Lutheran Church rather
than merely as 'Protestants'. The translation of Wolfgang Mommsen's ([1959]
1984:19) book on Weber's politics also employs the term 'Lutheran' Social Congress.
A variety of sources, both from insiders, e.g. P. Göhre, and other authors attempt
to provide insights into the origins, workings and effects of the *Kongress* which
continued to exist until 1940 (cf. Göhre, 1896; Eger, 1931; Herz, 1940; Kretschmar,
1972); or to analyze the broader question of the relation of the Protestant Church to
social policy issues (e.g. Ward, 1979; Kouri, 1984).

4   Few explicit hints allow us to precisely date the beginning of Weber's work on
Puritanism. In one passage, in the first version of the essay, he refers to a book by
Georg Jellinek, published in 1895, and the fact that it stimulated his interest in
Puritanism. At the same time, Weber ([1910] 1978b:150) reports, in one of his replies
to critics, the 'oral publication' of ideas related to *The Protestant Ethic* in 1897. In any
event, Marianne Weber ([1926] 1975:335) has noted an intimate relation between
Max Weber's work on the protestant ethic and his inner life: It was 'connected with
the deepest roots of his personality and in an undefinable way bears its stamp' (cf.
also Homans, 1989:242–50).

5   The reference here is of course to Merton's (e.g. 1977) important notion of the
self-exemplification of the social scientific analysis of social phenomena.

6   Beetham (1985) has taken pains to show that the key to a proper understanding
of Weber's sociology is not in the first instance his own personal or class situation and
beliefs but the nature of the academic context and traditions of the time.

7   The psycho-biographical approach 'rejected' is represented by Mitzman's
([1969] 1985:175–6) well-known study. For Mitzman the *Protestantische Ethik*
represents 'a new and much more sophisticated act of self-liberation on Weber's part,
in which he substitutes for the earlier naive identifications with the struggles of
oppressed rural workers against despotic paternalism a truly Nietzschean assault on
his own superego' and work in the period preceding the essay on the Protestant

ethic, as years shaped by the struggle 'to escape from and finally challenge the dominance in the Weber household of his father, a dominance which he identified subconsciously with the political hegemony of the Junkers over the landworkers in particular and the German people in general'. As a matter of fact, Max Weber himself has been described as struggling valiantly against such metaphysical conceptions (e.g. Honigsheim, 1926:271–2).

8   The general theoretical framework which Merton describes as the perspective which guided him in his thesis research is, one might argue, a Weberian perspective, or at least, one finds considerable support in Max Weber's work, particularly in the *Protestant Ethic* essay itself but even more so in various explanatory materials Weber wrote in reponse to criticisms of the essay or on the occasion of its republication in his *Gesammelte Aufsätze zur Religionssoziologie* (Weber, [1922] 1972). In the latter context, Weber stresses the extent to which the development of science derives its impetus also from the use to which its ideas are put in the context of the evolving capitalist economy. In other words, both the leading hypothesis of those parts of Merton's dissertation which deals with interrelation of the conditions for the emergence of modern science in seventeenth century England and the Puritan ethos as well as the general theoretical frame of reference of the entire study derive much of their intellectual mandate from Weber.

9   Max Weber ([1910] 1978b:169) describes the necessarily limited foci of his own inquiry into the impact of ascetic Protestantism on the emergence of the spirit of capitalism in a comment to a critique of that essay by Rachfahl: 'bei meinen Ausführungen handelte es sich darum, eine bestimmte konstitutive Komponente des *Lebensstils*, der an der Wiege des modernen Kapitalismus stand, an dem sie – mit zahlreichen anderen Mächten – mit gebaut hat, zu analysieren und in ihren Wandlungen und in ihrem Schwinden zu verfolgen. Ein solcher Versuch kann sich nicht die Aufgabe stellen, zu ermitteln, was zu *allen* Zeiten und überall, wo Kapitalismus existierte, vorhanden war, sondern sie hat gerade umgekehrt das *Spezifische* der einmaligen Entwicklung zu ermitteln.' Many of the subsequent criticisms of Merton's adaptation of the Weberian perspective, as far as I can see, were undertaken without the benefit of Max Weber's important set of metatheoretical reflections on his original essay. However, Merton's adaptation of Weber's perspective, it seems to me, reveals a much more careful reading and sense of the contingent and historically specific perspective advocated by the author of the *Protestant Ethic*. That is to say, one needs to compare a reading of Weber (but of all texts dealing with the *Protestant Ethic*) with the reading of Weber via Merton by many of the critics of Merton (Carroll, 1954; Hall, 1963; Mulligan, 1973; Feuer, 1963, 1979; Becker, 1984).

10   More specifically, belief in six categories of spiritual and material benefits of scientific activity are discerned by Merton ([1970] 1973:184), ranging from religious, economic, technological, military, self-development utilities to nationalistic usefulness of science as rationales for science.

11   I have not only restored Weber's emphasis of certain terms which the translator decided to omit but also changed the translation found in the excerpt of the response to Rachfehl published in the *American Journal of Sociology* (Weber, [1910] 1978c:1129).

12   Incidentally, it is in the same context that Weber ([1910] 1978a:324) provides Merton (cf. [1970] 1973:181) with an even more explicit 'mandate', compared to the closing section of the *Protestant Ethic*, for those parts of his dissertation which deal with the interrelation between the ethos of Puritanism and the evolving institution of

science, for it is here that Weber underlines that it would be entirely incorrect to regard 'that faith as such was an obstacle to the development of empirical science either at that time or later. The majority of the heroes in English natural science offer ample evidence to the contrary, from the seventeenth century up to Faraday and Maxwell, one of whom is known to have preached in his sect's church during the nineteenth century'.

13   In her biography of Max Weber, Marianne Weber ([1926] 1975:125) relates that his close personal ties to Otto Baumgarten and his mother Ida strongly supported Weber's evolving concern with 'the social question'.

14   Liebersohn (1986:14), for example, asserts that Weber's involvement is a reflection of his commitment to 'Christian socialism', a faith and doctrine shared by many of the prominent members of the Congress; 'this socialism guaranteed the physical and economic welfare of workers, protecting them from capitalist exploitation, returning working-class women to the family, enforcing Sunday rest, and extending working-class political rights'. In short, Liebersohn (1986:11–12) argues that the programme envisions a Kingdom of God in Germany. But as we will have occasion to observe later, the purely religious convictions which Weber adduces in legitimizing his own involvement in the activities of the Congress are in fact minimal. Mommsen ([1959] 1984:20) and Mitzman ([1969] 1985:173) suggest that Weber was neither then nor later a religious believer. In 1892, Weber (1892a:col.1104) describes his own position as that of a layman distanced from church life ('Ein dem kirchlichen Leben fernstehender Laie'). Aldenhoff (1987) analyzes the nature of the political convictions and goals which may have prompted Weber to engage in the activities of the Christian Social Movement in general and the Lutheran Social Congress in particular.

15   Based on the list of the occupations of participants found in the various volumes of the proceedings of the Congress, Liebersohn (1986:32) reports that clergymen accounted for roughly 40 per cent of the members of the Congress during the 1890s.

16   The extent to which higher civil servants in particular were among the participants of the Congress is in dispute; a number of contemporary accounts stress the attendance from among this group while later efforts to arrive at similar conclusions about the extent to which influential civil servants were drawn in large number to the Congress are far less certain that this was in fact the case (cf. e.g. Göhre, 1896 or Nobbe, 1897 and vom Bruch, 1980:268, n. 222). In an appendix, the annual proceedings of the Congress contain a list of participants. This list is based on self-reporting, that is, participants were asked to enter their names in lists provided for the purpose of counting the names and the occupations of those who attended. But as a note in the proceedings indicates, the validity of the information, including the occupation or profession listed, is far from accurate. None the less, the socially esteemed group of university professors and civil servants were represented and legitimized the Congress among the public at large (see also Schick, 1970:80).

17   Cf. Kretschmar, 1972:118–25 for a discussion of the topics covered during the entire existence of the Congress.

18   The questionnaire, initially developed by Paul Göhre and Max Weber but sanctioned by a committee of the Congress (cf. Weber, 1893c:col.536), is reproduced in the preface to Goldschmidt (1899) while a description of its structure and contents may be found in Weber (1893c).

19   Letter of 25 April 1887 to Hermann Baumgarten (Weber, 1936:233).

20   This term also appears in Weber's ([1895] 1921:26) inaugural lecture held at

the University of Freiburg just two years later, except that he refers in his lecture to the nature of the political conditions in Germany after unification.

21   Weber (1892a:cols.1107–8) defends the participatory study of his friend Göhre by emphasizing, 'It would appear, from my point of view as a layman, as a giant step ahead, if one could succeed in establishing a psychological link between the many varied demands made to the clerical profession by various classes of the population and their positions of economic and social interests.'

22   I have restored Weber's emphasis of certain terms which the translator decided to omit.

4
Economic Policy as Applied Social Science

Economics is a science of thinking in terms of models joined to the art of choosing models which are relevant to the real world.

John M. Keynes[1]

It is widely recognized that John Maynard Keynes's self-conception[2] as an economist was shaped, in the first instance, by his interest in economic policy. Eric J. Hobsbawm (Wattel, 1985:3) has recently summarized this view: 'From his dramatic entry on the public scene as a critic of the 1919 Versailles peace to his death, Keynes spent his time trying to save capitalism from itself' (also Schumpeter, 1946: 355–6; Robinson, 1956:11).[3] The thrust of this evaluation of Keynes corresponds to his own, hardly humble, self-judgement of the practical importance of his theoretical ideas. In 1936, he indicates for example that his doctrine offers, as a theoretical alternative to the neoclassical model, the only '**practical means** of avoiding destruction of existing economic forms . . . in its entirety' (Keynes, 1936:380; emphasis added). But his economic ideas also found followers among social democrats and active labor union leaders,[4] while some of his conservative critics condemned Keynes's ideas as advancing a socialist agenda (e.g. Coddington, 1974).

These diverse judgements indicate that the ways and means of the possible practical influence of Keynes's theories are quite complicated. The dissemination process and the possible practical effect of Keynesian ideas will hardly be limited and conform to a structure which follows the main outlines of political and ideological divisions in modern society. Yet, patterns of influence across political cleavages perhaps signal that his ideas were by no means, as a prerequisite for their overall influence, without their distinct theoretical looseness or ambivalence and therefore open to a range of interpretative possibilities.

The most important works of John Maynard Keynes, the *Treatise on Money* (1930) and *The General Theory of Employment, Interest and Money* (1936), in contrast to Marx's work, do not contain a universal history of capitalist development. The *General Theory* was published toward the end of the global economic crisis of the 1930s. Keynes began this work in 1932,[5] at the time when Great Britain had suffered, for more than a decade, from annual unemployment figures of at least 10 per cent. Keynes's *General Theory* was published after he had already participated actively in public debates on economic policies and purposes (cf. Chick, 1987). Tobin (1986:15) indicates that 'one evident purpose of the *General Theory* was to provide a professional analytical foundation for the policy positions he had been advocating in those debates'. That Tobin's interpretation is correct can also be gleaned from Keynes's own introduction to the *General Theory*, where he suggests that the book is primarily intended for his colleagues in economics. And he adds (Keynes, 1936:v) that the main purpose of the *General Theory* is intended to deal 'with difficult questions of theory, and only in the second place with applications of this theory to practice'. But despite Keynes's own testimony to the contrary, one can nevertheless concur with Adolph Lowe's (1977:218) observation that the *General Theory* represents the beginning of the end of pure economic theory[6] and the beginning of politically minded economic theory and that it constitutes the culmination of intensive reflection by Keynes about economic policy matters of the day (cf. Schumpeter, 1954:1157; Steindl, 1985:105–9). Though the treatise itself contains only few explicit suggestions for economic policies it none the less may be seen as the end product of Keynes's (1973:107) long-standing conviction that the orthodox *laissez-faire* doctrine was 'wholly inapplicable to such problems as those of unemployment and the trade cycle, or indeed, to any of the **day-to-day problems of ordinary life**' (emphasis added). In any event, as far as the retrospective and the contemporary interpretation of the nature of the *General Theory* is concerned, it is widely hailed as an eminent and exemplary piece of economic theory with practical intent.

The intellectual and socio-political circumstances which led to the *General Theory* confirm the observation that important theoretical innovations in social science often are a response to and develop as the result of intensive reflections about pressing contemporary events to which some kind of 'intuitive' solutions are proposed.

Keynes's *General Theory* amounts to a new paradigm for modern economic theory.[7] Keynes was convinced that his theory would have a revolutionary impact. In a letter to George Bernard Shaw, written before the completion of the *General Theory*, Keynes observes that he is writing a book 'on economic theory which will largely revolutionize – not, I suppose, at once but in the course of the next ten years – the way the world thinks about economic problems' ([1973] 1987:492–3). And very much in the sense of the meaning of the term paradigm, as proposed by Thomas Kuhn for the purpose of grasping the nature of intellectual *revolutions* in the history of the sciences, Keynes's radical innovation primarily consists of a 'displacement'[8] of central economic concepts and in a novel classification of economic phenomena (cf. Harrod, 1951:462–3; but see Lowe, 1977:217 who disagrees with this assessment).

That Keynes's main work was deeply rooted in the socio-economic and socio-political consequences of the Great Depression and was also based on his close involvement in policy discussions and his experience as speculator are pertinent for a number of reasons. That Keynes's economic diagnosis concerns the phase of the depression in the cycle of economic development, for example, is quite relevant for the kind of therapy which emerges from his analysis. Subsequent discussions and controversies about the 'universality' or generalizability of Keynesian ideas refer to the immediate intellectual impetus and aims of his inquiry and express doubt that Keynes's reflections can in fact be of great relevance and pertinent in different economic circumstances. At the same time, and in order to inquire into the conditions for and the features of practical knowledge, it is noteworthy that ideas in social science which are developed primarily in conjunction with pressing external problems rather than in the course of fashionable disciplinary theoretical controversies, may have a better chance to lead to workable solutions, though the range of situations in which such knowledge is perceived as relevant may turn out to be limited.

Keynes's economic theories represent the beginning of **macro**-economics as well as of the interest, which continues until this day, among economists in certain **aggregate** data of the economy of a society. Adolph Lowe (1977:220) observes that this kind of displacement in foci, in comparison to neoclassical economic theory alone, assures Keynesian theory a greater instrumentality, that is, 'by substituting for the innumerable micro-relations of the Walrasian model a few basic macro-relations, the *General Theory* arrives at propositions which easily lend themselves to statistical testing and, no less important, are handy tools for policy making'. The intelligibility of the economy no longer depends on an understanding of the rational decisions made by autonomous individual subjects. The object of reflection instead becomes the aggregate economy with its own independent dynamic; the subject in Keynes's analysis – namely the government or, even more precisely, the Treasury – remains outside the boundaries of inquiry (cf. Diesing, 1982:82–5). The shift in the theoretical interest from individual to objective collective features represents of course a transition which had its intellectual precursors in sociology and anthropology.[9]

A critique of the basic, harmonious assumption of neoclassical economics that advanced economic systems, organized in terms of capitalist principles, tend to achieve equilibrium at full employment levels, is usually seen as the characteristic starting point of Keynesian economic theory. Many interpretations of Keynes which stress this point fail to recognize, however, that Keynes is not only concerned about full employment but also with the unjust distribution of income and wealth. Keynes is convinced that his theory calls into question the core economic views typically employed to justify a skewed distribution of wealth. His own theory, he believes, will contribute to reduced social and economic inequality.

Keynes objects to the orthodox conception that the price mechanism alone assures the 'normal state' of full employment, that the distribution of income corresponds to the marginal utility of the means of production (that is, capital, labour and land) and that economic growth is a fairly assured prospect. The classical employment theory primarily is based on two assumptions:

1   As a function of the interest rate at full employment, the savings rate and investment decisions are in an equilibrium.
2   The equilibrium between demand and supply of labour is determined by the real cost of labour although its nominal downward flexibility is restricted.

The Keynesian conception of the process of economic action, in its most important attributes, especially of the psychological determinants and dynamics, also is quite different from the views of its neoclassical predecessors, particularly in regard to the latter's emphasis on rationalistic factors (*homo oeconomicus*) as a determinant of micro-economic behavior of individual and corporate actors. In short, Keynes chooses to stress the plasticity of economic action, its uncertainty, and the influence of a larger number of imponderables or 'irrational' motives (cf. Schmölders et al., 1956). Keynes's theory of economic action does not set aside the contingency of expectations, the importance of social conventions and the influence of speculative behavior on economic decisions.

In addition, the macro-economic theory Keynes advances in his *General Theory* differs from its neoclassical forerunner in the following details:[10]

1   Keynes's theory stresses the significance of investment decisions by businessmen for the rate of employment and growth. Investment decisions primarily are affected by uncertain or even speculative expectations about future economic data. The multiplicator of investments, in addition, stimulates demand. But instability is endogenous to capitalist economies. The rate of investment and the savings rate follows the economic decisions

of different actors[11] and a savings rate which is too high may impede potential investments.

2   The decisive economic dimension for Keynes is no longer the supply side. He instead stresses the **demand** side for economic processes and therefore inverts the emphasis of orthodox theorizing. In the context of Keynes's theory, consumption no longer is a function of supply, that is, supply does not generate its own demand, as it, for example, does in the case of Say's famous Law, but the supply is driven by demand. Commodities and services which are offered for sale are a function of the demand for such goods (Keynes, 1936:21–2; cf. Drucker, 1981b).

3   According to Keynes, **money** is more than merely a neutral medium of exchange. Keynes attempts to join value theory and a theory of money. The interest rate in an economy is determined, for example, by the demand/supply relation for money used for speculative purposes.

4   One of the key observations of Keynes's macro-economic theory concerns **employment**. He considers full employment to be a special case and is therefore prepared to accept the possibility that an economy may be in a state of equilibrium accompanied by unemployment. Unemployment is no longer the result, as still postulated by neoclassical theory, of a voluntary withdrawal from the labour market (that is, a segment of the proletariat refuses work because they consider the rate of real wages as too low), but is the outcome of the unique economic status of workers who are not in a position to determine the rate of real wages.

5   Finally, Keynes rejects the view of neoclassical theory that the income distribution in society occurs in accordance with the marginal utility of the various means of production.

The differences between Keynes's *General Theory* and neoclassical economic theory can also be seen to reflect a decisive change in the capitalist economy itself: until the early part of this century, the constitutive element of the economy was the interrelation between demand and supply for **commodities and services**, that is, the economy of goods. Demand and supply of goods and services represented the 'independent' variables of the economy. Later, and even more so in our own age, the capitalist economy is driven by monetary factors. Keynes (1936:vii) himself recognized the radical change and indicates that his theory, in contrast to neoclassical theory, revolves around the monetary or the 'symbolic' economy, that is, it is especially concerned with the supply of money, with credits, budget surpluses or deficits or interest rates. The Keynesian interpretation of economic facts offers a novel perspective: 'Instead of goods, services, and work – realities of the physical world and "things" – Keynes's economic realities are symbols: money and credit' (Drucker, 1981b:8). A theoretical perspective of this kind is only possible after the monetary economy has reached a certain measure of importance and independence and therefore becomes one of the significant determinants of economic activity generally. More recently, such monetarists as Milton Friedman have argued that these developments have accelerated and the real economy is today the monetary or symbolic economy. Keynesian economic theory in fact reflects these structural changes of the capitalist economy. The movement of capital and investment decisions become a market which is no longer dependent on the flow of goods and services (e.g. Drucker, 1971:56–9).

Politics and the economy

In examining the practical efficacy of Keynes's economic theory, it will first be necessary to indicate the features of the theory (and the policy measures) that might be used as standards. This task requires a general theory of the application of social science knowledge which transcends the orthodox model of instrumentality. As a matter of fact, the degree of 'helplessness' engendered by the model can be illustrated quite well if one asks what procedures and what answers the standard theory of the application of social science knowledge offers to the question of the possible utility of Keynes's economic ideas. The most sensible conclusion one would be forced to adopt, in this instance, is to indicate that any observable practical success of Keynes's economic theory amounts to being the result of accidental or fortuitous circumstances since Keynes's theory appears to be very far removed from the ideal social scientific theoretical model required by the orthodox view.

Although Keynes does signal, for example, even in the very title of his major work, that he aspires toward a *general* theory of employment, interest and money, his approach does not constitute, as one might therefore imagine, such a general theoretical model, especially when judged against widely supported and rather demanding methodological ideals about object-adequate social science knowledge. Keynes fails to enumerate and examine, as explanatory factors, the intricate interrelation of economic to innumerable other variables which all may affect the rate of employment, the value of money and the interest rate. The progress in knowledge represented by Keynes's ideas, when compared to neoclassical economic understanding of the dynamics of the modern economy, would surely have to be linked, to a significant degree, to a much more elaborate and comprehensive analysis of economic processes than that found in the *General Theory*. The disappointment, given such standards about adequate knowledge and advances in knowledge over time, could not be greater. Keynes's general theory of employment, money and interest, above all, is rather sketchy and parsimonious in regard to identifying relevant theoretical dimensions for reflection and inquiry. His theory refers to **but a few** attributes of economic action. As a matter of fact, for my purposes, Keynes's theory can even be summarized by asserting that his theory represents the discovery of the importance of **investment decisions** for the level of employment in the national economy. His theory is therefore far removed from attending or capturing, in Seymour M. Lipset's words, the 'total system behavior' of a major social phenomenon. On the contrary, Keynes's theory appears to be an intellectual 'throwback' to the fallacies of classical social science theorizing with its abundance of limited factor theories.

It is therefore useful to take account of Collingridge and Reeve's observation that there is the distinct possibility that access to impressive amounts of information and knowledge claims can be quite 'dysfunctional' in practical decision-making processes. Their observation is also intended to combat the prevailing view about certain qualities of rationality, in particular the thesis that the rationality of political decisions somehow improves, in an almost linear manner, with the quantity of information available to the actors. Collingridge and Reeve (1986:5) state 'it is simply not the case that a good decision can only be made once the uncertainties surrounding it have been reduced by gathering as much relevant information as possible. On the contrary, policy decisions may be made quite happily with the very scantiest information'.

Despite the fact that only a few pertinent attributes of economic action appear to have been examined and taken into consideration by Keynes in his *General Theory*, vigorous voices could be heard almost immediately after its publication and certainly a chorus in later years, praising Keynes's theory and insisting that it may well have very important practical implications and benefits for the economic affairs of a nation.

Knowledge for practice

'If we seek a science of that which is in the process of becoming, of practice and for practice,' Karl Mannheim stipulates in *Ideology and Utopia*, in the essay concerned with the foundations of **political**

knowledge or a science of politics, 'we can realize it only by discovering a new framework in which this kind of knowledge can find adequate expression' ([1929] 1936:152–3). However one may, in retrospect, assess Mannheim's own solution to employ the sociology of knowledge as an organon for a scientific politics, the starting point of his reflections remains most relevant to this day and retains its programmatic significance. But Mannheim's insight that knowledge for practice cannot be divorced from knowledge of practice, that is, the local constraints and possibilities of social action in a certain situation, must be translated into a meaningful general theory of the conditions which favor the application of social science knowledge. The greatest obstacle faced by social scientists in realizing the project of practical knowledge, that is, in being about an 'adequate representation of the relationships which concern us in the political sphere proper', is according to Mannheim ([1929] 1936:154) linked to an erroneous theoretical attitude displayed by researchers in relation to the context to which such knowledge is supposed to pertain in the first place. The predominant disposition of social scientists 'tends to destroy the **actual interrelations**' constitutive of specific situations and of particular interests local political actors may have (emphasis added).[12]

Initially, I would like to outline but a few of the basic assumptions of an alternative general theory of the application of social science knowledge. In accordance with Mannheim's observations, a theory of the pragmatic transformation of social science knowledge, as a capacity for action, should be based on the elementary insight that all social action is bound to specific situations and affected by local constraints. How local they may in fact be, is an empirical question. In addition, it can be assumed that such local, situational constraints and conditions may be interpreted, by the relevant actors, as either **open**, that is, in certain ways subject to their control and manipulation (used nonpejoratively here), or they may be apprehended, as **fixed**, that is, largely beyond their control. Since the constraints which issue from a given social context are both **subjective and objective** ones, the notion that constraints may be **apprehended** as open to action or as more or less unalterable, should not be interpreted to mean that the apprehension of pertinent constraints of action is merely a subjective matter, an idiosyncratic component of social action.

Not only the social definition of the nature of the situation decides which features, if any, of the context in question are fixed. Such a conception of situational components open to social action inevitably ignores what are often called 'objective' constraints of human conduct which facilitate social action or impose on it certain limits.

None the less, extraneous or structural constraints which issue from given social contexts may be interpreted in terms of 'sets of **feasible options**' open to individuals and groups (Giddens, 1990:107, emphasis added) because such structural constraints ultimately are the product of decisions of specific actors; it is, at the same time, a fact that in a very large number of instances, the ability of **many** to reproduce and effect such constraints is severely restricted. But in the final analysis, the point is, whatever the objective constraints, they are not beyond the control of **all** actors. These considerations require that the notion of features of specific social contexts as either relatively open or closed to social action should not be driven solely by a subjective definition of situational constraints but should recognize that actors may be largely unaware of constraints which are 'actionable' (cf. Merton, 1975:173–6). Individuals and groups may therefore be in need of and prepared to accept some form of enlightenment, a 'critical' function which could well be served by a practical social science by providing a cogent account of human agency as it is mediated by the specific contingencies of certain social contexts. In this sense, the function of social science is to open up those possibilities for social action which common sense often conceals or manages to close down (cf. Bauman, 1990:16).

In addition, the view that a specific situation is largely unalterable can also extend to the conviction that the status quo is acceptable, while the conviction that existing conditions are open to change may initially only pertain to the vague resolution that existential conditions have to be altered somehow. Friedrich Tenbruck's observation (1986:95) that human behavior should generally not be seen as determined by a given and limited repertoire of fixed patterns of action, triggered and enacted once certain conditions present themselves to the actors, adds to and elaborates the same notion. Of course, social action can at times take on an almost automatic and taken-for-granted quality, as described, for example, by Alfred Schutz. Many situations in everyday life involve action executed virtually without reflection whatsoever. But actors continually also tend to encounter new circumstances of action in which habitual patterns of response may not prove to be of much use. And what is of decisive importance for action evolving under circumstances of novel conditions and constraints is whether, and which, elements of the situation are considered to be **open**.

At the same time, the stipulation about the apprehended relative openness of the conditions of social action almost immediately raises questions about the reasons for interpreting circumstances of social action as relatively open or closed. This often is a matter of the local power structures, both within a certain context and its immediate environment, as well as the prevailing worldviews and beliefs found in that situation.

It is, in other words, rather easy to state that conditions of action should be classified as either open or fixed. Whether they are in fact open, is by no means easy and straightforward to ascertain. Conditions of action may be open to some but not others, they may be open today but not tomorrow, and they certainly do come pre-packaged and labelled as open or fixed constraints of social action. For the time being, however, the problematic of the conditions for the openness of a context and the leading situational beliefs, though important because they obviously affect the demand for and use of social science knowledge, and the ways in which one may determine 'openness', does not need to become the primary focus of the analysis. In the final analysis, this is an empirical question and not a matter to be determined and thereby arrested *a priori*. A definite calculus which without difficulty separates actionable from fixed conditions of social action is not at hand. And this may be fortunate, one should add. Nor is it necessary, I would maintain, to be swayed by the conclusion achieved by way of logic alone that the openness of a situation to social action can only be determined or examined *ex post facto*. It would be mistaken to draw the conclusion, on grounds of the primacy of logical considerations, that arguments and considerations about the degree of closure of social action lack any priority whatsoever and are entirely without meaning for social science discourse (cf. Meja and Stehr, 1988). But what can be stated with confidence is that a discussion of the **use** of knowledge must pay attention to situationally specific factors, whatever they may be and however contested their designation might be in practice, for they result in judgements which are related to both the self-definition(s) of a social context by its actors and/or to an assessment of the relative openness of structure and constraints as judged from a somewhat greater distance, for example, when examined by social science.

The fundamental question about the demand and the assessment of the adequacy or relevance of (additional) knowledge, produced in one context but employed in another one, now can be formulated to pertain to the **relation between knowledge and the local conditions of action**. And, if certain constraints and conditions of action in the context of application are apprehended as somehow open, the very demand for social science knowledge should be seen as prompted, driven and linked to these open conditions of action.

A brief example may serve as a first illustration of the basic question one may raise about all knowledge claims generated by social science. A rather common knowledge claim central to a number of theoretical traditions within sociology states that the degree of urbanization is closely related to the birth rate or the divorce rate. But such a knowledge claim does not pertain, in all likelihood, to conditions which are open to action. Even powerful politicians in a centralized state, concerned about reversing a decline in the birth rate or an increase in the divorce rate would consider such a claim highly irrelevant because the degree of urbanization is hardly an 'open' attribute or dimension even within their context of action. But that does not mean that the same context of action is void of attributes and conditions which are, in some sense, open and may in fact influence the rates under discussion. However, as we will see, these conditions may well have a much lower theoretical or disciplinary legitimacy.

Coleman (1972b) has suggested that 'discipline research' knows but two types of variables, 'independent' and 'dependent' dimensions of social action while social 'policy research' must attend to three classes of variables. There are 'policy outcomes', 'policy variables' and 'situational variables'. The latter are part of the circumstances of action and cannot be effected by it, while 'policy variables' correspond to what I have called attributes of action open to certain actors in a specific social context. Social policy research then is propelled by a consideration of 'policy variables', or begins with a problem that is formulated outside the discipline but is executed within it (Coleman, 1972b).

With the idea in mind that the use of social science knowledge pertains to the relation between knowledge and situationally determined conditions of action which may be, moreover, relatively open or fixed, I return to the literature concerned with the application of social science knowledge.

Previous discussions reflecting upon the relations between knowledge and the context of application, though few discussions addressing issues of 'applied social science' are directly concerned with this interrelation, allow us to distinguish a weak from a much stronger stipulation.

The **weak** (but more often ambivalent) stipulation that social science research somehow needs to be **oriented** toward, and coordinated with, the context of application may be found as advice for applied social science research in a number of sources (e.g. Freeman, 1963:150; Gans, [1971] 1975; Nowotny, 1975; Thomas and Tymon, 1982).[13] However, much of this type of advice is directed toward marketing gimmicks aimed, for example, at improving the **receptivity** for social science knowledge.

The **strong** stipulation, in contrast, may be found, at least implicitly, in the discussions of a few social scientists about the preconditions for the manufacture of practical knowledge. This stipulation states that the degree to which dimensions of action are subject to the control of actors should become a **criterion for selecting** 'variables' for social research and therefore should enter the construction of social science knowledge. Alvin Gouldner (1957:96), for example, reflecting about the criteria which govern the selection of 'independent variables' in applied and basic social research, comments: 'The applied social scientist inspects his independent variables to determine the extent to which they are accessible to control' (see also Dubin, 1976:37; Rossi, Wright and Wright, 1978:174; Cook, 1981:266). Similarly, one of the many but (from a theoretical point of view) uninformative empirical studies about the use of social science knowledge,[14] reports that the degree to which 'variables' are perceived as subject to manipulation or as having an 'action orientation' can affect the response to such social science knowledge as knowledge for action (Weiss, 1978:28–30; Weiss and Weiss, 1981:841).[15]

The perhaps most comprehensive and insightful theoretical and empirical analysis among adherents of the strong stipulation (which asserts that 'applied sociology' should follow rules for the construction of knowledge based on the considerations directly pertaining to the context of application) is Scott and Shore's comprehensive search for the reasons for the apparent failure of much of sociological research (1974;1979), though explicitly oriented toward policy purposes, to produce useful knowledge for **national public policy** in the United States. 'Useful' for Scott and Shore means that policy-makers pay thoughtful attention to sociological ideas and actually employ sociological concepts in attempts at solving the issues under discussion. Scott and Shore recognize that there are numerous other conceptions of the 'use' of sociological knowledge, some difficult to examine empirically. But given their definition of utilization, Scott and Shore's conclusion is that the main source of the widespread practical irrelevance of much applied sociology for policy-makers is related to the execution of such work within disciplinary rather than policy frames of mind. In other words, 'much of the research done by sociologists for purposes of governmental policy is, in fact, nothing more than conventional sociological research on practical problems in fields of applied work' (Scott and Shore, 1979:49). Policy research which would be germane and relevant must, in contrast, 'begin and end with policy concerns' (Scott and Shore, 1979:215). That is, social science knowledge is, for the most part, evaluated by policy-making bodies on the basis of the '**political feasibility**' of the implied changes. Scott and Shore (e.g. 1979:205) assume that the social conduct of corporate actors can reasonably be distinguished into means and purposes of social action and that a more policy-oriented applied sociology would proceed, first, from an improved understanding of the actual policy process to a production of knowledge which, secondly, directly addresses and pertains to that context.

Research would focus on dimensions of social action which are malleable, though the discovery of actionable 'dependent variables', or 'policy variables' (cf. Coleman, 1972b:5), is by no means a simple task (cf. Scott and Shore, 1974:52). At the present time, however, knowledge about the policy context, especially of its enduring features, among social scientists is rather limited and often based on idealized notions about planning and bureaucracy in public administration and politics. The common pattern of legislative enactment in the United States, for example, is 'piecemeal, incremental and disjointed' (Scott and Shore, 1979:208); as a rule, the changes that are feasible, at any given time, will be relatively minor. Changes will be incremental because of the constraints of the political process; however, change is also incremental because the policy process is a kind of self-correcting process. Changes generate related changes. The topics, issues and questions which may be raised with any hope for implementation must be, under these circumstances, less comprehensive, daring and perhaps interesting because they have to mesh with the contingencies of the policy process.

Concrete examples of the kind of interconnected questions which surface with regularity at various points in the deliberations to enact legislation are the matter of policy **goals**, **coverage**, **financing**, **administration**, **equity** and **time frame** of the program which could be enacted. In short, a better understanding of the contingencies of the policy process would enable social researchers to 'tailor' policy-oriented research, using proper procedures and tools, to these situational constraints, and do so even in advance of the predictable course of legislative deliberations.

In addition to the dimension enumerated by Scott and Shore, a further constraint upon the employment of social research in planning and political action derives from the discordant tempo of social inquiry and political decision-making (cf. Coleman, 1972b). That is, even if knowledge takes account of the special circumstances of the potential user, a dual temporal disjuncture between research and policy-formation may develop.

Under many circumstances, political decision-making is urgent, and out of step with the slow pace of social research. Urgency, the need to act and get on with things, can rightly be seen as one of the constitutive properties of the 'logic of practice', while scientific action transcends the temporality of social action and even considers it a virtue to do so (cf. Bourdieu, 1980; Stehr and Baldamus, 1983). Research can also generate troubling policy issues which public policy is slow to recognize as issues of public concern (cf. Merton, 1949; 1975:163). None the less, Scott and Shore's careful diagnosis of the shortcomings of applied social science driven by structured traditions and concerns within social scientific disciplines, strengthens the case for an 'applied sociology of knowledge' that must 'take note of such structurally patterned differences of what constitutes adequate evidence' (Merton, 1975:165), and more generally of conceptions and ways of constructing as well as assessing 'adequate knowledge claims' in social science and for social practice.

Conclusions analogous to Scott and Shore's findings about the desirability and the ways to develop practical social science knowledge, may be found in a study concerned with the 'usefulness' of the research organization which is part of the US Forest Service. David Lingwood (1979:361) concludes that the practical success of research and development projects appears to improve, once 'the knowledge-creation process is seen as a **response** to client needs as part of an overall problem-solving effort'. The results of this particular study do not, however, support such a thesis directly. The author focused not on the cognitive attributes of social science knowledge but exclusively on the personal and organizational conditions of relevant research. Nor can one infer with assurance from this inquiry whether the perception that research could be useful affects the evaluation of research results and the response to particular studies. But an empirical study by Carol H. Weiss (1980) designed to obtain information about the use of research findings in psychiatry indicates that client perceptions that results can somehow be implemented are positively related to perceptions of research as useful in practice.[16] Weiss (1980:57–91) also stresses that the professional competence of potential users of social science knowledge, in the context of application, in this case higher civil servants, apparently is not really a factor in the assessment of the usefulness of the judged research. But, then, the professional competence of the user need not, in any systematic way, be related to the openness of action components in practical situations.

And as illustrated by a comprehensive analysis of the failure of policy-makers of the World Bank, charged with allocating investment capital to promote economic development in less-developed countries, to employ an up-to-date methodology of 'social benefit-cost analysis' designed to determine investment policy and developed with the help of the advice of expert economists and consultants, because the 'model' was based on a view of the 'problem' which did not correspond to that of the policy-makers at the World Bank (Leff, 1988),[17] the sophistication of the research does not ensure its use in practice.

Finally, to conclude the brief review of analogous theoretical reflections and empirical findings toward an alternative, general model of application, Riecken (1969:110) has stressed, using the language of social research, that 'by fixing attention upon variables about which no action can be taken most sociologists provide theoretical and explanatory structures that have neither interest nor promise for the social problem-solver because he cannot use them as handles or levers'. As long as accounts or explanations, offered as the result of social science research, for example of deviant behavior or political preferences, mainly take recourse to variables such as childhood experiences, class position, age, gender, SES, ethnic background, educational attainment etc., one really should not be too surprised to discover that accounts which employ these attributes are widely perceived as irrelevant because it is virtually impossible, at least within a socially and politically feasible time, to influence these factors, let alone 'control' or 'manipulate' them in order to achieve a change in the observed phenomena. In fact, they cannot be controlled. Knowledge about the variation of political preferences by gender will be more than remote in efforts to reverse such preferences. Explanations and accounts which rely on what are mostly ascribed attributes inadvertently contribute to a reified perception of social relations. Thus, as Zaltman (1979:103) observes, if there 'is one factor that more than any other distinguishes successful from unsuccessful planned social change programs, it is a strong user orientation in which change agents and clients engage in an active exchange or transaction process' (also Lazarsfeld and Reitz, 1975:83–6).[18]

The social science literature generally and writings in the area of the methodology of the social sciences, scarcely contain any useful information about the identification and use of attributes of social action which may be open in specific situations, or are perceived by the relevant group of actors as open to their control. For example, when Lieberson (1985:227), in his recent critique of prevalent practices in social research, urges that 'there is a need for knowledge about a basic cause that is sufficiently strong to overcome the existing entropy and, of course, that will change the outcome in the direction desired', he does not provide the sympathetic researcher with any useful hints about how such a contribution to policy questions might be achieved in social research.

Within much of social science discourse, the decision about the factors or attributes to be selected as objects of theoretical reflection and empirical study is, as a rule, dependent on disciplinary traditions. The selection or choice of factors for data collection and analysis which are subject to control in practical situations becomes a matter of mundane theories, but, in contrast to scientific discourse, especially a question of the relative power of actors, *their* resources and resolve within *their* settings and with respect to the environment which also affects *their* context of action.

The fact is that many economic theories fail to address the question of power, resources and features of economic action beyond the control of the specific corporate actors. Indeed, economic discourse has eliminated such considerations as a matter of disciplinary reasoning, constituting, for some economists at least, an explanation of the relative practical impotence of economic theorizing (e.g. Rothschild, 1971). In other words, economists often seem to assume that virtually all factors which form part of their theoretical models are somehow open to action or that the ability of actors to engage in certain forms of economic action is more or less the same.

A critique of such a focus therefore speaks of an end of a cognitive focus within economics which more than fifty years ago still gave Karl Mannheim reasons to praise it as exemplary for the social sciences. Intellectual development in economics is, as Mannheim (1932:43) then observed, particularly advanced, compared to some of the other social science disciplines, as a result of the fact that it progresses from two poles simultaneously, namely theory and practice, and that both are transformed as the result of such reciprocal considerations.

Finally, I would like to repeat that some of the basic ideas which lead to a model of application radically opposed to the model of instrumentality can already be found in observations among the classical sociologists. Mannheim's notion of a 'political knowledge' is programmatic in this instance, though it really was not developed satisfactorily.

But one also finds observations in Simmel's essays on the structure of modern culture which appear quite suggestive and helpful. Simmel (1919:247) refers to the increasing production of superfluous scientific knowledge. What he has in mind is an increasing growth in the volume of knowledge which displays quite closely the abstract standards of science but which none the less is alien to the 'real' purpose of scientific research. The alienated and superfluous scientific knowledge Simmel has in mind is knowledge which is somehow useless with respect to specific 'external' purposes. It is knowledge which is largely meaningless in terms of certain intellectual and cultural purposes. Among the prerequisites for the possibility of the manufacture of such useless knowledge are a supply of scientific talent, an immense output of work by a growing pool of scientists, and a largely in-house evaluation of scientific results which amounts practically to a kind of conspiracy among scientists. Simmel observes that an emphasis on methodological achievements, on stringency in particular, results in the fetish-like character of scientific knowledge. The scientific value of research is presumably assured once a specific method finds application. An analogous situation may be observed in the world of art. As long as technical ability is somehow recognized as good enough, an artist may well be able to ignore the 'general purpose of art' (Simmel, 1919:248). Both developments are manifestations of a nearly universal 'tragedy of culture' in modern societies, in which means are substituted or are mistaken for ends and become independent from their creators, only to resist a subsequent personal re-integration.

Correspondence versus identity

The general criteria for the model of application which so far has only been sketched do not necessarily imply that a social science knowledge which is, in its development, driven by hopes of being useful and considerations of the contingent context of use, results in a mere duplication or 'doubling' of the practical situation. In the case of a pragmatic social science, such knowledge, in the end, does not and cannot become identical with the political system, for example, nor does power fully determine what constitutes adequate practical knowledge.

In the case of modern society, any analytical model which assumes the hegemony or subordination of particular societal institutions, be it science or the state, and therefore postulates for example that the state is virtually dependent on scientific knowledge, produced in the fully autonomous scientific community, must be rejected as wholly inadequate (cf. Furner and Supple, 1990b). Terms such as contingency, competition and interdependence constitute a much more realistic and powerful perspective. Thus, social science knowledge which aims to incorporate dimensions of social action which are open, could well be a form of critical knowledge because as knowledge in action it is likely to contribute to changes in the context of application.

It is possible that a kind of 'practical dialectical process' (*Realdialektik*), as Mannheim calls is, develops between science and practical situations which leaves neither theory nor practice intact (see Mannheim ([1929] 1936:112). The practical dialectical process signifies that 'we cannot calculate *a priori* what a thing should be like and what it will take . . . The dialectical relationship between theory and practice consists in the fact that, first of all, theory arising out of a definite social impulse clarifies the situation. And in the process of clarification reality undergoes a change. We thereby enter a new situation out of which a new theory emerges.' One of the decisive features of Mannheim's characterization of the reciprocal and dynamic interrelationship between theory and practice is that knowledge is produced with respect to a certain situation and not merely with a view to conforming to certain internal methodological standards and theoretical concerns. Moreover, practical knowledge can change a situation which then requires, in turn, a fresh examination of the same social context etc.

But the manufacture of such critical knowledge requires, it goes without saying, a flexible approach to methodology, data collection and analysis as well as theory.[19] For Mannheim, what counts above all is the next concrete step and political thought which illuminates a specific situation, not merely acting and doing.

In other words, a strict correspondence between forms of knowledge and language in social science and practical situations is neither possible nor desirable. For example, Blume (1978:46) has suggested that the 'deliberate utilization of social scientific knowledge will depend upon the extent to which a particular social scientific orientation seems to be in accordance with a given policy-orientation (or paradigm)'. The requirement for such a duplication of premises of social science knowledge and knowledge in practical contexts is not only unrealistic but also dysfunctional. Gouldner (1957:95) argues that it is necessary for applied social science research to translate its conceptional apparatus, and not merely some of its research tools, into the language of everyday life to ensure that its research findings will resonate with existing ideological conceptions. In other words, the translation of social scientific language into everyday language is a necessary preliminary step for the application, especially if 'use' is defined as use within the context of discursive practices (cf. Lau and Beck, 1989:29). But in the end, there is the danger that identity of one form of knowledge meshes with the identity of another, and is therefore lost. If one were to take such demands and advice seriously, then the lament that certain forms of social science knowledge not only duplicate everyday knowledge but also legitimize the status quo, would be quite an appropriate criticism of social science.

Moreover, if one chooses to mirror the apprehended structure and consciousness of concrete situations in social research as accurately as possible, then one necessarily is confined, with all its consequences, to a context of social action which is for the most part fixed and closed. For the typical mundane portrait of social life tends to be one which describes and assesses it and its own role in this context as immutable. Therefore, even from the point of aiming for comprehensiveness, one could argue, it would be better to search for and focus on social action dimensions which are open and not reified by the actors.

In contrast to technological systems, constructed outside the laboratory often with a view to maximizing elements and processes which are fixed or closed to intervention and which clearly highlight elements of the situation subject to manipulation to achieve a desired effect, in 'natural' social situations it is often difficult to diagnose those factors which are fixed and those which are open. But this does not mean that a designation of factors as open is virtually impossible, as Hoos (1969:14) for instance seems to suggest: 'In the social sphere, the crucial elements often defy definition and control and do not behave according to a set of rules.' What is crucial to practical knowledge is not necessarily an identification of the 'crucial' elements, for example, in the sense of orthodox data analysis, namely of elements explaining the greatest variance, but the identification of elements which can be affected in some way and therefore can make a difference.

The openness of conditions of action, the extent to which situational factors can be manipulated and the availability of resources, including knowledge for action, is not only a matter of intellectual work and the transparency of the context but also a question of the concrete ability of actors to change and of the costs associated with any transformations. It might well be one of the most critical functions of knowledge as a capacity for action to illuminate the context in a way which allows actors to apprehend that certain factors and conditions of action in fact are under their control. It is a legitimate function of social science to examine existing interpretations of social reality; it may even be the purpose of sociology, as René König (1979:362) has indicated, that sociological knowledge contributes to an extension of collective consciousness and therefore to an improvement in the degree of understanding in practical circumstances.[20]

Similarly, William Foot Whyte's (1982) program for the discovery, description and analysis of **social inventions** may be seen to constitute another example of social research which is closely attuned to the practicalities of specific social contexts, yet is by no means merely engaged in efforts to faithfully duplicate the status quo of such situations.[21] At the same time, one should not underestimate the practical difficulties of advocating social inventions; as Rossi (1987:75) reminds us, the 'ruling paradigms of social problems are difficult to upset because existing programs are often based upon them, and new paradigms might upset current organizational forms and procedures'.

That social science also is able to differentiate, perhaps even arbitrate, as Offe (1977) more optimistically maintains, between competing interpretations of social reality, would appear to be a somewhat dubious proposition, at least if formulated in such an ambivalent yet authoritative manner. The practical-political outcome of such a promise might well be that the social sciences create expectations which they will not be able to satisfy. It is difficult to imagine that the social sciences will be capable of adjudicating competing interpretations of social reality and of gaining assent for the outcomes of such labor. Excessive and unrealistic claims can only add to a lack of public credibility.

A pragmatic social science, it seems to me, reduces the degree of differentiation between social science discourse and mundane accounts, but it does not altogether eliminate it. The difference between science and politics for example will not vanish as the result of programmatic claims about practical knowledge and how best to construct such knowledge in social science. The differentiation will persist, even if these claims about practical knowledge are executed successfully. It certainly makes a difference whether the contingencies of social action are the object of analysis or the basis for social action (cf. Beck and Bonss, 1989a:9). Even a pragmatic social science cannot dispose of the need to engage in, and subsequently to carry out, such an analysis, in an attempt to reach understandings based on everyday communicative practices and in the context of situational contingencies of social action. A kind of authoritarian or 'scientistic' conception of science may claim that scientific and practical solutions to practical problems are identical. Extreme demands and optimistic claims such as these indicate, however, that the intellectual relationship between science and external social institutions is also a matter of the political attitude of scientists and the scientific community. Social scientists must maintain distance while displaying interest and concern for situation-specific issues of individual and corporate actors in order to help bring about a measure of practical understanding.[22]

Social science knowledge which does not aspire to displace and be a substitute for cognitive practices and ideas in everyday life almost instantly and fully, also does not pretend to be able to offer knowledge for action which can be translated into action virtually unchanged and unmediated, as the model of instrumentality appears to promise. Social science knowledge does not become effective in practice without any accommodation. The mediation between context of production and context of application in all cases, needs to be **accomplished** by individual or corporate actors. The work of individuals, for example, critical self-reflection and interaction in practical situations, is not displaced and cannot be eliminated in principle (cf. Ulrich, 1987:332). Nor is it possible for social science knowledge to somehow remove the peculiar contingencies of practical situations (cf. Dahrendorf, 1989:8) which affect its implementation.

A mere duplication of societal knowledge by social science conversely implies that social science knowledge becomes 'socialized', that is, that the boundaries between forms of knowledge vanish almost completely with the result that the knowledge of social science is replaced by everyday knowledge and by the knowledge of corporate actors. Mies (1986:11), for example, observes, though he does not produce any evidence, that contemporary West German social science is governed by criteria of relevancy, topics of research and research strategies which are generated and determined by political processes and actors rather than by social science itself. The cognitive differentiation of social science requires socio-structural support. The practical success of social science depends also on the social differentiation of a pragmatic social science. Social scientific reflection about social problems has its own dynamic *vis-à-vis* the social condition and the interests which may have prompted reflection and study in the first place. Inquiry is self-propelled and therefore has a measure of intellectual independence if such reflection is able to draw on a repertoire of cognitive traditions. There is of course always the danger that the agenda of individual and corporate actors outside of social science, especially in the case of applied work, can influence, even dominate the agenda. The model of instrumentality does not offer any special provisions and protection to exclude such possibilities. But it is doubtful whether influence in setting the agenda in terms of researchable issues means simultaneously that external actors also can influence the conceptual apparatus, the methods of data collection and analysis, and the interpretation of findings. Any direct political influence on the intellectual agenda of social science requires a political context for social science in which autonomy and independence are threatened by force. In countries where a junta, the government or a powerful political élite initiates and sanctions social science research, any differentiation between social science knowledge and the ruling ideology may indeed vanish (cf. Lubasz, 1981). The model of instrumentality offers, under these circumstances, no protection whatsoever. It may even be justified to serve those in power and claim to do so without compromising ethical standards. But in societies in which the capacity of corporate actors to enforce their will is limited, this danger is little more than a potential danger. Thus, the question whether modern industrial societies are increasingly characterized by a 'powerlessness of politics'[23] becomes a highly relevant issue. As always, the nature of the historical context makes a difference, in this instance as well.

The specific relationship between knowledge and the situationally contingent social factors which ought to be achieved in the construction of practical knowledge perhaps can best be described as a **pragmatic** correspondence rather than a **logical** relation.[24] In contrast to the model of instrumentality, therefore, a general model of application stresses a kind of active as well as contingent connection between context of manufacture and application of knowledge. The 'solution' to application cannot be forced or built in with any certainly found *a priori* in the production of social science knowledge but must be recovered again and again. After all, social science knowledge is merely a capacity for action and not identical with social action. One simply cannot even assume with any confidence that social science knowledge will in fact be **perceived** as relevant, and such assurance is lacking even once research is conducted with the contingencies of specific social contexts in mind. But what may be said with some confidence is that the chance that social science knowledge will be considered irrelevant grows with the differentiation of the social sciences from other societal institutions unless accidental circumstances and developments transcend such alienation.[25] Social science knowledge largely generated on the basis of disciplinary traditions may acquire social significance as the result of largely fortuitous circumstances and, in addition, on the basis of considerable effort by social scientists. As Gunnar Myrdal (1972:357) for example notes, when 'we want our ideas and knowledge translated into action for the welfare of society we have therefore, first, to convince our colleagues, so that we can form a fairly united front and, second, to win the support in the lay society for the social reforms that can embody our inventions'. Social science knowledge may even become quite powerful, for example as an ideological current in society. As indicated, I will discuss Helmut Schelsky's lament about the inordinate influence of social science generally and sociology in particular on the collective consciousness of modern society in a separate section.

Social science cannot be assured, however, that its ideas will achieve such intellectual authority in society with ease and certainty. Moreover, such ideological effects will occur without any control about the nature of its influence being exercised by social scientists. It is unlikely that social scientists will be able to design knowledge precisely for such a 'journey' of ideas and specific impacts their views may have on the self-conception of individual and corporate actors. Disciplinary knowledge will have to contend, in any event, with competing 'lay accounts' of social reality (cf. Lammers, 1974). For example, Meehan's pessimistic view that economic theory today is without practical impact (1982:117–73), is based on the observation that economic thought is closely bound to disciplinary considerations.[26] Yet, Meehan's general assessment might well also be mistaken if (professional) economic theory, for more or less accidental, that is, unintended reasons resonates with certain practical contingencies, therefore acquiring the character of practical knowledge. Such convergence would not be by design. It does not directly or logically follow from a particular knowledge claim that it will have this or that effect on practice. Social science knowledge can indeed undermine, strengthen or shape practice (Taylor, 1983:73), but whether it will do this cannot be deduced with certainty from the knowledge itself. In any event, the subject-ive intentions of social science discourses and their objective consequences are often very much at odds (cf. Merton, 1963:87).

Georg Simmel's warnings about the growing irrelevance of science as a result of its increasing differentiation contradicts the thesis about the functionality of the growing autonomy of science or the significance of the resistance scientists have to offer against external appeals and pressures to respond to pressing public issues.

The institution of science, just like any other social institution, is inclined to defend its autonomy. In science, this autonomy finds expression in the 'free' choice of researchable issues, the auto-nomous selection of dimensions to be investigated and the absence of external constraints in the interpretation of findings. A character-istic attribute of the role of the scientist, in this context, is the **resistance** against external guidance and attempts to influence data collection and data interpretation. External controls contradict the norms of the scientific community (cf. Merton, 1963:88). As a result, scientists appear to favor basic research inasmuch as such research best symbolizes the autonomy of the scientific community. Any science policy which fails to recognize these facts, according to Merton (1963:88), runs the risk of failure from the outset.

One can take a skeptical attitude toward this kind of description of the autonomy of the scientific community and ask whether the description is not a prescription designed to postulate or to legitim-ize the autonomy of science in order to obscure the fact that a defense of the autonomy of the scientific community has multiple functions. It is doubtful that autonomy breeds objectivity and objectivity ensures practicality. Nor is it evident that the extent of the societal steering of science, including unintended forms of control, the control of its resources and personnel, even in democratic societies, is adequately represented in this conception. None the less, Merton's reflections make evident that one cannot simply dismiss the possible resistance of scientists and science against attempts to influence intellectual priorities, and, therefore, the loss of cognitive autonomy within science. Any conception of a pragmatic social science will have to face the question of the dialectics of intellectual independence and dependence in matters of establishing a new relation between theoretical knowledge and practice.

At this point, I will not develop the various implications of this position in any detail; however, it needs to be emphasized, since it might be concluded from what has been said so far that contemporary social science is condemned to be largely irrelevant and ineffective, that this is by no means the case. Social science knowledge is only severely limited in its practical efficacy if one confines one's conception of what is efficacious to the restrictive notions propagated by the model of instrumentality. Social science may well be most effective in practice in the form of knowledge which functions in the first instance as a means of practical **orientation** and **interpretation**. None the less, the exact manner and therefore the precise degree of influence the social sciences may have today in different countries as a source of social meaning, that is, as a mode of public orientation and justification, is very difficult to estimate empirically and to assess with any precision and certainty (cf. Giesen, 1983; Beck and Bonss, 1984; Lau, 1984:427).[27] In other words, the demand for social science knowledge by certain groups and in certain contexts can occur in the form of a demand for interpretative 'knowledge' and not merely for rational-instrumental forms of knowledge. The demand for knowledge is not necessarily restricted to information about means of action for predetermined goals.[28] Social scientists have (as often very visible language-users, cf. Schelsky, 1975; Tenbruck, 1984; Gergen, 1986:153–5) a considerable influence on the cultural and symbolic repertoires of a society. Sociological language has affected public discourse as well as numerous specialized intellectual communities and disciplines in many countries (cf. Bressler, 1967).

Keynes himself was convinced that ideas can carry a great deal of authority and influence. He suggests that history may well be written as the history of economic concepts and the ideas of political philosophers: 'The ideas of economists and political philosophers, both when they are right and when they are wrong, are more powerful than is commonly understood. Indeed the world is ruled by little else' (1936:383). One might of course in turn suggest that Keynes's views display excessive doses of self-confidence, a vice not all that rare among intellectuals and scientists, but Keynes's notion that the societal authority of ideas may be independent of their professional certification is worth examining and has, moreover, some interesting predecessors in the history of ideas.

Practical knowledge

It is desirable, as already indicated in my earlier discussion of knowledge as a 'capacity for action', to distinguish between 'practical knowledge' (or, knowledge for action) and 'knowledge which has been translated into action' since the practical relevance of knowledge does not itself determine whether knowledge for action becomes knowledge in action.

If one follows, in this context, the strategic insights of Karl Mannheim, whose goal was a 'scientific politics', it becomes evident that reflections about the 'use' of knowledge in social contexts of application require an understanding of the fact that one does not encounter in such (practical) realms something akin to a theoretical, distancing attitude toward social action nor, the conditions for the possibility to take on such a contemplative perspective. Constitutive of practical situations, the context of application is always an essential **meshing** of interest, evaluation, worldviews and the product of thought ('*Willensimpuls, Wertung und Weltanschauung*' and '*Denkergebnis*'; cf. Mannheim [1929] 1936:143) and the pressure to get on with things. Mannheim ([1929] 1936:150) explicates these observations about the relations between interests, worldviews and knowledge in practical-political[29] circumstances by suggesting that such contexts require a special type of knowledge, namely **practical knowledge**. That is, in the realm of politics,

> in which everything is in process of becoming and where the collective element in us, as knowing subjects, helps to shape the process of becoming, where thought is **not contemplation** from the point of view of a spectator, but rather the active participation and reshaping of the process itself, **a new type of knowledge** [emphasis added] seems to emerge, namely a knowledge in which **decision and standpoint** are inseparably bound up together. In these realms, there is no such thing as a purely theoretical outlook on the part of the observer. It is precisely an actor's purposes that give him his vision, even though his interests only partially illuminate that segment of the totality in which he himself is enmeshed, and toward which he is oriented by virtue of his essential social purposes.[30]

It is quite evident that Mannheim stipulates for the project of practical knowledge a linkage between worldviews, interests, evaluation, contextual contingencies etc. and knowledge claims which do not merely enter into the equation in the way social science knowledge 'enters' the context of application; Mannheim sees such a linkage as occurring earlier, namely at the point of the manufacture of social science knowledge that aims to become practical knowledge. Thus, the differentiation Mannheim proposes between types of knowledge does not just amount to a reiteration of the orthodox stipulation of a gap between the production of scientific knowledge and its practical implementation as a means of social action in situations in which the purposes of action already are or will be determined virtually independent of social science knowledge claims. That Mannheim is interested in depicting and developing a structured relationship between knowledge and politics already becomes evident by virtue of his designation of 'ideologies' or 'worldviews' as a form of knowledge, as political knowledge or as 'active knowledge for orientation' (*'aktivem Orientierungswissen'*). Mannheim views these means of action orientation as a special type of knowledge which differs, in a number of respects, from 'theoretical' knowledge. At the same time, these unique attributes of political knowledge produce, for example, its special effectiveness as knowledge for action. As a result there cannot be a linear transformation of knowledge into practical knowledge and then into knowledge in action. Knowledge has to be linked to the value-laden situational environment. The transformation of knowledge for action into knowledge in action requires, according to Mannheim, that theoretical knowledge takes on features which constitute the conditions for practical knowledge as a special type of knowledge. This means that theoretical knowledge needs to be **re-attached** to the social context; its relations to situational interests, purposes and worldviews, from which it had been detached for the purposes of theoretical reflection, must be re-established. Various attempts to establish a structured relationship between politics and knowledge obviously will differ markedly as to the concepts and issues which appear to be central, as to the approaches which might be adequate, and as to the criteria for correct answers to the questions raised.

Economic knowledge

> Our final task might be to select those variables which can be deliberately controlled or managed by central authority in the kind of system in which we actually live.

> John Maynard Keynes (1936:247)

The practical economic lessons drawn from Keynesian economic theory constitute a 'system of political control over economic life' (Skidelsky, 1979:55). More specifically, a careful reading of the *General Theory* shows clearly that Keynes explicitly tried to devise practically sound answers for economic problems which were constructed with a certain corporate actor in mind: the British Treasury.

Keynes's theory is above all characterized by the fact that it consciously stresses the importance of only a few **aggregate** quantities of the national economy. But on the basis of these dimensions, it is possible to point to the decisive determinants of the employment level, or to the conditions which **set** (un)employment **in motion**. More precisely, Keynes is concerned with the annual total or aggregate production of goods and services of the economy, the aggregate demand for these goods and services and the aggregate income which can be distributed and which forms the basis for aggregate investments and demand. The determinants of the employment level can then be ascertained on the basis of these aggregate quantities. In other words, Keynes stipulates a relation between the national income level and employment; the relation is mediated by **five** endogenous and **one** exogenous economic variables. In addition, the analysis is based on a number of mostly static assumptions which, taken together, indicate that Keynes's theory surely cannot claim anything approaching 'completeness' or 'comprehensiveness' in reflecting the intricate empirical nature of national economic relations.[31] If the propensity for consumption (or the ability to consume) and the readiness of entrepreneurs to invest are insufficient to use national economic resources to the fullest extent, and if both cannot be expected to rise in light of the prevailing economic data, the state should step in and stimulate the economy with additional expenditures.

As a rule, additional state expenditures have to be financed by the central bank or by way of money raised in the capital market because a tax increase, the other potential source for additional revenue, would result in a decline of demand and therefore achieve the opposite effect. But an economic policy committed to these means implies, in the anticyclical case, that the goal of the balanced budget has to be sacrificed and since a continuation of compensatory state spending incurs a continually rising indebtedness, it is not surprising that proponents of 'solid' and carefully drafted budgets have always resisted those policies supported by Keynes (cf. Spahn, 1976:216).

In contrast to the occasionally vigorous opposition of economists and politicians to state intervention, especially in the United States, it is precisely an **activist** conception of economic policies of the state which is a characteristic feature of Keynesian economic policies. Keynes (1936:379) even refers to the necessity of greatly expanding the traditional functions of the state in order to secure full employment. In a significant passage from his *General Theory*, Keynes discusses in broad terms the propensity to invest and suggests that 'in conditions of *laissez-faire* the avoidance of wide fluctuations in employment may . . . prove impossible without a far-reaching change in the psychology of investment markets such as there is no reason to expect. I conclude that the duty of ordering the current volume of investment cannot safely be left in private hands' (1936:320). In other words, the fundamental presupposition, in direct contrast to neoclassical theory as well as the currently favored monetarism, that the state is capable of constructively intervening in the economy, becomes a taken-for-granted feature of his theory and Keynesian economic policies. However, such compensatory state activity today is no longer readily accepted because the so-called self-healing abilities of markets are again emphasized by many economists and politicians. As a result, the primary economic function of the state is seen to concern policies which protect competition and the free market.

In the following section I will show how Keynes's theoretical conceptions meet ideological and socio-structural conditions, that is, either resonate or fail to converge with such circumstances of action which make it probable that such a perspective will be translated into economic policies or not. The aim therefore is not to demonstrate that Keynes has an intellectual monopoly and priority for state interventionist economic policies. Indeed, a variety of politicians and economists before and after Keynes, without referring to him, advocated such action by the state in favor of specific social classes and economic goals.[32] But quite independent of the question of the intellectual genesis of certain ideas and any priority disputes, the problematic at issue here requires us to discover indications that a particular theoretical perspective incorporates social conditions which are actionable. Such resonance between theory and practice should not be mistaken to signal that a particular theoretical conception is **logically** implicated or that it has been established empirically without doubt that certain processes and subsequent developments can only be the result of such a linkage or parentage. As a rule, societal conditions rarely if ever allow for such definitive responsibility of ideas. But this is by no means reason for despair. On the contrary, one has to be aware of the virtue that society is quite resistant in this regard.

The state as entrepreneur

In 1929, unemployment in England stood (and remained unchanged for a decade) at approximately 1,500,000 million and was about to reach the 10 per cent level (see figure 4.1). The rate of unemployment became, not surprisingly, an important political issue in England and figured prominently in the parliamentary campaign of the Liberal and Conservative political parties. The Liberals, under the leadership of Lloyd George, promised in a March 1929 political manifesto that, should they assume the role of government, they would reduce unemployment to a 'normal level' by way of a government-financed program to create employment, especially in the field of transportation and housing. The programme was opposed by the governing Conservative Party. Lloyd George had already supported such a platform for economic initiatives of the state in 1924. The official government position at the time was equally clear. As Winston Churchill expressed it so forcefully in his 1929 budget speech, 'it is orthodox Treasury dogma, steadfastly held, that whatever might be the political or social advantages, very little additional employment can, in fact, and as a general rule, be created by State borrowing and expenditure' (see Winch, 1972:111).

Keynes participated in the public debate following the election promises of the Liberals. In a campaign flyer, written in collaboration with Hubert Henderson, Keynes ([1929] 1984)[33] directly intervened in the campaign on behalf of the Liberals. He tried to justify Lloyd George's election promises and attempted to refute the arguments of his political opponents. The outcome of the election must have been quite disappointing for Keynes because the Liberals only managed to finish third. The Liberal Party, however, was able to assume the role of power broker since neither the Conservatives nor Labour won a majority of the seats. Ultimately, the Labour Party formed a minority government.

Here and in other essays written in the 1920s and early 1930s (Keynes, [1926] 1984; [1930] 1984), Keynes voices his commitment to specific economic policies in a much more insistent and explicit fashion than might be found in his more academic or scientific writings, including the *General Theory*. He argues for certain fiscal and monetary measures, in particular for an increase in government spending on the basis of either a reduction in the interest rate or an intensification of public expenditures for investment purposes.[34]

Don Patinkin (1982:200–20) has examined in detail the development of Keynes's conceptions of economic policy measures and the apparent contradictions in his economic policy recommendations. One of the foci of Patinkin's analysis is the question of when and

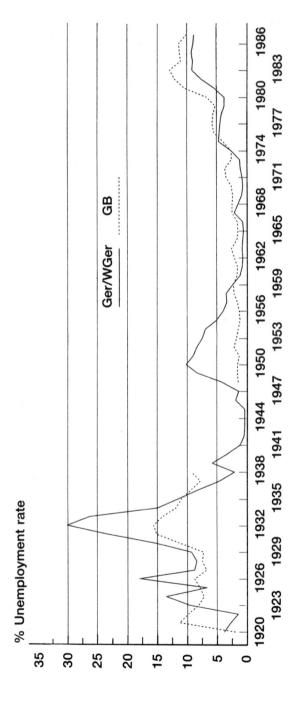

Source: Liesner (1985) and IMF International Financial Statistics

Figure 4.1   *Unemployment rate for Great Britain and Germany/West Germany, 1920–87*

why Keynes favors **monetary** over **fiscal** policies. In his *Treatise on Money* or in statements published in newspapers at the same time, Keynes recommends, in response to the prevailing economic conditions, both monetary as well as fiscal measures of the state. Patinkin does not believe that the emphasis on different policy instruments involves a contradiction. The stress on a reduction in the interest rate, on the one hand, and an expansion in state expenditures, on the other, reflects the different roles Keynes assumed at this time. In the *Treatise on Money*, he takes on the role of a 'pure' scientist and attempts to formulate 'universally' valid claims. In his interventions in the public debates of the day, however, Keynes tries to contribute, as the best-known economist of his country, ideas for the economic policy of **Great Britain** in response to her unique economic conditions (cf. Patinkin, 1982:208–9). Keynes suggests economic measures which could be enacted under these conditions and which appeared to be in the interest of the country (cf. Lekachman, 1968:65–6).

The more polemical essays of the 1920s and early 1930s and the academic writings of the same time were written, in other words, for a very different kind of audience. None the less, the explicit advocacy in these essays for economic policies designed to reduce unemployment was quite compatible with the more reserved and usually implicit policy recommendations of the more academic work. In both cases the general idea was to expand aggregate demand.

Keynes offered a straightforward, pragmatic calculation, intending to demonstrate that an increase in state expenditures and therefore the expansion in demand were in the interest of all citizens and less costly to the economy than a continuation of high unemployment. The Liberal Party had promised in its election platform to create an additional 400,000 to 500,000 jobs and calculated that the state would have to spend £1 million for each additional 5000 positions. Keynes actually considered these figures to be conservative since the indirect effects had not yet been taken into consideration. The indirect, cumulative effects, later known as the multiplier effect, of additional state expenditures should have a much greater effect on the national level of employment (Keynes, [1929] 1984:106). Additional expenditures were supposed to be financed through a public borrowing program. It was assumed that the interest to be paid would effect the budget only in a minor way.

In the context of this kind of economic advice, political questions such as, should the state become economically active at all, should the state become an entrepreneur, is inactivity or are the self-healing powers of the market insufficient to resolve the economic crisis (cf. Keynes, [1929] 1984:117–19), and do 'collective' policy measures in fact undermine the nature of the economy as a capitalist economy, move of course toward the top of the political agenda. Keynes rejected all these arguments and expectations. Neither will the capitalist economy be undermined, nor are the self-healing powers of the market sufficient to cope with recession. In the past, war was often required to lift an economy out of a deep depression. As Keynes ([1931] 1982:60) observes with a measure of resignation, 'formerly, there was no expenditure out of the proceeds of borrowing which was thought proper for the State to incur, except war. In the past, therefore, we have not infrequently had to wait for a war to terminate a major depression. I hope that in the future we shall not adhere to this purist financial attitude, and that we shall be ready to spend on the enterprises of peace what the financial maxims of the past would only allow us to spend on the devastations of war.' But beyond these fundamental factors, most of the infrastructure of society (roads, housing, communication) was owned by the state and the quality of these structures constituted a decisive resource for private business. Keynes also pointed out that credit funds raised by the state did not compete with private investment activities; on the contrary, since the profit expectation of business was lacking, the propensity to invest among entrepreneurs must be stimulated by way of a growing national income. A high level of savings is not automatically translated into significant investment activity by business. For as Keynes ([1929] 1984:123) stresses, 'the object of urging people to save is **in order** to be able to build houses and roads and the like. Therefore a policy of trying to lower the rate of interest by suspending new capital improvements and so stopping up outlets and purposes of our savings is simply suicidal.' Moreover, an expansion in the credit volume and the investment of these funds during a recession, does not automatically go hand-in-hand with an increase in inflation. The sum total of state investments and the general consequences of state economic activity changes by no means, Keynes predicts ([1926] 1984:292–3), the essential features of a capitalist economic system. Moreover, he adds, 'I think that capitalism, wisely managed, can probably be made more efficient for attaining economic ends than any alternative system yet in sight, but that in itself it is in many ways extremely objectionable' ([1926] 1984:294).

When the minority Labour government in 1931 embarked upon the opposite course of action to reduce unemployment, Keynes reacted with irony and disappointment. State expenditures were reduced; for example, teacher salaries were cut and taxes increased.

According to Keynes, such policies were destined to tragically worsen the economic situation. His appeal that 'something must take the form of activity, of doing things, of spending, of setting great enterprises afoot' (Keynes, [1931] 1984a:139) did not register and his advice was not heeded. The unemployment rate continued to increase.

Keynes changed the substance of his policy advice once more, as it became evident in the early 1930s that the rate of unemployment did not decline despite a fall in the interest rate (cf. figure 4.1). In light of the new situation, Keynes advised the government that both a fall in the interest rate and additional state expenditures were required to reduce unemployment (e.g. Keynes, [1933] 1972a:353–5). A change in Britain's foreign exchange policy assured, moreover, that such a concerted policy would not lead to a flight of capital from the country. Keynes ultimately also favored such a combination of policies in his *General Theory* (e.g. 1936:164, 378).

These episodes in the development and the reaction to Keynes's policy advice to realize certain economic goals in Britain at the end of the 1920s and the early 1930s show quite clearly that the manufacture and publication of social science knowledge do not automatically assure that such a capacity for action is in fact translated into action. The opposite seems to be true, at least in this case. One might ask, therefore, if it is possible to discern certain more general factors, factors transcending the specifics of the English political situation which might account for the disappointment and failure personally experienced by Keynes.

One could ask, for example, if the advice Keynes offered to the government, both in private and in public, to combat mass unemployment already constituted a concrete enough capacity for action or whether it still had to be translated into 'instruments', as Smith (1987) indicates, which allowed the advice to be translated into action? Perhaps it also is possible to discover other general preconditions, for example, in the form of national economic statistics which might show that Keynes's advice in fact failed to discern economic factors which properly could be influenced with the type of means available to the government of the day, and whether it was possible to gain any insights as to the likely effects of the measures? In any event, it is not surprising to see that there is little agreement on the reasons, aside from the politically motivated opposition, as to why Keynes's advice found such little acceptance in Britain at the time.

That a certain form of economic thought, in particular among the dominant circle of academic and government-based economists, in conjunction with ideological reservations, contributes to protracted

and successful resistance to alternate economic policies, and therefore forestalls the transformation of an economic doctrine into
knowledge in action, can be documented by way of the example of
the discussion of Keynesian ideas and policy recommendations
among economists and politicians in the Weimar Republic, at a
crucial juncture of its short history.[35]

During the great depression, Keynes not only engages in efforts
to persuade English politicians about the merits of his diagnosis and
therapy. In the memoirs of Heinrich Brüning, one finds a brief
account of a one-hour meeting between Keynes and the then
German chancellor Brüning on 11 January 1932 in Berlin.[36] Brüning (1970:506), who was head of the government in the Weimar
Republic from March 1930 to May 1932, recalls that Keynes tried to
convince him that the chancellor's 'propagation of an inflationary
technique stifles any reasonable fiscal policy in Germany'. Brüning
adds the observation that the audience of a lecture to the International Economic Society in Hamburg on 8 January 1932, which
carried the title 'The economic prospects 1932' (cf. Keynes,
1982:39–48) erroneously assumed that the British government
shared Keynes's economic policy prescriptions. Keynes's visit to
Hamburg and Berlin coincided with the announcement of the
German government that it would henceforth stop further repara-
tion payments.[37]

The position toward the economy favored and implemented by
Brüning, in particular the fiscal and economic policy efforts of his
government designed to operate in a pro-cyclical and deflationary
manner, corresponded closely to the interests of business but also
found support among the Social Democratic Party (Landfried,
1976). These policies reflected and were supported with vigor by the
majority of economic experts and advisors during this economic
crisis in the Weimar Republic (e.g. von Mises, 1931; Röpke, 1932;
A. Weber, 1932:169; Kroll, 1958:131–93; C.-D. Krohn, 1981:142–9;
Landmann, 1981).[38] Most economists and practitioners in Germany, just as in Britain, were confident that the 'natural healing'
powers of the market would ease the burden of chronic high
unemployment. High unemployment rates for them were the result
of excessive wages which impeded the accumulation and formation
of investment funds. Imbalance in the demand and supply of labour
ultimately should depress wages and interest rates and contribute to
a self-healing of the economy. Thus, Alfred Weber (1931:29), in a
lecture addressing the annual meeting of the *Verein für Sozialpolitik*
in September 1930 in Königsberg and devoted in part to praising the
virtues of the capitalist economic order, suggests that there is a
consensus among fellow economists. Weber observes that the

preconditions for substantial increases in investment funds can never be consumption but an injection of new capital. Unleashing consumption in fact can never, according to Weber and his colleagues, result in anything beneficial economically. On the contrary, supporters of a 'primitive theory of demand', for example certain labor union leaders in Germany, or Henry Ford, are victims of an almost tragic error which can only lead to a collapse of the economy (cf. A. Weber, 1931:32).

No economist, Alfred Weber proclaims (1931:58), who investigates this issue without prejudice and in a disinterested manner, thereby only serving the search for clarity and truth, can possibly reach, after an objective assessment of the crisis situation, the conclusion that a solution would be possible **without** a temporary reduction in the level of wages (cf. A. Weber, 1931:40). Such a conclusion implies, of course, that policies which involve borrowing of capital by the state for the purpose of relief-works are at best meaningless and, at worst, dangerous.

German economists are in virtual agreement, despite differences in worldviews and different methodological preferences, as Weber reports with pride in his lecture, that their theoretical diagnosis of the crisis and their prescriptions for policy are correct. Only marginal or eccentric members of the discipline violate the broad professional consensus. These deviant members do so out of self-evident psychological motives. But they are dangerous none the less. They are a danger to the profession and the public at large with their support of superficial and non-scientific views (A. Weber, 1931:56).

Alfred Weber's judgement is representative of the kind of expert advice from economists received by the German government toward the end of the Weimar Republic.[39] The advice strengthened Brüning's resolve to follow deflationary policies and reduce public spending as an answer to the economic crisis in general and the fear of inflation in particular.

With these goals in mind, the German government increased taxes, fees and duties, for example the income tax and the value added tax. Since these fiscal policies did not result in increased public income, expenditures were slashed broadly in order to achieve a balanced budget. The result of these measures was a kind of cumulative and self-sustained recessionary process.

When Keynes ([1932] 1982b:61) complains, at about this time, that the responsibility for widely ineffective economic policies of the state designed to combat the economic crisis must be linked to a **lack of knowledge** of economists and politicians, he undoubtedly displays a far more accurate sense of the reasons for the practical impotence of the economic policies of the day than his many skeptical critics. Keynes stresses that he continues to believe that:

> we still could, if we would, be the masters of our fate. The obstacles to recovery are not material. They reside in the state of knowledge, judgement, and opinion of those who stir in the seats of authority. Unluckily the traditional and ingrained beliefs of those who hold responsible positions throughout the world grew out of experiences which contained no parallel to the present, and are often the opposite of what one would wish them to believe today.

The effects of the opposite strategy, namely an active economic policy, were widely unknown. But such an active policy, favored by Keynes in the early 1930s, was by no means impossible in the Weimar Republic. Even foreign policy constraints would not have constituted serious obstacles to an active economic policy (e.g. Sanmann, 1965:125; Landmann, 1981:217).

The great influence of Keynesian ideas on economic policy in the United States in the wake of the 1938 recession (cf. Salant, 1989), affirms the Weimar diagnosis. This influence in the United States was further strengthened during the Second World War. After the war, Keynesian ideas were successfully exported to other Western countries by the emergent American superpower. These developments led Hirschman (1989:4) to conclude that the dissemination of economic ideas and their implementation as policy is fostered considerably if the theories are first embraced by the élite of a country. If that country happens to achieve global political influence and the élite finds occasion to disseminate these ideas, then such ideas will achieve considerable practical importance.

The policy conception Keynes advocated was characterized by its simplicity and flexibility, though different concrete policy measures were consistent with its overall thrust.[40] But Keynes's economic views and his policy conception must be distinguished from the kinds of macro-economic instruments and goals which emerged, especially in the post-war era in the United States, but none the less were widely perceived to be Keynesian ideas and policies. Keynes (1936:ix) himself describes his *General Theory* as a perspective which is much less 'based on narrow pre-conceptions than is the case for orthodox theory and can therefore be applied with greater ease to a wider range of circumstances'.[41]

Keynes's theory and policy measures advocate the intervention of the state in an effort to balance the disequilibria of the capitalist economy. Specifically, these interventions should (1) create institutional conditions which lead to lower interest rates and contribute to expectations about economic growth which in turn should stimulate investments. (2) The state should support demand by increasing public expenditures.[42] A crucial, perhaps decisive, premise of Keynes's advocacy of such economic policies is the **ability of the state to act** in the desired manner (cf. Feuer, 1954:683–4; Lindblom, 1972:3–4).

But it took some time before Keynes's ideas found acceptance and were carefully implemented in some countries. Initially, his economic policies were met with considerable skepticism among politicians, civil servants and by business. The war years and the economic consequences of the Second World War affected the outlook of politicians and economists and eventually led to a fully fledged acceptance and practice of Keynesian ideas in Britain, the United States (Full Employment Act, 1946), in West Germany (the so-called law concerning economic stability and growth, 1967), and in most other Western nations, even in the charter of the United Nations. Keynes's economic theories and the policies they inspired became the new orthodoxy (e.g. Kaldor, 1983:29–30).

Only twenty-five years later, in the 1970s, it became evident that economic policy measures inspired by Keynes to secure full employment no longer worked and economists were confronted, first, with the largely novel phenomenon of stagflation and, later, its opposite. Keynesian policies are now increasingly assumed to be inadequate in the face of new realities, and economic goals of a pre-Keynesian era, for example inflation as the basic ill of an economy and efforts to direct and control the supply of money, acquire central importance.

Even if it were possible to distinguish between a level of full employment which might be achieved with the aid of genuine Keynesian policies, a notion advanced by John Hicks (1985:23), and the residual portion of the unemployed, it remains a puzzle why the Keynesian rate of employment has constantly declined in the past two decades.

As an inspection of the information reproduced in table 4.1 about the export ratio for three selected countries indicates, one of the more dramatic consequences of the worldwide recession in the early 1930s was an enormous reduction in exports and imports. The proportion of the GNP exported has, however, rebounded and continues to increase with each passing year in the post-war era. By the mid-1980s the ratio for (West) Germany, for example had begun to approach the level of the late 1920s, while it had already exceeded it in the mid-1970s in the case of Great Britain and earlier still for the United States.

The trends reflected in the growing export ratios provide a first approximate indication of the changing ability of the state to affect the development of its economy on the basis of economic policies

Table 4.1 *Exports as a percentage of Gross National Product expressed in market prices for selected countries, 1928–84*

Year	Ger/WGer	GB	USA
1928(9)	33·24	22·75	(5·29)
1936	12·00	16·36	3·79
1950	9·33	17·55	4·41
1954	13·83	16·69	4·51
1960	16·02	17·33	5·21
1964	15·71	17·27	5·74
1970	19·91	21·55	6·49
1974	23·32	24·89	8·70
1980	23·47	27·50	10·79
1984(3)	25·19	(26·41)	(9·09)

Sources: The reported ratios for Germany/West Germany, Great Britain and the United States were computed on the basis of information found in Liesner (1985).

directed toward national developments. In other words, the effectiveness of Keynesian economic policies varies with the ability of the state to influence economic goals (cf. Feuer, 1954). For countries with high export ratios, economic policies are much less effective than in countries which generate a lower proportion of their economic wealth abroad – assuming that many of the other economic ties and effects which originate from outside the boundaries of the nation-state can be largely discarded. Of course, such an assumption is increasingly unrealistic.[43]

Modern society, as Daniel Bell (1987:2) observes, is embedded in a **world** economy, while the 'political orders are still **national**'. In other words, much of the political work and framework which attempts to respond to changes induced by global processes, for the most part, continues to be affected by national institutions and responses. In the case of multi-national organizations, especially the European Community, coordinated political efforts are designed to respond to globally induced economic changes. Yet, these developments mean that the range and the instruments of national, sovereign economic policy are reduced. Economic discourse also continues to reflects this contradiction; even a few years ago, the nation-state was always regarded as **the** most meaningful unit of economic analysis (e.g. Kuznets, 1971).[44]

A few interpreters of the work of Keynes do maintain that his *General Theory* is by no means premised on the existence of a more or less closed and therefore largely autonomous nation-state but instead has as its general reference point a global economy (e.g. Hicks, 1985:22). In the *General Theory* Keynes does not explicitly refer to international trade. However, whether such a deliberate omission can be interpreted to mean that Keynesian theorizing had as one of its primary empirical points of reference the global economy remains highly dubious.

The growing interdependence in the industrialized states of national economic developments raises the question whether such change represents a historically new configuration. An answer can perhaps be best gleaned from a comparative analysis of economic trends.

A comparison over time of the developments of certain macro-economic indicators, for example economic growth, unemployment rates or long-term interest rates, should display the following structured pattern if the thesis about a growing lack of differentiation of present economic developments is in fact accurate. Nationally unique movements in such trends, especially after the depression in the 1930s and in the aftermath of the Second World War until about the early 1960s, should diminish and, as a result, in recent decades, national macro-economic indicators increasingly ought to converge to begin to form a common pattern. The convergence should be reflected in closer and closer correlation coefficients between national economic indicators. Tables 4.2–4.4 summarize such a comparative analysis for the United States, Canada, Great Britain and Germany (West Germany). The detrended (by quadratic time trend) data for each of the four countries are used as the basis for the computation of simple correlation coefficients among pairs of countries. The reported correlations refer to three periods of time: 1920–38, 1948–62 and 1963–87.

The three periods chosen correspond to the most frequently noted broad socio-economic and socio-political eras in the literature in international economic developments among industrialized nations. If one compares the resulting correlation coefficients, first

Table 4.2 *Correlation coefficients between (detrended) growth of Gross National Product for selected countries, 1920–38, 1948–62 and 1963–87*

Countries	1920–38	1948–62	1963–87
USA/Can	−0.63	0.82	−0.05
USA/UK	0.56	−0.04	0.68
USA/Ger	−0.11	−0.52	0.59
UK/Ger	0.70	0.33	0.83
UK/Can	0.20	−0.24	−0.29
Ger/Can	0.82	−0.81	−0.60

Sources: The raw data on which this table is based as well as the sources for the information may be found in the Appendix.

Table 4.3   *Correlation coefficients between (detrended) rate of unemployment for selected countries, 1920–38, 1948–62 and 1963–87*

Countries	1920–38	1948–62	1963–87
USA/Can	0.97	0.81	0.84
USA/UK	0.56	b 0.54	0.77
USA/Ger	0.92	0.38	0.55
UK/Ger	0.73	b 0.33	0.74
UK/Can	0.68	b 0.75	0.79
Ger/Can	0.94	0.63	0.83

Sources: The raw data on which this table is based as well as the sources for the information may be found in the Appendix.

Table 4.4   *Correlation coefficients between (detrended) long-term interest rates for selected countries, 1920–38, 1948–62 and 1963–87*

Countries	1920–38	1948–62	1963–87
USA/Can	0.87	0.88	0.83
USA/UK	0.32	0.32	0.03
USA/Ger	na	b 0.56	0.38
UK/Ger	na	b 0.14	0.29
UK/Can	0.08	0.08	0.22
Ger/Can	na	b 0.48	0.26

Sources: The raw data on which this table is based as well as the sources for the information may be found in the Appendix.

for the two most recent periods which coincide with the division in the adoption and then rejection of Keynesian economic policies in most of these countries, it is possible to conclude that the comparisons appear to confirm the expected results. Aside from a small number of exceptions, the vast plurality of pairwise comparisons between the USA, Canada, Great Britain and Germany for the periods 1948–62 and 1963–87 indicate that the correlation among these major economic indicators are the highest in the present-day period.

   The data also indicate that the relatively greater 'sovereignty' – and therefore the conditions for the possible success of Keynesian economic policies – in the post-war years were perhaps to a large extent the outcome of the major dislocations brought about by the war. Such an interpretation gains plausibility as one observes the rather close correlation between certain economic developments in the USA, Canada, Great Britain and Germany between 1920 and 1938. The correlation coefficients for the level of unemployment in these countries during this period are rather substantial and as close as in the most recent observational period.

On the surface, the data summarized in tables 4.2–4.4 reflect the fact that the rather significant 'interdependence' among nations reached during the first part of this century – which was particularly high prior to the First World War – took a considerable number of years before it was re-established after the Great Depression and the Second World War. As a matter of fact, the conclusion could be reached that the degree of economic autonomy of different nation-states at the present time is even more substantial than was perhaps the case at the beginning of the century. However, such a conclusion would be a misinterpretation of the data. The reciprocal dependence of the major trading nations today is much greater than fifty years ago.

Even though the export ratio in the case of some countries still has not reached previous record levels, the structure and extent of economic interdependence among nations has grown as the underlying structural factors have changed. While the mere 'physical' dependence of one nation on other nations may in fact have declined over the past few decades, the autonomy of nations has been undermined in other significant respects (cf. Rich, 1983).

In order to demonstrate these differences in mutual dependency relations among the economies of the industrialized nations, it is necessary to examine the different flows of commodities and services, the kinds of imported and exported goods and services as well as the flow of capital and investments, the convertibility of currencies, the exchange of knowledge, patents, education, skills, inventions and, generally, the growing importance of the 'symbolic' economy, for example, of exchange and interest rate differentials. Political developments both enable and inhibit the flow of these tangible and not so tangible commodities. The growth of multinational corporations is both a motor and an expression of these developments. Production in different countries by the same firm reduces the need to export and reduces the risks associated with exports. Direct investments have the result, as Rosencrance (1987:163) stresses, that national barriers to investment opportunities produce a common interest in the success of each investment which originates in the period after the First World War.

Both the economic and the political consequences of the present interdependence of national economies is different from earlier interdependences, such as the dependence of nations as expressed in high export ratios in the decade of the 1920s. Mutual dependence forces nation-states into cooperation. Any attempt to uncouple a nation from the global economy is bound to have serious economic and political repercussions. Compartmentalized economic policies are a strategy of the past. National economic goals can paradoxically only be achieved on the basis of international coordination and integration which inevitably lead to a loss of sovereignty.

The conditions for the crisis of Keynesian economic policy

The purpose of my inquiry is not to show that the limits to effective economic policy measures which may be derived from the *General Theory* are identical with the limits of the *General Theory*. No doubt there are such limits. But there also are limits to effective economic policies which derive from a change in existing economic conditions. The 'scientific' and logical limits of Keynes's *General Theory* have been examined frequently and by competent critics (e.g. Hansen, 1952; Kaldor, 1983). My interest focuses, in contrast, on the practical opportunities offered by and the limits associated with social science knowledge as such knowledge confronts specific sociohistorical circumstances. This implies, it seems to me, that attention must center not on the internal, for example in the sense of the 'logical' or 'scientific' limits to the *General Theory* but on the 'historical', that is in the sense of the actual practical limits of Keynes's economic accounts.

For the most part, economists and others for whom these issues are relevant, for example politicians, now appear to accept the view that economic policies inspired by Keynesian economics are, under present economic conditions, especially since the mid-1960s, no longer as effective as they once were. But this general consensus about the evident practical limits of Keynesian economic policies under current economic conditions has its ambivalent features as well. There is a wide range of at times contradictory accounts designed to explain the diminished practical force of such economic policies. Among these is the suggestion that in many Western countries economists and politicians have always approached Keynes with considerable skepticism and that his economic advice has often been heeded and translated into practice only half-heartedly (e.g. Steindl, 1985:116–18). It has also been argued that Keynesian policies were 'misused' in the 1970s because their effectiveness is limited to a specific 'Keynesian situation' (cf. Schiller, 1987). Still other critics were never convinced that Keynes had produced economic ideas capable of translation into practice. Alfred Weber ([1935] 1956:42), for example, maintained his opposition to Keynes even after the war, arguing that while 'Keynes's epigones have been busy asserting that the ideas of the master represent a **general** theory of macro-economics, they also are generally responsible for the serious difficulties from which much of the free world now suffers'.

The ability of the state as any other economic actor to act effectively must be brought into relation with those dynamic factors which determine the evolution of the economy, especially economic expansion, under changing socio-political and socio-economic conditions.

As a result, the need for an alternative to classical economic theory arises, according to Keynes (1936:1), first and foremost because classical theory is inadequate in the face of changed economic conditions. Classical economic theory covers the special case of a full employment economy. It would therefore be misleading and even dangerous to apply it to the case of involuntary unemployment. To apply classical theory to changed economic conditions in fact amounts to employing Euclidian geometry in a non-Euclidian world. It is necessary to develop a non-Euclidian mathematics. Keynes assesses his own theory in these terms and expects that it will contribute to a much closer integration of theory and practice. But Keynes's own account in responding to unique socio-economic conditions is bound to be subject to 'the same fate.

Among the conditions or factors which are significant for present-day economies but figure neither in neoclassical theories nor in Keynes's theoretical program are, for example, scientific and technical developments and inventions (Freeman, 1977). While Schumpeter ([1912] 1951) stresses the significance of innovations for the expansion of the economy,[45] there is no comparable discussion of the importance of innovations in Keynes's *General Theory*.[46]

As is well known, from most vantage points and certainly from the perspective of a nation-state, technological inventions and change cannot be planned, controlled or limited. In any event, Schumpeter is convinced that Keynes's analysis only applies to a restricted and temporary set of conditions since the elimination of the dimension of technological change as a dynamic variable means the limited 'applicability of this analysis to a few years at most – perhaps the duration of the "40 months cycle" – and in terms of phenomena, to the factors that **would** govern the greater or the smaller utilization of an industrial apparatus **if** the latter remains unchanged. All the phenomena incident to the creation and change in this apparatus, that is to say, the phenomena that dominate the capitalist process, are thus excluded from consideration' (1952:283).

There can be little doubt that the limited practical relevance of Keynes's theoretical perspective, if such a restricted usefulness can indeed be demonstrated, is linked to the kinds of policy goals, especially the possibility of full employment,[47] and economic 'variables' selected by him for analysis. By the same token, limits to its effectiveness therefore are associated with the neglect of other variables or means of action. In economic discourse, the selection of specific conceptions of economic goals, dimensions of economic conduct and concrete economic indicators is governed both by intellectual concerns internal to the profession of economics, its theoretical and methodological standards and preoccupations, and by prevailing economic conditions within a primary socio-political and socio-economic context of reference, for example, the nation-state.

The Keynesian analysis does not, for example, explicitly address the question of **productivity**. On the one hand, such analysis should be expected from Keynes because productivity is widely seen as an important indicator and reference point pertaining to the supply side of economic conduct. On the other hand, the neglect of the 'productivity' dimension reflects existing economic conditions. That is, the period 1900–20 in particular saw one of the most significant improvements in productivity ever. These facts most likely gave rise to the optimistic expectation that the scarcity of economic resources which had always been emphasized in the writings of the classical economic theorists represents a much less serious limiting issue for economic conduct in modern societies than the classics thought. Drucker (1981b:10) therefore stresses that the reversal of the 'theory of productivity from one that postulated a built-in tendency towards diminishing returns to one that postulated a steady increase, was a major factor in the Keynesian "scientific revolution"' because it made the switch from 'supply-focus to demand-focus – that is, to the belief that production tends inherently to surplus rather than to scarcity'.

Among the factors which currently influence economic developments in advanced societies are well-known attributes of economic conduct and contextual constraints. While those were already regarded by Keynes as relevant, they have since been considerably transformed. An important example is the role of **expectations** of economic actors. Present-day economic actors must react immediately and much more directly to changes in economic and political conditions or, more precisely, in the assessment of such conditions by a variety of groups participating in discourse about economic affairs today. Economic conditions today are much less **robust** and recalcitrant than a few decades ago. Economic actors are consequently much more certain today that the future is uncertain and that disappointments are probably the rule. Rumors, rapid changes in sentiments and opinions, fluctuating expectations about future developments are all highly characteristic dimensions of economic affairs.[48] But as the conviction among economic actors that economic conditions lack robustness becomes common knowledge, and as the belief that prompt and rapid responses are the only meaningful and effective reaction to fast changes in conditions becomes widely entrenched, the very lack of recalcitrance in the economy is reinforced and compounded.

Finally, the enumeration of some of the reasons responsible for the present-day decline in the practical usefulness of Keynesian economic thinking cannot ignore the distinct possibility that it has been the very success of Keynesian policies that has affected their future effectiveness. Keynesian economic policies may well represent a peculiar case of self-elimination.

Keynes did not anticipate that his theories would become part of economic common sense. Nor was he able to foresee the transformation of economic realities as the result of the wide use of economic policies inspired by his theoretical ideas throughout the world.

Among the conditions for the effectiveness of economic policies suggested by Keynes are, for example, the possibility of effectively influencing demand. But once economic actors anticipate attempts by the state to influence demand, for instance with the aid of fiscal policies in order to bring about a reduction in unemployment rates, such policies can be undermined by inflationary pressures (e.g. Scherf, 1986:132). The extent to which a successful employment of Keynesian policies has been undermined by the very success of Keynesian policies, of course, is the result of fundamental structural change and cannot merely be attributed to the cognitive anticipation of state-initiated economic policies by various economic actors. The fundamental structural features of the modern economy itself have indeed changed considerably and this transformation is in some ways also the result of the application of Keynes's economic ideas.

Successful economic policies demand economic theories which take these changes explicitly into account. As a result, Alfred Marshall's ([1890] 1948:30–1) observation about the fate of economic doctrines remains valid: 'Though economic analysis and general reasoning are of wide application, . . . every country has its own problems; and every change in social conditions is likely to require a new development of economic doctrines.'

Keynes's self-assessment of the status of his critique of neoclassical doctrines confirms Marshall's views, for Keynes (1936:378) indicates that his own critique is not principally a critique of certain logical or methodological problems of classical theories. His critique is rather based on a fundamental disagreement with certain unrealistic premises of classical theory concerning the structure and the nature of the modern economy. It is these unrealistic assumptions of classical theories, that led to the failure of economic policy derived from these premises. More concretely, Keynes (1936:382) attempts to point out in his *General Theory* that 'under the system of *laissez-faire* and an international gold standard such as was orthodox in the latter half of the nineteenth century, there was no means open to a government whereby to mitigate economic distress at home except through the competitive struggle for markets. For all measures helpful to a state of chronic or intermittent under-employment were ruled out, except measures to improve the balance of trade on income account.' And, as indicated, Keynes's own ideas of course are by no means immune from his general observation.

Notes

1   John M. Keynes letter to Roy Harrod 4 July 1938; cf. Keynes ([1930] 1971:296).

2   It is not desirable to merely hint at the outlines of Keynes's economic theory and the intellectual and socio-economic context in which his ideas originated. However, while I will sketch many of the details of Keynesian theory, a description of 'Keynesianism', that is, an account of the many economic policies in different countries attributed to and justified with reference to Keynes is not necessary (but see Bombach et al., 1983). Nor will it be required to take account of what has come to be known as 'Keynesian economics', a largely formalistic and highly technical economic literature, divided into a variety of groups of economists over the past thirty years (cf. Davidson, 1978; Diesing, 1982:114–19) all claiming to have explicated and developed assumptions and ideas which may be attributed to Keynes. I will refer instead directly to the writings of Keynes and not engage in a discussion of the complex debates they engendered among fellow economists and the development or dilutions his program may have subsequently experienced at the hand of the same fraternity, however urgent and justified these amendments and deviations might have been. A more intensive and detailed critical discussion of Keynesian ideas, the economic policies they inspired, the thick and possibly opaque crust of interpretations they have generated or the changes his ideas have undergone in the meantime as a result of such vigorous interpretative work, are proper, for example, within a discussion of the history of economic ideas, but not necessarily within the context of a study of the practical efficiency of Keynes's economic doctrines.

3   Schumpeter (1946:356) observes that it was the 'ideological element' in Keynes's economic thought that gave impetus to his ideas because 'new departures' in science are impossible without it and accounts for its appeal at the time. He describes the ideological component in Keynes as 'the vision of decaying capitalism that located the cause for the decay in one out of a number of large features of latter-day society.'

4   The labor union movement continues to be primarily impressed by economic theories which stress underconsumption because such ideas appear to have greater strategic significance in struggles to raise wages. At the same time, such views also function as evidence for a kind of disinterested, that is, objective legitimation of the

goals of unions. However, it is not justified, it seems to me, to draw the dubious conclusion from an elective affinity between Keynesian ideas and the labor union movement, as O'Connor (1984:202) for example has done; for him Keynes's theory is 'the unintentional **result** of working-class struggle' and therefore not only 'a doctrine to legitimate working-class demands' [emphasis added].

5　See the letter from Keynes and the editorial comments by Donald Moggridge in Keynes's collected works ([1973] 1987:172, 243, 337) for further information. Moggridge refers to two 'external' reasons why Keynes may have started work on the *General Theory*. First, the reception of the *Treatise* among fellow economists and, secondly, a discussion, also connected with the same work, among younger students of economics in the so-called *Cambridge Circus* at the University of Cambridge (cf. Keynes, [1973] 1987:338–43).

6　Economic theory no longer merely refers to 'situations where there is no practical need for theoretical guidance, since the automatism of the system ensures that all goes well' (Lowe, 1965:98).

7　The view that Keynes's theory constitutes a radical break in economic theorizing is, of course, not shared throughout the community of professional economists; some suggest that he failed to be radical enough (e.g Brothwell, 1988) while others do not detect an intellectual break of any significance which would warrant the label of revolutionary.

8　Compare the important notion of the 'displacement of concepts' proposed by Schon (1963) as a central category for a general understanding of the conditions for and the process of theoretical innovation and imagination.

9　These attributes and the stress on non-rational elements in economic decision-making of Keynes's theory have also led to criticisms that his work is too 'socio-logical' (e.g. Brunner and Meltzer, 1977).

10　Compare the first and classical description of these differences by Hicks, 1937.

11　Keynes's ([1930] 1971) initial observations on this matter, partly at least, for example in his *Treatise of Money*, resonate with more conventional views: 'An act of saving by an individual may result either in increased investment or in increased consumption by the individuals who make up the rest of the community.'

12　In his later work, Mannheim (1940:164–90) shifts, as is well known, to a preoccupation with planning. The 'tension' between scientific discourse and practical thinking continues to concern him. However, his treatment of these issues in *Man and Society in an Age of Reconstruction* is, in my view, less sensitive and sophisticated than in his earlier work. Though there are evident resemblances in his discussion of the disjuncture between theory and practice, he now stresses the partiality and remoteness to practical affairs which comes with the ideal (and the practice?) of abstractness of theoretical social scientific discourse. Moreover, as Mannheim stresses, the methodological and substantive specialization of research further compounds the partial nature of scientific thinking. The remedies he invokes at this juncture are less cognizant of a practical calculus of attributes of social situations which should be addressed and, paradoxically perhaps, more obscure than is the case in *Ideology and Utopia*. The notion of *principia media* is the analytical key to particular worlds within with conduct takes place and must be understood as well as controlled.

13　Coleman (1978:677) categorizes sociological inquiry which is designed to have **some impact** upon the functioning of society as 'social policy research'. The contrasting orientation aims at 'discipline research' (cf. Coleman, 1972b).

14　The majority of the findings of empirical studies concerned with the application of sociological knowledge are self-exemplifying, that is, they exemplify the confusion among social scientists about the reasons for a failure or a success of such knowledge in practice (cf. Lazarsfeld et al., 1967; Beyer and Trice, 1982).

15   An analogous case can perhaps be found in the case of the evaluation of social programs, at least if one follows a suggestion by Cook (1981), which would focus on the particulars of local projects rather than national programs as the unit of assessment. As a result, evaluation might be used, for example, to 'assess whether some successful practices can be selected from among manipulable, policy-relevant activities that occur within a program and that stand a reasonable chance of being implemented elsewhere' (Cook, 1981:259).

16   More concretely, the research design requires that higher civil servants in the United States Department of Health assess research studies, commissioned by the government department, and summarize the results in two pages, according to a number of criteria. Such a design perhaps constitutes at best a first explorative assessment attempting to obtain attributes of social science knowledge which somehow affect the usefulness of such knowledge in particular contexts. The artificial context in which the civil servants were expected to evaluate the research studies can hardly serve as a substitute for the kinds of conditions which may impinge upon such an assessment under less simulated constraints. In any event, Weiss (1980:92) reports that her findings indicate that the perceived chance that findings can be implemented influence the judgement of her subjects about the relevance of the research they commissioned.

17   As Leff (1988:84) describes it, 'practitioners needed a decision mode that was heuristic rather than algorithmic in nature; they also required an approach that paid attention to considerations of overall development strategy'. The social benefit-cost analysis it seems was not able to satisfy either requirement.

18   It is perhaps worth noting in this context that Blalock (1979) refers, but only in a marginal note, in an essay primarily devoted to strategies of theory building in social science, to the possibility of assessing the **usefulness** of social theories in much the same sense. He enumerates additional criteria for the (external) utility of theories, for example, the social importance (i.e. what is the societal prestige of a particular theoretical problematic), the amount of information a theory contains and the generalizability of a theory. However, Blalock does not pause to reflect in any detail on the importance of the criteria for the task of constructing social theories. He merely enumerates the standards of evaluation.

19   William Foote Whyte (1986:557) gives an account of a series of research projects which he characterizes as quite successful in practice. What is particularly striking is how Whyte describes the role of social scientists: 'The social scientists have not been playing the conventional role of the professional expert who stands aside and submits his ideas at the same time as he writes research reports, so as to claim academic ownership. The social scientists have learned from the practitioners in management and labor, just as the practitioners learned from the social scientists. Furthermore, in trying to understand and effect organizational changes, social scientists have had to learn enough about engineering, architectural design, and business administration to integrate their contribution into the research and development process' (see also Whyte, 1984). The ideas advanced by social scientists in these instances with some success were governed and explicitly linked to a decisive extent to the contingencies of the social situations the researchers were asked to examine in the first place.

20   König suggests that sociology therefore acquires at least a dual theoretical-

practical function, since it may be both participatory and assume some distance in its intellectual work to practical situations.

21   A social invention according to Whyte (1982:1) may be a 'new element in organizational structure or interorganizational relations, new sets of procedures for shaping human interactions and activities and the relations of humans to the natural and social environment, a new policy in action (that is, not just on paper), or a new role or a new set of roles.'

22   Karl-Otto Apel has examined some of the methodological issues and has developed ideas designed to lead to a theoretical model which assist in mediating between everyday and scientific communication (cf. Apel, 1973a:95; 1973b:256).

23   cf. Jänicke, 1986.

24   Compare the analogous distinction between the logical and pragmatic implication of language in Grice, 1975; Cavell, 1969.

25   Compare Kuhn's (1970:164) discussion of the beneficial function of the differentiation of the **scientific community** in the case of the natural sciences.

26   Meehan (1982:125) offers the following general and apt observations about the self-referential or discipline-bound nature of modern economic thought: 'Most theoretical studies focus narrowly on the logical dimensions of formal models ignoring constraints, limitations in application, or adequacy of assumptions. References to events in the real world frequently, and perhaps nearly always, involve an improper transfer of a nominally defined term to the world of experience. When such procedures are used to generate policy suggestions, acceptance and use are not warranted. The cognitive status of economic theories is at best uncertain. To the question, "How much credence should be attached to policy recommendations developed from contemporary economic theory?" the weight of evidence clearly suggests the answer must be "None!".'

27   As Morris Janowitz (1978:405) stresses, 'social science is a language which has deeply penetrated the *Zeitgeist* of the United States' but there is no 'careful research which points up to the consequences of this flow of communication and its effect on societal change'.

28   This is not to deny, as Max Weber for example stressed repeatedly, the importance of empirical social research or the 'objectivity' for politics. Weber (e.g. [1921] 1958:258) stresses the significance of 'matter-of-factness' (*Sachlichkeit*) in political debates and struggle as a precondition for effective political action (see also von Schelting, 1934:9; Beetham, 1985). Such *Sachlichkeit* is surely a virtue. Nonetheless, 'correct' or adequate empirical analyses do not constitute a sufficient condition for effective political conduct. Knowledge of the facts is therefore not the decisive component in political conduct, even for Weber.

29   The term 'political', in its broadest sense, Mannheim ([1928] 1952) urges, should be taken to refer to all activity 'aiming at the transformation of the world' in accordance with a 'structured will'.

30   I have restored, to the translation of this passage, the emphases from the original which are not part of the translation of the text into English and tried to improve the readability of the translation.

31   Cf. for example Schumpeter (1954:1175–6, 1183–4).

32   Wagner (1990:301) underlines, for example, that the theoretical perspective which prompted and legitimized continental European élites to intervene more strongly, after the crisis of 1929, in economic affairs was linked less to any Keynesian conception than to the old intellectual opponents of liberal theory from the era of the urgency of the so-called 'social question' and role of the state in socio-economic

issues, especially at the turn of the century in Europe. After the war, however, even on the continent, the linkage of economic policies to Keynes was quite explicit.

33   In Keynes's own collection of his most important essays and statements about contemporary economic policies, first published in 1931 under the title of *Essays in Persuasion*, the statement still carries the programmatic title 'A programme for expansion', while the same essay is retitled in Keynes's *Collected Writings* as 'Can Lloyd George do it?' (cf. Keynes, [1929] 1984). The latter version has been expanded by a few passages compared to the essay authorized by Keynes for his *Essays in Persuasion*.

34   In an essay, written in 1926, 'The end of laissez-faire' (Keynes ([1926] 1984:292), as well as in his *Treatise on Money*, Keynes favors certain monetary policies to combat unemployment in Britain, specifically, a flexible interest rate policy of the Bank of England. He also recommends a reduction in the interest rate to the United States at the end of the 1920s.

35   A discussion of the much broader history and problems of the implementation of economic policies indebted to Keynes's theory in the post-war era in West Germany, in the United States and in the United Kingdom may be found in a study by Spahn (1976).

36   The meeting between the chancellor and Keynes most likely was arranged by Keynes's friend Carl Melchior who also served as an advisor to Brüning (cf. Johnson and Johnson, 1978:59). Keynes's recollections (1978:366–9) about his friend Melchior may be found in his *Collected Writings*.

37   Keynes analyses the problem of the reparations payments, based on his recent experience and observations in Germany, in a newspaper article published in mid-January 1932 in the *New Statesman and Nation*. He favors a moratorium and therefore supports the position taken by Brüning in this instance (cf. Keynes, 1978:366–9).

38   Historians of this era in Germany tend to conclude, in light of the convergence of the views of politicians and economists, that the economic and fiscal measure adopted by the government of chancellor Brüning constituted, on the whole, a meaningful, even adequate response to the conditions the government had to face while economists, judging on the basis of current knowledge, are more likely to conclude that the same policies were an erroneous response to the same set of contingencies (cf. Sanmann, 1965:110).

39   The economic doctrines which Alfred Weber and his colleagues represented did not exhaust economic discourse at the time. However, a group of younger economists around Adolph Lowe, Gerhard Colms, Eduard Heimann and Emil Lederer, did not have much intellectual influence and institutional support to ensure that their analysis of the crisis – which reflected upon and incorporated British contemporary economic theories and their policy advice – gained much credence during the days of the Weimar Republic. As a matter of fact, most of these social scientists were soon forced to leave Germany. Claus-Dieter Krohn (1981; 1987) has presented a detailed account of the views of these economists and their personal fate.

40   The great appeal of Keynes's *General Theory* generated among economists is, in all likelihood, also linked to its relatively uncomplicated but persuasive explanatory scheme. Keynes's straightforward account of the imbalances generated by the capitalist economy **and** the unambivalent economic advice to the state as an economic actor the theory generates represent considerable intellectual assets of his reflections. Bleaney (1985:37) observes therefore that Keynes's theory 'was a theoretically sophisticated exposure of the weaknesses of neoclassical pure theory,

which by introducing the principle of effective demand yielded **a very simple** explanation of the problems of the Great Depression' (emphasis added).

41 These observations by Keynes may be found in his introduction written especially for the translation of his *General Theory* into German. The German edition was published in 1936. Keynes's own stress, in his introduction, on the relative flexibility and relevance of his theory to a wide range of circumstances is also intended to suggest that his ideas, though formulated, in the first instance, for the case of *laissez-faire* economic orders, may in fact be applied to economic conditions in which the extent of 'state intervention is much more significant'.

42 Sometimes the suggestion is advanced that Keynes is a savior of the capitalist system. This view is based on the argument that the non-productive programs of public expenditures Keynes advocated help to solve the capitalist problem of underconsumption or overproduction. During the 1920s, output increased despite a decline in the amount of capital and labor used in production. Keynesian policy measures deal with these developments on two levels: on the one hand, the use of even more efficient means of production is slowed as a consequence of higher state expenditures because the economy is drained of investment funds. On the other hand, these expenditures produce additional demand which balances surplus supply of goods and services. Of course, the survival of the capitalist economy is only temporary according to some neo-marxists (cf. Block and Hirschhorn, 1979:370–1).

43 Highly relevant is for example the comprehensive analysis by Peter Drucker (1986:768) – though it advances much beyond issues of immediate relevance here – who stresses that the global economy generates most of the decisive economic effects in the contemporary world and not 'the macroeconomics of the nation state on which most economic theory still exclusively focuses' (also Lipsey, 1992).

44 What consequences the growing integration of national economies appears to have, for example for the governability of the nation-state, national cultural and social policies, is a wide field for often politicially motivated speculations and accusations. Is it the case, to refer to but one issue in greater detail, that growing international competition, as Hotz-Hart (1983:313) maintains, will significantly reduce the ability of a state to maintain social policies unique to a country because there inevitably will arise a conflict between the logic of the market and the logic of the welfare state?

45 Schumpeter's conception of innovations is not restricted to scientific and technical innovations. He uses it in a much broader sense in order to stress the occurrence of (progressive) discontinuities of various sorts in the course of economic development.

46 More precisely perhaps, a discussion of the role of innovations is no longer contained in the *General Theory*. Keynes ([1930] 1971:85–6) discusses innovations in his *Treatise on Money*. He still explicitly follows Schumpeter's lead in an essay published in the same year and refers to the significance of technological change and inventions for economic growth, fluctuating investment decisions by industry, changing interest rates and the immense capital accumulation in the modern age (cf. Keynes, [1930] 1984a).

47 It should be noted, however, that Keynes (1936:38) considers unemployment as a kind of permanent affliction of the capitalist economic system. That is to say, the aim of permanent full employment is not merely unattainable as the result of present-day technical developments but is a structural feature of the overall economic system. None the less, the consensus on the desirability of full employment as a goal of state sponsored economic policies, irrespective of political ideology, has been

considerable for decades in the West and East. It is only now that the political and economic premises facilitating the consensus about full employment or, the 'right to work', begin to fall into disrepute (cf. Gorz, [1980] 1982]; Keane and Owens, 1986; Keane, 1988:69–100).

48   Robert Heilbronner's response to the question why economists today have much greater difficulty anticipating future economic developments is linked, it seems to me, to a similar diagnosis of the growing lack of recalcitrance of the structure of economic phenomena: 'It may be that this [prediction] is less possible than it was, because the economy itself now is so much more a creature of decision making, and so much less the outcome of sheer interplay of impersonal forces, that prediction becomes inherently more difficult' (quoted in Greene, 1974:64).

5
Pragmatic Knowledge

A plea, and the demand, for knowledge produced but not oriented fully by criteria internal to the social science community, can be criticized on the basis of at least two significant considerations. The first, and more credible argument, would maintain that the progress of knowledge in social science is impeded by the cognitive aims of a pragmatic social science. Secondly, it might be argued that the production of social science knowledge propelled not solely by internal criteria and modes of orientation, possibly produces a form of 'practical' social science but also engenders serious political and ethical dilemmas for the social community. More specifically, one could object, for example, that practical social science knowledge undermines one of the essential characteristics of human conduct, namely its spontaneity and the positive function such spontaneity generally may be seen to have for the course of social conduct.

I will discuss each of these counter-positions and the intellectual traditions on which they draw in the next section and will attempt to show that they indeed constitute important but not fatal objections to the position for a practical social science knowledge presented here.

One variant of the second objection would try to highlight the political implications of my conception in even stronger terms and perhaps conclude that a pragmatic social science, in the final analysis, amounts to a version of positivist social science despite its own explicit disclaimers. Is it not the case, one could point out for example, that both in the context of the model of instrumentality and in the context of a pragmatic social science the actual translation of knowledge into action constitutes a process which is external to the social science communities and its legitimate activities and that social science knowledge can be employed in the interest of a considerable **range** of political conceptions? A pragmatic social science does not really offer any effective solution to the dilemma of the deliberate abstention and alleged neutrality the model of instrumentality embraces. I will try to deal with this type of objection directly but not immediately. I will address it in the context of the discussion of the advantages and costs of a pragmatic social science.

First, I would like to examine the objection that a practical focus somehow impedes the general progress of social science knowledge and should be avoided, possibly at all cost.

Knowledge guiding interests and practice

My case study concerned with the success and failure of economic policies, based on Keynes's economic theory, allows for a number of additional lessons which can be utilized in the context of a discussion of the conditions that would make possible a practical social science knowledge.

First of all, it can be concluded that the development of (social) scientific knowledge in highly differentiated science communities and societal institutions – as is the case in modern social science and the political or economic system for example – may well proceed in 'opposite' directions. The dominant social scientific knowledge guiding interests represent, in virtually all cases, an interest in the extension or the improvement of cognitive work on **disciplinary theoretical traditions**. In a similar way, Kaufmann (1977:45) observes that sociology's cognitive interests are predominantly theoretical cognitive interests designed to advance the development of sociological theories. The practical relevance and the conditions for the possible use of such theories are rarely made part of any explicit consideration: 'The dominant cognitive interests of sociology consider social policy matters for example not because of any direct interest in social policy but examine them . . . as social conditions in need of an explanation, as material for the purpose of confirming certain theories or as the basis for the falsification of hypotheses.' The cognitive interests pursued in 'discipline research' (Coleman, 1972b:2) are the interests of particular scientists who, in most cases, are constrained to work on specific scientific traditions since rewards and advancement in the scientific community are rarely offered for contributions toward structured themata and acceptable solutions which are not 'internal' to the intellectual traditions of disciplines or specialties.

There are important epistemological and methodological reasons which allow one to interpret any deliberate and direct abstinence against practical cognitive interests as a distinct virtue.[1] The exclusion of pragmatic considerations promises more reliable and speedier progress in the development of 'objective' social science knowledge.

A restricted but clear epistemological demand and justification of this kind may be found in Mannheim's significant essay on the 'Prospects of Scientific Politics' in his *Ideology and Utopia* ([1929]

1936). Mannheim addresses the inevitable linkage of social scientists to the fields of politics and political decision-making. If the scientist is to be able to formulate valid knowledge claims, his intellectual activity must be, at least in formulating the foundations of social science thought, independent *vis-à-vis* the domain of political struggle. For Mannheim, the epistemological demand for **reflection-at-a-distance** results last but not least from the political goals his program for a sociology of knowledge offers in contrast to competing political-historical forms of thought, especially in work which may produce a practically viable and helpful synthesis of political views. Such a synthesis of political conceptions of course is not possible from the vantage point a particular political party is able to offer (cf. Kettler et al., 1984).

It is especially useful in this context to refer to much more detailed considerations by Emile Durkheim ([1895] 1964:141–6), found in his *The Rules of Sociological Method*. In the *Rules*, Durkheim defends with considerable eloquence the need for a radical abstinence of social scientists from the demands of practical contexts in the course of the development of sociological knowledge.[2]

The basic purpose Durkheim defends is the need that sociology should confine itself to sociological activities. This demand has been echoed since by a number of social scientists at different periods in this century, for example, quite strongly in the post-war era for (West) German sociology by René König ([1958] 1967:8). König agrees with Durkheim that progress in the development of sociological knowledge can only be guaranteed as long as sociology restricts itself to being nothing but adequate sociology.

One must stress of course that the goal of a 'pure' sociology is, both in the case of Durkheim and later for König, legitimated by way of arguing for the elimination of a range of issues from sociology as non-sociological concerns. For König this is the purge of what he considers to be properly philosophical perspectives and issues from disciplinary discourse in sociology, in particular questions connected with the philosophy of history and social philosophy. These perspectives contain, for the most part, issues not amendable to empirical work or offer claims which are not based on empirical research. 'Speculative' theories which effectively resist, and are not really amenable to empirical test, should at best be employed as a source of hypotheses to be tested subsequently. But without such empirical tests they remain inadequate and totally unreliable claims (König, 1961:81).

In addition, König is in favor of a separation of sociology from 'practical' disciplines. If practical disciplines or considerations are allowed to enter sociological discourse, it would lead to an undesirable mixture of cognitive interests. König ([1958] 1967:10) sums up his considerations by suggesting that sociology does not oppose the need for a proper intellectual development and advance of practical disciplines but it should reject, on **scientific** grounds, that practical perspectives and considerations directly enter into the manufacture of social science knowledge.[3] In other words, the differentiation of purposes does not imply the elimination of practical issues from social science discourse. But work on such matters best follows the peculiar intellectual order and norms of scientific discourse. If such cognitive demarcation and rules should not be observed, it is possible that the development of objective knowledge would suffer or be seriously deflected. As a result, König pleads for a strict differentiation of sociology from disciplines centered around practical issues, for example, from social ethics, social reform and social policy. In short, and as Durkheim ([1895] 1964:145) tries to argue as well, 'sociology is . . . not an auxiliary of any other science; it is itself a distinct and autonomous science, and the feeling of the specificity of social reality is indeed so necessary to the sociologist that only distinctly sociological training can prepare him to grasp social facts intelligently.' This thesis of course does not necessarily imply a strict abstinence from practical issues and contexts. But for Durkheim ([1895] 1964:142) it does.

> With reference to practical social doctrines, our method permits and commands the same independence. Sociology thus understood will be neither individualistic, communistic, nor socialistic in the sense commonly given these words. On principle, it will ignore these theories, in which it could not recognize any scientific value, since they tend not to describe or interpret, but to reform, social organization.

The role of sociologists and sociological discourse primarily is directed toward an emancipation from political parties. As a result, intellectual activities within sociology acquire a special attitude toward social problems. Science alone justifies and provides the required distance.

Durkheim ([1895] 1964:146) views himself and other sociologists who follow his example as rather lonely and unpopular heroes-cum-scientists because

> the time has come for sociology to spurn popular success . . . and to assume the exacting character befitting every science. It will then gain in dignity and authority what it will perhaps lose in popularity. For, so long as it remains involved in partisan struggles, is content to expound common ideas with more logic than the layman, and, consequently, presumes no special competence, it has no right to speak loudly enough to silence passions and prejudices.

Durkheim demands a sociology for experts which has the will to be unpopular and unheroic but as a result is a dignified scientific and professional activity.

The unanticipated and unintended consequence of the methodological position advocating distance to practical problems and contexts is that an intellectually autonomous social science **may** well be destined to be irrelevant in practice. Paradoxically, such irrelevance increases as internally set criteria defining what constitutes precise and objective knowledge are more and more approximated in the social science community. Knowledge claims which conform to such standards may be of little interest to anyone outside the social sciences – and may be virtually impossible to comprehend (cf. Stehr and Simmons, 1979).

The methodological objections which are advanced against the construction of practical knowledge are primarily directed at the social and cognitive affairs of the social science community of the day. They are often only relevant for the purposes of internal politics of the social science community and the conduct of its ordinary activities. But as long as the defense of knowledge claims produced at a distance from practical affairs has considerable appeal and support in the social community it is rather difficult to sustain efforts to focus research activities on the construction of practical knowledge.

Social science research which is not explicitly designed to generate practical knowledge may in fact succeed in producing such knowledge. But efforts which are from the beginning aimed at producing such knowledge claims have a much better chance to succeed because such research efforts do not have to rely on fortuitous 'local' circumstances in order to achieve a fit with practical conditions of action.

Though every kind of knowledge as knowledge of reality represents, at least in principle, a capacity for action and therefore constitutes the potential to construct reality on the basis of theoretical knowledge (cf. Krohn and Rammert, 1985:419), the chances of translating knowledge for action into knowledge in action are immeasurably improved once it is recognized that the probability to realize knowledge is dependent on context specific social, political and economic conditions. If one incorporates these conditions at once, then the likelihood for practical knowledge is considerably enhanced. Knowledge claims constructed with the aim of eliminating any reference to time and place in all likelihood will turn out to be entities mainly relevant to disciplinary discourse and its limited public.

A rather intriguing and challenging argument opposed to a

pragmatic social science and the kind of cognitive orientation it requires, but also to a social science in strict mechanical analogy to a form of technological practice, has been developed and defended by the economist and social philosopher Friedrich von Hayek. He explicates his ideas (which can already be found sketched in his book *The Counter-Revolution of Science*, 1952), in greater detail in 1974, a time of high inflation, in Stockholm in his acceptance speech for the Nobel prize for economic sciences.

Hayek outlines and exemplifies his objection to the dominant philosophical and methodological conceptions of 'proper' social science in direct opposition to one of his favorite intellectual targets, namely John Maynard Keynes, by rejecting both his diagnosis of and therapy for high unemployment in developed economies. Hayek dismisses the widely held notion that high unemployment rates are a reflection of a lagging **demand** for goods and services. Economic policies premised on such a 'fatal' diagnosis are obviously wrong as well and have ill effects for the health of the economy. Attempts by the state to stimulate demand lead to a massive disallocation of economic resources and unintended increases in unemployment.

Hayek observes that the validity of Keynes's diagnosis can be verified empirically; but paradoxically, it is mistaken. According to Hayek, the proper explanation for high unemployment, formulated prior to Keynes's writings on the subject, indicates that a disequilibrium of the **relative** prices of the factors of production is responsible for unemployment. However, this explanation cannot be verified empirically (cf. Hayek, 1975b:19).

But what is the relevance of these considerations for a pragmatic social science and why does the success of economic policies inspired by Keynes's theories constitute a valid argument against a social science driven by practical concerns? The importance of the substance of Hayek's ideas is straightforward. But an answer to the question posed requires a slight detour via epistemological terrain.

The subject matter of the social sciences, in contrast to the natural sciences, may be characterized according to Hayek as 'essentially complex' phenomena. The defining or characteristic attributes as social processes can only be modelled adequately, as Lipset and many other social scientists who adhere to the model of instrumentality stress repeatedly, with the help of a large – too large – number of variables.[4]

The communication medium 'market' is an appropriate case in point for the complexity of economic processes. The nature of the complexity of the market makes it difficult, if not impossible, to directly observe and quantify. Yet, 'Competition, for example, is a process which will produce certain results only if it proceeds among a fairly **large** number of persons' (Hayek, [1974] 1975a:33). We are in a position to comprehend market-processes in a general sense but specific market developments can only be apprehended, let alone predicted, once detailed knowledge of the organized complexity of the market is at hand. But such a goal is impossible to realize according to Hayek ([1974] 1975a:41).[5]

Local knowledge, for example knowledge of economic agents intimately linked to a particular time and place, cannot be safely added up, cumulated or abstracted without severe qualitative loss for the observing economist or the planner interested in formulating general claims or policies. It is against the 'nature' of such knowledge to enter into statistics (cf. Hayek, [1945] 1969:83). And since economic processes are based on the rapid adaptation to local circumstances with the help of knowledge bound to the peculiar features of time and place, it follows that only **decentralized** decisions assure efficient responses by economic subjects. As a result, social scientists who base their judgement about what are theoretically significant economic dimensions on the potential quantifiability of social phenomena and processes, commit a methodological fallacy. Such a position ignores or neglects the influence of social factors which are difficult, often impossible to measure in quantitative terms.

In the case of the explanation of unemployment rates favored by Hayek but rejected by Keynes this means concretely that the exact prices and wages which would exist in an equilibrium condition produced by market forces cannot be measured and therefore predicted in a quantitative manner (Hayek, [1974] 1975a:33).

Though Hayek's argument is perhaps not tautological, it is not too difficult to conclude that it is formally constructed in such a manner that the premises he employs – social processes have a large number of participants, therefore are complex and require for any adequate theoretical reconstruction the enumeration of a large number of variables – invariably lead to the conclusion that any effort to operate with but a limited number of variables leads to knowledge claims which restrict social action and, what might be even more fatal, result in taking sides on behalf of inefficiency. If only a large assemblage of actors is capable of achieving favorable consequences it is self-evident that any other concrete configuration of demand and supply must be unable to do so.

None the less, the methodological barrier represents an economic, perhaps even a political-normative advantage: the **spontaneous** interaction of many unimpeded decisions is especially efficient and represents the foundation for the distinct advantages of a well-functioning economic market. The ideal of uninhibited competition is turned into an epistemological norm. In other words, it is mistaken to attempt to 'scientifically' cope with market forces, that is, to control and manipulate the market since any attempt to do so achieves its opposite goal and leads to a destruction of the essential spontaneity of forces and to the elimination of its special economic accomplishments.

Any effort to control and plan practical social circumstances is, following Hayek's conception, evidence for false consciousness. The conviction that social **science** knowledge cannot only be produced but translated, not unlike natural science knowledge, into action is an arrogant belief. Humans will have to live with the perhaps unsatisfactory fact that the control of social situations with the aid of a **comprehensive** understanding of such contexts is impossible in principle.

Hayek's conclusions do not really differ from the reasons for a pragmatic social science I have tried to advance. But the foundations for the common conclusion, especially for the rejection of the notion that a scientifically grounded technical social science – based on a comprehensive reflection of the essential complexity of social phenomena – can be very successful in practice, but diverge because they are based on very different considerations.

In my view, opposition to a technical or instrumental social science is based on the observation that most social contexts are characterized by a certain stratification of whatever attributes one might consider significant and that it is by no means accidental and dependent on fortuitous circumstances that a certain process of adaptation or innovation is set in motion or not. As I have tried to show, the knowledge claims Keynes advances for the reasons of and possible remedies for high unemployment in developed nations do not in any way contain a full enumeration of most attributes of economic processes. Nor are all the relevant individual or corporate actors, as further evidence for the stratification of the time and place in question, participants of equal stature and similar interest in the process. One of the corporate actors, the state, presumably plays a special role and has a unique function in arresting high unemployment rates. Thus, as long as Hayek describes the dynamics of the market as one which is set in motion and altered as the result of the action of **individual** market participants who are generally quite weak within the aggregate process – given their status, interests and resources as individual entities – he underestimates the deviation of market forces from the ideal, atomistic structure (cf. Hayek, [1945] 1969:86). One is therefore able to agree with Hayek's polemic against a social science which is both committed to a complete and mirror-like description of social processes and proclaims that only such knowledge can be effective in practice, without agreeing with his highly individualistic premises and his favored intellectual enemies.

Knowing and doing

If social science discourse, whose restricted qualities Simmel ([1907] 1978:430) describes as a mere awareness of the world's content or as a completely indifferent mirror of reality, acquires, despite these bare features, any practical significance, then one of the reasons for its limited use value has to be found in a profoundly transformed economic or political structure, at least this is how the generation of Max Weber saw it.

In the closing chapter to the *Philosophy of Money*, Simmel perceptively analyzes the increase in the number of lengthened means which form the content of our action as a result of the money economy in and the growing intellectualization of the modern world.[6] This means, everyday life becomes increasing dominated by considerations pertaining to the means of social action. Straightforward purposes of life are transformed and extended into multiple and roundabout series of means. The satisfaction of interests is deferred, at times, beyond the horizon of the individual. The calculation of means is the accomplishment of the intellectualization of life. 'Wherever the intellect leads us, we are completely dependent, since it leads us solely through the actual connections between things' (Simmel, [1907] 1978:430). The role of impulse and emotions linked to the purposes of action is displaced. Among the consequences of the lengthening of the series of social action is not only the disappearance of emotional elements from action but also the growing transformation of all features of life into means and the increasing (scientific) penetration of objective intelligence into all practical spheres of life. All conceivable elements of social action 'become objectively and subjectively calculable rational relationships and in so doing progressively eliminate the emotional reactions and decisions which only attach themselves to the turning points of life, to the final purposes' (Simmel, [1907] 1978:431). Simmel's pessimistic vision is animated by his dichotomous conception of reason and emotions. The spiritual energy which circulates and corresponds to the peculiar nature of the money economy is rationality. The standard currency in an age of money is not emotion.

The life world of reason, the world of **universality** and the life world of emotion, the world of **particularity**, are neither of equal value nor is the 'knowledge' circulating in each identical. On the contrary, one world increasingly displaces the other context of living. The power of the 'superior intelligence rests upon the communistic character of its quality because, in terms of its content, intelligence is universally valid and everywhere effective and recognized, the mere quantity of intellectual endowment of the individual confers a more unconditional advantage than can any more individual possession, which, because of its individuality cannot be universally used or cannot find the domain for itself anywhere in the practical world' (Simmel, [1907] 1978:438). What elevates the culture of objects and the objective culture to its social superiority over the culture of individuals is 'unity and the autonomous self sufficiency' it has reached in modern times (Simmel, e.g. [1907] 1978:503).

One must ask, despite the apparent persuasiveness and widely shared imagery of Simmel's account of and warning against the transformative capacity of objective knowledge, is his conception of why and how scientific knowledge becomes efficacious outside the boundaries of scientific discourse really adequate?

Local knowledge and practice

> In general it is only by the use of artificial experimental isolation that one can predict physical events.
>
> Karl R. Popper[7]

Is it also true, one may ask in response to Popper's observation, that the **use** of physical knowledge in practice, requires the 'experimental isolation' of that physical event or effect? Can one set such a physical event in motion without isolating it?

On the basis of what has been said so far about the limits and possibilities of effectively employing social science knowledge in practice, one could easily reach the conclusion that these considerations apply with particular, even exclusive force to the special case of social science knowledge. But this would be a mistaken conclusion. In close analogy to the limits of the usefulness of social science knowledge, there are limits to the application of natural science knowledge, produced in scientific laboratories, outside its immediate context of manufacture, for example as the result of certain material and cognitive conditions which made the observation of the physical event or effect in the laboratory possible in the first place.

As indicated, I am referring to physical effects or processes that are first observed as the result of 'scientific action', initially for example in the scientific laboratory based on a configuration of particular conditions. It follows that the re-production of laboratory effects, **outside** the context of the laboratory, can only occur under exactly the same circumstances which allowed for the possibility of the original effect. Unless one is prepared to accept the fact that knowledge produced under specific laboratory conditions remains 'irrelevant' or 'impractical' knowledge, the transfer of laboratory observations (and effects) into other contexts is possible only on the basis of a transfer or a re-creation of the conditions of the production of the effect (cf. Latour, 1983; MacKenzie, 1987; Rouse, 1987). What is conceivable also is that the (experimental) knowledge is modified and converted in ways which allow its adaptation to local, external circumstances. In other words, the experimental conditions are constitutive for the knowledge generated by a scientific experiment. What determines the transfer and a re-creation of experimental circumstances are, in most instances, however, interests such as economic or political aims.

It would appear that Popper concurs; though he only indicates that physical effects can be predicted by way of artificial experimental isolation, he does not explicitly describe how the predicted effects can be reproduced, if at all, outside the conditions of artificial experimental isolation.

More generally, how can scientific predictions be realized? For Popper ([1957] 1972:139) the answer is quite straightforward: predictions cannot be realized in concrete or practical circumstances because 'we are very far from being able to predict, even in physics, the precise results of a **concrete** situation, such as a thunderstorm, or a fire'.

In order to achieve a certain result in the laboratory, one has to screen out, simplify or reduce for example the complex impact of the natural environment on a process. Only then is one able to clearly determine or identify a specific relation. The transfer and implementation of such a laboratory result into practice is of course encumbered with considerable difficulties, not to speak of various risks (cf. Krohn and Weyer, 1989) which follow from the transformation of society into a laboratory and which might contaminate the effect or make it impossible to repeat it outside the laboratory. It is very likely that unanticipated intervening factors could occur, even with a certain delay which might jeopardize any effort to repeat the effect observed in the laboratory.

It is of course possible to conceive of scientific knowledge as entirely independent of the ability to manipulate and control processes in **concrete situations**, for example outside the artificial isolation of the laboratory. However, Rouse (1987:234) argues that it is not meaningful to conceptualize scientific knowledge as independent in principle of the practical capacities to produce a phenomenon or set in motion a process. Rouse refers in this instance to the practical abilities of scientists to produce laboratory effects and not so much to the issue of the transfer, especially the ability to extend the laboratory and realize the observed results in other, external contexts. The practical ability to achieve certain effects or set a process in motion indeed is closely linked to knowledge as a capacity for action and the translation of such knowledge into practice requires that conditions prevail which allow for the execution of these practical abilities. The capability to produce a result must not be undermined by the circumstances which prevail in the 'new' situation. This means that the conditions which allow for the production of knowledge must be transferred to the other contexts as well. As a consequence, Rouse (1987:234) stresses that 'generalizing . . . local knowledge is more a matter of extending specific practical skills and reconstructing or reconceptualizing new situations to make them amenable to the extension than of discovering and applying universal laws'.

This conception of both the nature of natural science and its realization outside the context of science is very much at odds with the more conventional understanding of scientific knowledge, especially the notion that natural scientific knowledge must be viewed as independent of the material world. As Giddens (1984:348) puts it well, 'the theories and findings of the natural sciences are separate from the universe of objects and events which they concern. This ensures that the relation between scientific knowledge and the object world remains a "technological" one, in which accumulated knowledge is "applied" to an independently constituted set of phenomena.' Of course, if this is not the case what remains of the allegedly solid demarcation between social and natural science, especially when it comes to the practical implementation of social and natural science knowledge?

Social and natural science knowledge in action

The precarious consensus which emerged among social scientists in recent decades about the distinctiveness of social science knowledge is considerable when judged against the background of the cognitive dissensus in the social science community about what constitutes adequate knowledge and how one may generate and validate such knowledge claims. But the consensus about the many **unique** problems faced by social science because of its subject matter and the lack of recalcitrance it appears to offer to the observer, does not always extend to the question of the kind of social science knowledge and the ways in which it may prove to be effective in practice.

The model to which many social scientists continue to adhere, as described in some detail earlier, is the model of instrumentality. Inasmuch as that model is supposed to represent the conditions which affect the proper manufacture of social scientific knowledge and of such knowledge in action, any claims about the distinctiveness of social science knowledge should be reflected within the model. It turns out that the enabling features social science offers in practice converge closely with those promised by natural science knowledge.

Since I have tried to argue that the model of instrumentality is erroneous because of its mistaken universalistic premises, and since I have now attempted to argue that natural science knowledge too, if it is effective in practice at all, must be a kind of local knowledge, the matter of the distinctiveness of social and natural science knowledge in action should be taken up briefly once more.

Based on the considerations about implementation advanced so far, the point which can be made with some confidence about both natural and social science in action is that their use may present distinctive 'problems' only because of the unique 'resistance' practical circumstances may offer to attempts to **realize** experimental conditions, or, in the case of social science, thought experiments. That is to say, it is quite adequate to assume that social science knowledge, as a capacity of action, can be translated into action in analogy to natural science knowledge, as long as social scientists, or their willing agents, are prepared to control and erect conditions in practice which would allow individual or corporate actors to set such knowledge claims in motion. Since the ability of social scientists to manipulate and control the social environment in ways required to set their ideas in motion is more than limited, social science and natural science knowledge differ considerably when it comes to enacting such knowledge in practice.

But what produces the distinctiveness of these forms of knowledge if it is not constitutive of the knowledge claims? The difference of natural and social science knowledge is associated with the 'present' nature of external social and political reality which such knowledge claims confront. While the socio-political context in the case of the natural sciences is often enabling, it virtually always issues inhibiting constraints for the realization of social science knowledge claims. Comte and Marx could be expert witnesses.

It is as a result of this profound difference that only a pragmatic social science can, as long as these conditions prevail – and one would hope that they will continue to dominate in the case of the domain of the social sciences – anticipate to generate knowledge which may be called practical knowledge.

Notes

1   This is in addition to more latent social functions of such an epistemological position, which I will not consider in any detail, for example in terms of its legitimation of a professional ethic of scientific activity which ascribes greater value to pure rather than applied research, greater intellectual significance to theoretical discourse rather than empirical or historical research and greater moral value to an ethic of political neutrality (cf. Kaufmann, 1969:72).

2   Toward the end of the decade of the 1950s, Talcott Parsons advocates a somewhat less radical variant of Durkheim's position. Parsons (1959:559) demands that American sociologists primarily should concentrate in their work on the development of social **scientific** knowledge and should advance the function of the professional social scientist oriented toward the needs of the **discipline**. Parsons's demands for disciplinary work are connected to the warning that one ought not to focus primarily on practical issues, for 'it should never be forgotten that the central task of a scientific profession is the development of its discipline and the training of its successors in carrying on that function. Increasing involvement in popular ideological discussions and in applied functions **could** readily divert attention from these functions, although of course here there need be no intense conflict.'

3   In the immediate post-war years, König (1952:36) published a methods collection in order to familiarize social scientists and social science students in Germany with research techniques developed in North America; in his introduction, he stresses emphatically that social research **ultimately** responds to and is concerned with practical matters (cf. also König, 1987:14).

4   And consistent with this premise, Hayek ([1974] 1975:40) observes, referring to the reasons for and the patterns of the expeditious development of natural science knowledge that 'the chief point we must remember is that the vast and rapid advance of the physical sciences took place in fields where it proved that explanation and prediction could be based on laws which accounted for the observed phenomena as functions of comparatively **few** variables – either particular facts or relative frequencies of events'.

5   Hayek maintains that Popper's falsification criterion is not invalidated as a result of his conclusion about the difficulties of anticipating social events because restricted predictions are possible.

6   'The number of means and the length of their series which form the content of our activity . . . develop in proportion to intellectuality as the subjective representative of the objective world order' (Simmel, [1907] 1978:430).

7   Popper, [1957] 1972:139.

Excursus
Sociology as Enlightenment

The political, or more precisely the **ideological** significance of sociology for the prevailing self-conception of individual and corporate
actors of modern society may well come as a surprise to those who
are firmly convinced that the model of instrumentality accurately
captures the process. Having accepted the model and consequently
the limits to the power of sociological knowledge in society it may
seem a dubious assertion to them. However, even proponents of the
model of instrumentality, as found for example among the classics
of sociological theory, were always confident in an ambivalent sense
perhaps, and at times even quite certain that the political impact of
their serious and sober intellectual efforts would not be limited to
the obviously rather modest possibilities instrumental rationality
signals. They harbored the suspicion, from time to time, that the
influence of their work might filter into society on much more
circuitous and less visible avenues. For example, when Talcott
Parsons (1959:554) speaks of the present period as the age of
sociology, he is obviously not merely referring to the consolidation
of sociology as a scientific discipline and perhaps as a profession, but
also to the ideological impact of the sociological imagination on
society. If one follows Parsons's observations, the ideological
demand for theoretical models produced by sociology – that is
collectively meaningful accounts of social events – is a response to a
cognitive deficit rather than a response prompted by structural or
'material' transformations of society and is produced by a loss in
relevance and significance of once dominant self-conceptions of
industrial society. More specifically, Parsons suggests that the
'psychological' era is displaced by the sociological era since the
former has been exhausted as a meaningful point of reference.
Parsons (1959:553) indicates in a somewhat ambivalent fashion that
it 'became apparent that the understanding of the complexities and
changes of our large-scale society and its "mass" phenomena
require more than analysis of individual phenomena'. As a result,
sociology begins to emerge as the relevant intellectual resource,
expert and partner for society. Apparently sociologists fashion, that
is Parsons's feeling, the kind of answers pertinent to the intellectual
challenges produced by important private and public problems of

modern society. It is evident, however, that Parsons is only alluding to the possibility of such a development. He never analyzed in detail any of the probable opportunities, limits or dangers for sociology connected with such a prominent role in present-day society. He may have shied away from more comprehensive reflections about the ideological 'function' of sociology because he clearly favored the view that such a socio-political role represents a dubious purpose for sociology, perhaps even a dangerous distinction for professional sociology. Even if sociological ideas resonate with worldviews and values of individual and corporate actors, they also come into potential conflict with the norm of objectivity internal to the scientific community (Parsons, 1959:555). Moreover, Parsons sees the primary function of a profession in the development of, and attention to, professional matters; it, therefore, does not extend to concerns about its external impact or image. None the less, despite his evident misgivings, Parsons's cautious observations about the possible **ideological** impact of sociology in modern society, which C. Wright Mills ([1959] 1970:91–6) stressed much more affirmatively in the same year, are noteworthy and suggestive. I will try to pursue these leads in greater detail.

One controversial, detailed and very pertinent response to the challenge of Parsons's observations was issued some fifteen years later, occurring, though, as a reaction to different socio-political developments and having been triggered in response to distinct intellectual inducements. However, the account in question dealing with the reasons for and the ways in which sociological ideas may travel and effect individuals and corporate actors takes up the suggestions found in Parsons's earlier reflections about the possibility that sociology is more than a limited provider of instrumental rationality for individuals and institutions. The account I have in mind can be found in a book by the late German sociologist Helmut Schelsky. The almost immediate controversy it elicited did not explicitly revolve around the practical impact of sociology, especially around the ways in which such influence is occurring. Schelsky's polemical observations were read instead as a conservative political manifesto and lament on the nature of modern society and the possibility for planning a more human socio-political structure. While I will make reference to the reception of the book, at the time, my primary intention is to present and interpret Schelsky's ideas as a contribution to the theory/praxis debate within social science. None the less, there is ample evidence for a close affinity between Schelsky's anti-sociological rhetoric and a conservative disenchantment with certain manifestations of modernity which goes beyond the mere concern that sociology, in the post-war era, had become 'the folk-science of liberal reformers' (Ravetz, 1971:397). In a narrower sense, Schelsky's critique of sociology also highlights the often deliberate distancing of political conservatives from sociological discourse and their intellectual difficulties with it which in itself may be observed as a reaction to the earliest efforts to establish sociology as an academic discipline (cf. Rehberg, 1986).

If nothing else, Schelsky's views stand out as an intriguing and challenging position in the generally somewhat bland spectrum of the theory/praxis debate. His notions were first developed in the mid-1970s in West Germany, that is only a few years after the intellectual reign of critical writings in the late 1960s, often inspired by social science conceptions and social movements against entrenched and apparently rigid modern social structures, for example, in the political system or the university. Schelsky's efforts were immediately denounced by his many critics as the polemical and misguided attempt by a neoconservative intellectual to get even with his opponents. Schelsky's main thesis and insistent warning, labeled anti-sociological by him, is directed against what he fears is the impending rule of a new caste of priests and the danger of a takeover by a new class of intellectuals, made up first and foremost of social scientists, especially sociologists, which will rule modern society in the guise of a kind of theoretical élite or *Reflexionselite*.[1]

Given the means of their authority and the kind of power they exercise, the study of this new élite according to Schelsky requires a sociological analysis, a social psychology and sociology of knowledge of the claims to authority relevant to the analysis of the rule of clerics in mediaeval times. But Schelsky's thesis also is nothing less than a radical reversal of the classical sociological view of the real sources of social and political power in society. Schelsky talks about the power of ideas. His observations represent, in addition, a dramatic departure from his warnings about the impending emergence of a 'technical state' which he had outlined in the context of his theory of a 'scientific-technical civilization' (cf. Schelsky, 1961). That is to say, the power of technical necessities or the rule of instrumental rationality, which he had seen as constitutive of advanced society only a few years earlier, now appear to be defeated as the result of what he at that time considered to be the only effective weapon against the progressive march toward dominance by modern technology and science in society, namely heroic intellectual resistance.

These provocative observations, Schelsky's opposition to the priestlike rule of intellectuals over the business of society and individual consciousness, can be found in his treatise which carries the programmatic title, 'The others do the work' (*Die Arbeit tun die*

anderen). The book also is a fully fledged critique of dominant
sociological perspectives and ideas. It was first published in 1971
and then reissued in 1975 with a postscript in which Schelsky tries to
respond to this generally hostile reception. Though his views are
especially challenging, it ought to be stressed that they represent
nothing more than a diagnosis of the special influence of social
science on modern society. They are by no means idiosyncratic. In
the 1970s, analyses about the historically unique and inordinate
influence of social science on public life and public policy can be
found in countries other than West Germany as well. In the case of
the United States, Daniel P. Moynihan (1970:2), for example,
points to the exceptional power and authority of university professors of social science: 'There is no place on earth where the
professor reigns, or has done up until very recently, as in the United
States. For the past thirty years in our society the intellectuals – the
professors – have influenced almost without precedent in history.'

The primary social and political reasons which give rise to the
possibility that sociologists will become the new rulers of society
are, according to Schelsky, the result of the gradual decline in social
differences and inequalities within modern society. In all industrial
societies, at least in those influenced by and patterned on Europe,
class conflict and degree of class based on the inequality of
proletariat and bourgeoisie diminishes, perhaps even disappears.
The reduction in social inequality results from the increasing
employment of the new means of production, from technical
progress in general and welfare policies. However, it is the institution of political democracy which is primarily responsible, and the
balancing social power labor unions acquire in these societies. In
place of the old class divisions, a new kind of 'class conflict', based
on the emergence of a new class, surfaces in advanced society. The
new class is made up of the educated, and among those the
academically educated in particular, who deal in and represent
certain cognitive positions and commitments. This segment of the
population is often neglected in Marxist-based class analyses of
modern societies. The same group was responsible for the age of the
enlightenment and therefore for many of the developments which
have helped to reduce the old style class conflict (Schelsky,
1975:13).

Schelsky concedes that he is by no means the first theorist to
stress the importance of intellectuals. After all, Alfred Weber and
Karl Mannheim did so in the 1920s. In the late 1970s, Alvin
Gouldner (1979) analyzed the same phenomenon for Western
industrial societies, while George Konrád and Ivan Szelényi (1979)
did so for state socialist countries. None the less, Schelsky main-

tains, especially in contrast to the notion of the free-floating intellectuals developed by Weber and Mannheim, that certain societal or material developments are responsible as preconditions for the possibility that the educated gradually assume more influence in modern society. The growing significance of the transmission and interpretation of information, of scientific knowledge, of knowledge required for training and educational purposes and of the means of orientation in a complex society with an intricate network of corporate actors forms the basis for the influence and importance of this segment of the labor force.

Schelsky's observation about the changing nature of advanced society can be reduced to the thesis that the special significance of **knowledge** for the reproduction of modern society constitutes the basis of power and authority for groups monopolizing these instruments of power. These groups are expected to issue demands for a share in the control of society. The control of knowledge allows these groups to form a class. This class finds itself in opposition to all those employed in the production of commodities for the satisfaction of basic individual needs, the maintenance of the standard of living and the functioning of society. Schelsky (1975:14) labels the emerging group of knowledge-producers and knowledge-disseminators the class of the 'distributors and mediators of meaning and purposes' (*Sinn- and Heilsvermittler*). However, it is not in the interest of the new class that knowledge of its rule should enter public consciousness. Since it tends to dominate education, the media, and the public relations field – in short, all those spheres in modern society which somehow have to do with the formation of the public's consciousness and identity – it is relatively easy for this class to deceive the public about its inordinate influence and its interests. One of the most effective strategies employed in this deceptive process is the maintenance of the old myth about the continued existence of the old class conflict between proletariat and capitalist.

Based on a historical perspective, these general observations about the emergence of a new class suggest, according to Schelsky, that this change in the structure of social inequality of advanced society amounts to a **regressive process**. As a matter of fact it constitutes a kind of 're-primitivization' compared to the social and political achievements reached in the wake of the enlightenment, especially the successful abolition of the rule of priests and of the church. A new kind of intellectual clergy now launches the attempt to gain control over secular events and is poised to influence developments in society according to its own image. The original opponents of the enlightenment have been stripped of their influence and power in society. A critical-aggressive stance, taken by the emergent power-brokers and without a real opponent to fear, transforms itself 'almost automatically into a demand for power which lives off past illusions and artificial reference to old antagonisms' (Schelsky, 1975:16).

However, this description of the impending rule by a new class of meaning producers and disseminators remains somewhat schematic and empty because it refers to few, if any, reasons for the apparent readiness and willingness of those who are subject to their domination to accept the interpretations these groups have to offer as legitimate. In addition, Schelsky's account appears to be somewhat vague when it comes to the description of the kinds of modern social and political conditions which allow for the rule of the new élite and the unusual means of domination the secular clergy employ in its rule.

Since Schelsky's polemic in this context is interpreted as engaging the question of the possible practical efficacy of social science knowledge, the details of his observations which are of particular interest concern, of course, the substance of the ideas and views of the educated élite and the reasons for the practical success (especially) of sociological knowledge. Sociological knowledge becomes after all, according to Schelsky, one of the most important sources of meaning for social action in advanced society.

Schelsky's views on the nature of domination follow, for the most part, Max Weber's theory of authority relations. That is, Schelsky assumes with Weber that the exercise of domination need not rely on a monopoly of physical force but that the behavior of others may be controlled by influencing their value orientations, their belief in the legitimacy of commands and similar convictions. The exercise of authority which is able to rely on beliefs about the legitimacy of domination is a form of internalized social control or psychological constraint. The type of control generally concerns the meaning individuals attach to life. Schelsky considers therefore authority relations which are based on broad, socially imposed and effective patterns of meaning as a form of 'intellectual domination or rule based on meaning' (Schelsky, 1975:40). The imposition of meaning may be achieved through various conceptions and value orientations designed to explain life and the nature of the world and to set purposes for life which individuals then follow in order to fulfill these aims as their goals in life. An intellectual system which aspires to rule and which individuals and corporate actors follow in their action brings about order to their beliefs, frees them from possible contradictions and indecisiveness, allows them to somehow conquer the disorienting and complex realities of life as well as uncertainty and chance which they are forced to confront in their world (cf. Schelsky, 1975:41). From an ideal-typical perspective, the use of force and the imposition of meaning do not differ. Both are means of social control and authority. Schelsky therefore is convinced that he does not advance a contradictory observation when he refers to the possibility of social and political domination based on the imposition of meaning.

As far as the substance of the beliefs which serve as justifications for forms of life is concerned, Schelsky sees a range of new 'social religions' emerging which substitute a worldly promise of salvation for an otherworldly one. This worldly promise feeds the expectation of a kind, perfect, and harmonious state of society in which 'fear and suffering, violence and fate, deprivation and abuse, poverty and illness, domination and exploitation' (Schelsky, 1975:77) have been eliminated. Even on the basis of such a limited characterization of the new social religion, it becomes evident that Schelsky is primarily aiming to describe the secular message of a particular political movement which he suspects will become the leading or dominant political force in society, namely progressive or socialist political parties. At the intellectual level, he is aiming to describe the programmatic political beliefs of Marxism or critical theory.

But how and by what means is this kind of social religion going to assume intellectual dominance throughout society? Why do precisely these beliefs achieve pre-eminence and not some set of other ideals and commitments? Schelsky is convinced that modern social religions practice and employ with great success the methods for the production of knowledge and the forms of knowledge, especially those developed by the philosophy of the enlightenment, for the purpose of transmitting beliefs. Unfortunately, even such a suggestion remains somewhat ambivalent. Nor does Schelsky's thesis about the new religions' relentless success in persuading modern individuals to become followers offer any firmer and more concrete evidence. As the proper instrument of thought he refers to a 'critical philosophy' which achieves dominance and, with it, a much more skeptical attitude toward existing conditions as well as a monopoly of reason, yet fails to explicate these suggestions based on sociological considerations. Generally, a critical attitude governs social action and praxis is reduced, as Schelsky (1975:92) resignedly puts it, to the execution of autocratic theory. Certain fixed theoretical purposes and goals are declared to represent practical aims. Reality has to adjust and subject itself to theoretically derived desires. In short, the new class of meaning producers and disseminators usurps and increasingly monopolizes the interpretation of the modern world, especially in the form of a monopoly in determining the standards for rationality and reasoned conduct, a critique of the suffering of the world and a determination and interpretation of the ultimate purposes of existence.

But what are the societal conditions which, aside from the appeal of the substance of the new religions, allow the new class to assume power over the beliefs of society and ultimately domination over virtually all aspects of life in society?

The preconditions for the rule of the new élite

From a sociological point of view, one not only needs to ask what are the socio-structural conditions responsible for the rise of the new class in modern society but also who is expected to assume leadership among the new élite and what specific beliefs has the latter group to offer in the struggle for intellectual domination.

As indicated already, in analogy to a sociological analysis of the domination of the medieval clergy, Schelsky suggests that the modern successors to this clergy will again monopolize interpretations of the meaning of life and exercise power over the majority. The possibility of the rise of the new clergy rests, at the most general level of modern social conditions, on the 'growing and irreversible complexity of all social points of reference' (Schelsky, 1975:119) in advanced society. More precisely, this implies that

> modern superstructures are anonymous and that social relations, often located beyond the ability of individuals to experience them first hand, which become the foundation of societal existence and determine the nature of all their work and production, administration and political decisions, leisure and education, invariably produce a heightened sense of 'abstraction' of social relations in the minds of individuals attempting to comprehend these relations (Schelsky, 1975:119).

Such a heightened complexity of modern social relations, as the result of increasing social differentiation, has, of course, been observed by most sociologists. According to Schelsky, most have tried to capture its meaning with the help of dichotomous terms such as 'society vs. community' (Toennies), 'secondary system vs. primary groups' (Freyer), while others generally refer to the increased complexity in modern social systems.

The theories of modern society listed by Schelsky have indeed emphasized that the increased complexity of social life requires, in order to lessen the disorientation it may generate, for example, a 'reduction of the complexity' (Luhmann) in all spheres of social life and personal circumstances. However, the same theorists tend to stress that the ability to reduce the complexity of data, references, goals, relations and means of action constitutes an anthropological constant and a necessity of human existence. In the tradition of philosophical anthropology, a reduction in the complexity of points of reference, possible courses of action and interpretations is indispensable. Relief and discharge from complexity is required at all times in all social formations and is therefore not necessarily a modern phenomenon. Modern societies may indeed present actors with an even greater range of possible courses of action but the ability to achieve a reduction in the complexity in order to act is by no means a novel task faced only by contemporary individual and corporate actors. In short, Schelsky's reference to the complexity or even the heightened complexity of modern existence cannot serve as a sufficient reason for the domination of a new secular minded clergy. For this reason perhaps, Schelsky hints that another process might be responsible for the emergence of the new class of meaning producers and disseminators. He maintains that over time meaning inevitably is subject to obsolescence. At the same time, the reduction in the complexity of life demanded in modern societies simply cannot revert to the beliefs and meanings useful in the past. Schelsky observes that there is a convergence between the forms of culture and social structure. The meanings which come into use in advanced society are subject to the same forces which increase the complexity of social reality in general, that is, concepts and motives will be more abstract as well. The elevation in the degree of conceptual abstraction to which beliefs and motives which provide meaning in everyday life are subject, corresponds to increasingly abstract and decreasingly transparent social relations. The convergence between cultural forms and social structure occurs, according to Schelsky's thesis, on multiple levels.

The **first** level is linked to the 'retreat to practical or "technological" efforts to master' the complicated situations of modern civilization (Schelsky, 1975:119). The result is that the ability to engage in action is facilitated by a form of avoidance strategy. The need to engage in discussions of purposes and goals of social action is reduced or even eliminated because technology and the knowledge of production processes, that is, technical knowledge, is elevated to a type of 'governing knowledge' ('*Herrschaftswissen*'). Constitutive for such knowledge is that desired goals are realized without conscious reflection and discussion. But technical knowledge – and here Schelsky follows the conventional conception of technology – is not really meaningful and able to inform the self-conception of the individual. On the contrary, the greater the success of technical knowledge and its artifacts, the larger the deficit in the social meanings it produces. In short, at the first level of the growing abstractness of modern social life, a generalization of the knowledge of the world of work to other spheres of life can be observed.

As a consequence, on a **second** level, general worldviews (or '*Orientierungswissen*'), that is, normative goals as purposes of action, are elevated to the same degree of abstractness. Organizations and entire social institutions which produce and offer these broad value-orientations, as for example the family and education, which allow individuals to 'lead' a certain life, increasingly dominate the identity individuals acquire. Schelsky also is convinced that the control over normative orientations is structurally more important for the distribution of domination in modern society than is the control over the means of production.

On the **third** level of the increase in the abstractness of social existence, the new élite of meaning producers and disseminators construct global patterns of orientation or normative patterns concerning the whole of society. At this level, Schelsky refers to the social and emancipatory knowledge of salvation or global conceptions about human happiness, and the meaning of a more perfect existence. In analogy to Max Weber's sociology of religion Schelsky proposes to develop a level of otherworldliness found in this new abstract structure of normative orientations. For Weber, such a sphere of otherworldly conceptions is constitutive of all religions and religious forms of domination since otherworldliness is the very foundation for religious beliefs and therefore the authority of the clergy.

What remains to be explicated, finally, is the nature and the composition of the groups who acquire authority as a result of their ability to manufacture the meaning it takes to live in modern society. Apparently, the new clergy cannot be recruited from the scientific community because, as Schelsky (1975:125) argues, there is no scientific discipline which is capable of offering effective and superior normative orientations for the majority of individuals in modern society. A vacuum in normative leadership is the result. Intellectuals, initially vaguely perceived as the producers of culture and ideological visions, begin to fill the vacuum and gradually assume authority. But the basis of their power and of the advantages they begin to acquire in the struggle for domination is not linked to the superior cognitive achievement of this group. What allows intellectuals to assume and retain power is above all a matter of their control of the **means of leadership**, especially their domination of the information apparatus (mass communication) and their control over education and training at all levels in society. Such power ultimately amounts to a control of public opinion. If today there still is something approaching public opinion or a '"*volonté générale*", then it is dominated and manufactured by the "communicators" and "socialization agents" of society' (Schelsky, 1975:133). The élite of meaning producers exercises, at the same time, a kind of class domination which comes about as the result of the development of class antagonism between the classes of the producers of commodities and meaning. A new structure of societal inequality is constituted which is of course no longer based on private property.

The discipline of sociology acquires a special position within the élite of meaning producers and disseminators. As a matter of fact, for Schelsky sociology becomes the 'key science' of modernity. Although many of Schelsky's examples and targets are to be found in the West German society of his day, he claims to have observed that sociology acquires the same intellectual status in all modern societies. Even state socialist countries are not immune because all 'ideological-totalitarian socialist' countries are dominated with the crucial help of sociological ideas (Schelsky, 1976:171). Last but not least, sociology becomes the key science because in advanced societies much of the curriculum for the training and the generic knowledge of many occupational and professional groups is increasingly dominated by sociological conceptions. Schelsky refers to teachers, theologians, journalists, writers etc. forming the core of the users of sociological ideas.

What is the nature of the sociological ideas which acquire dominance and in what ways do they differ from meaning structures they are assumed to replace? In the most general sense this question can be answered in a straightforward fashion: the normative authority of sociological ideas implies that a conception which stresses the social nature of human beings prevails. As a result, individual identities are governed primarily by views which stress the social embeddedness of the conduct and the beliefs of individual actors.

According to Schelsky the discipline of sociology fulfills three specific functions: (1) sociology produces systematic theory; (2) it carries out empirical research; and (3) it supplies means of orientation for practical circumstances. The new clergy relies mainly on the third function of sociology. The scientific basis and legitimacy of those formulae produced by sociology which have a normative status in society are not primarily at issue. For Schelsky such conceptions are effective in practice and sufficient for practice as a result of the problematization of social issues from a sociological perspective and with the help of sociological concepts.

Again and again, Schelsky refers to critical theory and its topics and views as a particularly efficacious and practical means of normative orientation. Critical theory offers a critique of capitalism, of the prevailing power structure, and of prevailing political ideologies and patterns of popular culture and consumption. In each instance, the purpose of these analyses is not so much to change underlying social structure, as it is to influence the collective and individual consciousness. Once the collective consciousness has been transformed the world of social facts might be transformed as well (Schelsky, 1975:267). The enlightenment about modern society which sociology therefore offers to the public is, as far as Schelsky is concerned, nothing but a highly selective or politicized set of normative interpretations. 'Genuine' rather than 'deceptive' enlightenment always implies the dissemination of knowledge which is self-explanatory, which each individual is capable of understanding, and which does not directly rely on scientific justifications and a comprehension of social problems driven by scientific reasoning. Genuine enlightenment emancipates individuals from reliance on, and from domination by, specific institutions and individuals. Sociological enlightenment, as widely practiced according to Schelsky, finds itself enmeshed and trapped in a self-contradiction. For in the consciousness of the individual sociology struggles against the authority of the other sciences but fails to do so in its own case (cf. Schelsky, 1975:161). Moreover, social science theories are particularly suited to fall victim to such a self-contradiction since they are especially prone to appear (or pretend to be able) to represent, at least among non-specialists, the whole of the means of modern orientation. They claim to increase the intellectual transparency, when in fact they are not impartial. Thus, the influence of sociology is based not so much on the topics and problems it tackles in its theorizing and research and the insights it generates, but rather on the basis of its conceptual apparatus, the meanings of its peculiar vocabulary and its unique point of view and perspective of individual and social conditions.

Sociology becomes visible and is considered important through its language. Status, role, function, community, mobility, social change, group, team, stress, frustration etc. are simplified formulae which convey not merely 'information' but meaning and orientation. The influence of sociology rests not with its research findings. More systematically, in Schelsky's diagnosis, intellectuals convey a common message despite internal cognitive divisions, namely the end or the dissolution of the person and its self-obligations manifest in social action (cf. Schelsky, 1976:178–82). The cognitive traditions of sociology convey the notion that traditional, individually centered orientations first developed in the

Renaissance, then continued in the French enlightenment and the political idealism of the nineteenth century are obsolete. In particular, reference to all forms of social action which invoke the **individual**, or the single person with unique inner convictions and a sense of responsibility, is considered antiquated. The notion of an individual soul and conscience is discredited by sociology and the philosophical perspectives it supports. The idea of 'personal conscience' falls into disrepute and is eliminated as socially irrelevant which implies the possibility of a sociologically informed morality. Sociological concepts and ideas separated from their disciplinary contexts and references become popular formal guidelines for political and individual conduct. The ultimate outcome is a kind of 'sociological' collective consciousness (Schelsky, 1975:269).

As remarkable as Schelsky's euphoric praise of the practical accomplishments of sociology may be, even more remarkable is perhaps how rapidly the thrust of the assessment of this science's practical influence can be reversed. Today, the social sciences are plagued by self-doubt and the perception of a distinct lack of public credibility, whereas the natural sciences, for instance, have never been subject to such rapid fluctuations in their self-evaluation and public confidence. At the present time, Ralf Dahrendorf's observations and conclusions (1989) about the intellectual and societal status of the social sciences are much more to the point. In the developed world the decade of the 1980s was a time of innovations, most of which were clearly not the outcome of social science research or theory. Dahrendorf even voices the suspicion that these social innovations, such as a decrease in the importance of the welfare state, a reduction in taxes, the encouragement toward credit based consumption, the deregulation of a number of spheres of life, are in fact transformations which were initiated and set in motion **against** the social sciences. At least the widespread skepticism toward the social sciences among politicians seems to suggest to him that such a conclusion is warranted. The practical success of the social sciences in general and sociology in particular therefore may be seen to find expression in the consolidation rather than in the acceleration of societal trends. Dahrendorf (1989:8) concludes his assessment of the actual practical efficacy of sociology in the present period by indicating that sociology functions more like a brake limiting the speed of social transformations.

But then the speed with which judgements about the 'real' practical impact of social science are reversed appears to have gone largely unchecked. As a matter of fact, the speed might be accelerating. Almost fifty years ago, in an essay on patterns of self-assessment among social scientists, Schumpeter (1946:345) felt he had to go back at least 100 years to find a period in which economists were as optimistic as they were in the late 1940s.

Disadvantages and benefits of a pragmatic social science

> If economists could manage to get themselves thought of as humble, competent people, on a level with dentists, that would be splendid.
>
> John M. Keynes[2]

When examined from the perspective of knowledge about economic discourse available at the present, John Maynard Keynes appears to have had the precariously utopian hope that economics one day will be able to compare itself and therefore evolve into a science which enjoys the same social prestige, ease of administration and painless recognition as does the 'science' of dentistry, while it can also claim to produce the same kind of useful service to individuals and society. Keynes's view expresses the 'powerful faith that social science could solve problems which in the past had brought about the downfall of nations and civilizations' (Skidelsky, 1979:57).

Many economists have interpreted Keynes's observation as supporting a strictly value-free economics and as evidence that he shared their aspiration for economics to generate a kind of soulless expert knowledge. Whether such an interpretation is warranted may be questioned (e.g. Fitzgibbons, 1988:45). What is less controversial is that economics has not lived up to expectations which would put its practical success on a footing equal to dentistry. As a matter of fact, it has not even come close to this goal in the past sixty years. Whether economic discourse – and by implication social science generally – is able to or should in principle attempt to reach the goal outlined by Keynes, and what the associated 'opportunity costs' might be, is the topic of the following section.

Many observers would stress, and I will emphasize in my review, that a pragmatic social science knowledge comes at a price (cf. Ravetz, 1971). Keynes did not appear to have any ethical or epistemological reservations against a discipline of economics which conceives of directly generating practical knowledge as a fairly normal state of affairs. But it is precisely the prospect of such a state of normality for social science which causes other social scientists to become quite concerned.

The infamous Project Camelot which was halted in June of 1965 by the US defense secretary, Robert McNamara, after the Norwegian social scientist Johan Galtung had informed Chilean politicians and intellectuals about the research plans, surely is an instructive but also ambivalent example of the potential dangers of a 'pragmatic' orientation for the social science community. The research, supported and endorsed by the United States Army, was designed to inquire according to official pronouncements into the conditions for the possibility of internal political conflicts and the response of government to disturbances of this kind in Latin American countries. It was interpreted by critics as an attempt to obtain sensitive intelligence for the purposes of destabilizing and ultimately overthrowing political regimes hostile to the United States, or for that matter, obtain knowledge about ways in which revolutions inspired by the left could be prevented. But Galtung's account and interpretations of the purposes of the project are already contested by collaborators and co-investigators of the research plan. Their claim is that Project Camelot represented a case of basic social and political research. Since the project collapsed at the end of 1964, it really is only possible, at this time, to examine the response of social scientists to a hypothetical situation. One is, for example, able to examine in the case of Project Camelot, both among its critics and its proponents, the then predominant but mistaken judgement about the power of social science knowledge. At the same time, it is evident that many saw the autonomy of the social science community in general and of the investigators in particular jeopardized. Irving L. Horowitz (1965:46) stresses that the 'autonomous character of the social science disciplines – their own criteria of worthwhile scholarship – should not be abandoned'. Gideon Sjoberg (1967:152) arrives at a similar conclusion, based on the apparent identification of the investigators with the goals and means of the foreign policy of the Army or the American government: 'The major problem social scientists faced in Project Camelot, and encounter in many other research projects as well, is the inability to achieve a sufficient degree of autonomy *vis-à-vis* the administrative-control sector of the social system that supports these research efforts.'

The question which follows almost immediately is what strategic measures and forms of conduct can in fact assure that the autonomy of the social science community is guaranteed, how much dependence and in what areas is perhaps unavoidable? Obviously these are not easy questions to answer. A satisfactory response generally depends on the nature of the local conditions faced by the social science community at a specific time and place.

But as the discussion about Project Camelot also shows, reflections and disputes about the practical usefulness of social science are often carried out in a polemical tone and for polemical purposes. Frequently, even the willingness of social scientists to take part in, or work on practical matters for someone, is denounced, without hesitation, as 'ideological work' or as simply wrongheaded and without merit, in particular if there is indication that this appears to be work for the wrong side of some kind of dispute. Paradoxically, vigorous opponents of social science discourse with a practical intent overestimate its efficacy. A pragmatic social science cannot hope to usurp practical decisions. Only a kind technocratic science mistakenly claims and aspires to be able to do just that.

One alleged moral and political dilemma invariably invoked in such emotionally charged discussions is the suggestion that social scientists face the choice of either serving the powerful as experts and therefore of facing the risk of undermining and corrupting the ethos of science, or if one deliberately takes on a role-at-a-distance, the risk of losing any influence on the course of political events. In reality, however, the situations and the range of choices are much more varied (cf. Wilensky, 1971).

Keynes and his economic ideas of course were not immune to these ethical and political dilemmas. It is thus unavoidable that Keynes's theoretical program and his economic advice became linked to certain dimensions of the entrenched value-free debate in social science discourse. But Keynes (1936:380) was aware that he would not be able to escape such countervailing forces:

> whilst . . . the enlargement of functions of the state . . . would seem to a nineteenth-century publicist or to a contemporary American financier to be a terrific encroachment on individualism, I defend it, on the contrary, both as the only practicable means of avoiding the destruction of existing economic forms in their entirety and as the condition of the successful functioning of individual freedom.

Instead of the relatively ambivalent, perhaps even empty goals (*Leerformeln*) and essentially contestable political purposes of classical economic theory, such as freedom, equality, wealth or justice, Keynes substitutes with full employment, economic growth and low inflation, much more concrete socio-economic aims. But in the wake of defining more concrete policy goals and of calculating possible successes and failures of economic policies more directly, a significant political transformation of economic discourse has taken place as well. Political goals which cannot be directly deduced from and justified by Keynes's theory are displaced from discourse. Although a program for a pragmatic social science is unlikely ever to become the dominating component of the social science community, such a transformation of discourse represents an advantage but also has its costs.

The social relations of power in a society determine what is possible in society. This applies to the practical realization of natural science knowledge, the development of technical artifacts (cf. Noble, 1984), but also to social science knowledge as a capacity for action and the chances of its realization. What is possible is governed, in the case of both forms of knowledge, by the nature of social reality. Social reality assures (or deflects) the possibility of controlling certain conditions, of realizing specific effects or minimizing the impact of others. All of this of course implies as indicated that existing power relations play a decisive role in the realization of technical designs but also in the practical reconstruction of social scientific models. At the same time, any deliberate and successful attempt, as social scientists have demanded from time to time, to 'abstain' from any active involvement in social and political affairs, also amounts to a specific political and moral stance and is by no means without its own practical consequences. And, each side in the debate on the merits of detachment and involvement of science invokes ethical and political considerations on its own behalf; C. Wright Mills, in his *The Sociological Imagination* ([1959] 1970), for example, demands and insistently points to the moral and professional obligation of social scientists to try to influence political decision-making with the help of their research findings while a much more sizeable and influential part of the social science community strongly opposes such engagement as an inherently alien stance for scientists.

The demand for a strict separation of science and politics is based on the conviction and unease that a merging of knowledge and belief would be the inevitable outcome. After all, critics of a close linkage between reason and politics can point to numerous and grave historical examples: fascism in Germany and Stalinism in the Soviet Union are, though in the latter instance the experiment lost much of its legitimacy after the death of Stalin (cf. Kneen, 1984), two of the most serious and frightful recent cases of enforced efforts to join science and politics.

The potential intellectual, moral and political distance from what I have called a pragmatic social science to a social science which is based on mere immediate utilitarian concerns is perhaps but a short and hazardous journey. A pragmatic social science is bound to encounter a dilemma which all science that aspires to be useful and is successful in this effort must face: 'The usefulness of science confers a new kind of societal stability but threatens also its autonomy' (W. Krohn, 1988:178).

However, the dangers, under present social and political circumstances and institutional arrangements, are easily exaggerated. Modern scientific disciplines are not homogeneous communities nor are they national institutions. Science cannot easily be subjected to control, even if the political will to do so is present. The balance sheet of efforts in different nations to subjugate science is for the most part not very encouraging to those contemplating the assumption of cognitive and institutional control.

On an individual basis, scholars who become the willing instruments of the rulers, corporations, political parties and interest groups lose their claim to be legitimate members of the scientific community and can no longer rely on their membership status. The advocacy and execution of a pragmatic social science, hand-in-hand with a built-in critical political stance and engagement for stringent ethical standards, are not at odds in principle. In this world, as Bulmer (1978) observes with justification, I believe there really cannot be more than a handful of 'social scientists' who more or less mechanically live up to the expectations of their 'masters' and execute their desires to the letter. A pragmatic social science, in any event, is not and need not be distinguished by blind political partisanship. Such a stance, as is the case for its extreme opposite, can only lead to social science knowledge which is, at best, only useful as the result of fortuitous circumstances.

At the institutional level, contemporary social science, in contrast for example to the social science community during the 1920s and 1930s, or even the 1950s, has reached a critical mass of practitioners. The socialization of social scientists under present conditions is to a much larger extent a matter controlled by the science community itself and not external forces in the form of external ideologies, institutions and therefore pre-existing qualities of recruits to science. Socialization in science opens access to status and reputation in the scientific community and not political conformity or timidity.

The influential role Keynes played between the wars, both in public and in private, is a position which would be very difficult, if not impossible to attain under present conditions in the modern scientific community or the public administration of the state (cf. Scherf, 1986:88). The institution of contemporary social science represents a highly differentiated social organization in which a multitude of legitimate theories and intellectual traditions are developed and in which important social networks of cognitive influence are international in nature. The danger that the social sciences as a whole or important parts of the social science community should fall under the control of purely utilitarian thought-categories and convictions and thereby lose their critical distance, or their institutionalized skepticism, is unrealistic.

What critics of social science, especially an allegedly political conformist social science, forget is the now well-established social and not merely intellectual foundation of distance, autonomy and even remoteness of the social science community. As long as the present, highly differentiated international social and intellectual organization of social science does not change dramatically, the chance that the social science community suddenly and decisively will be governed wholesale by external constraints, must be rated very small indeed. On the contrary, it is entirely possible that the opposite development continues to be strengthened, including a dependency of economic and political contexts on those parts of social science discourse which prove to be successful in practice. An increase in the usefulness of science can go hand-in-hand with an increase in the societal dependence on science. As a matter of fact, most theories of post-industrial society or of knowledge societies (Bell, 1973; Böhme and Stehr, 1990; Stehr, 1992) postulate just such a development for many spheres of modern society as they are increasingly penetrated by scientific and technological knowledge. Correspondingly, the increased socio-political autonomy science gains might well be accompanied by a consolidation of the social and intellectual independence, distance and remoteness in certain spheres of social science discourse. Yet, these developments do not alter the possibility that individual social scientists will continue to be enticed, and be vulnerable, to offer knowledge claims which suit specific interest groups in society.

Among the costs of a pragmatic social science is, finally, the possibility that social science knowledge oriented to specific practical circumstances, though it may be able to alert individual and corporate actors to concrete opportunities for action and may even be able to set such action in motion, could simultaneously deflect attention away from important social problems because it happens to define these issues as unaccessible, at least for the actors who form the primary audience for it. Of course, specific social scientists today rarely have a monopoly in providing knowledge about specific circumstances. Intellectual competition is the more likely scenario. Among the opportunity costs of competition among advice from social science is a reduction in the potential disadvantages of a reliance on a single voice.

Aside from concerns expressed by social scientists from time to time about the danger that external demands and purpose may unduly affect the intellectual development of social science discourse, laments about the growing distance between social science and its potential users – for example in the form of a talking past each other and of researching at odds with each other – may be found with some regularity in observations of social scientists who have devoted at least part of their work to practical issues or spent time in organizations outside of academia (e.g. Platt, 1976:178–9; Wenger, 1987). By the same token, social scientists who have tried to interest practitioners in prospective research know only too well that these conversations and petitions for support are quickly embedded in a sense of mutual mistrust, misunderstanding or the expressed doubt that social science knowledge is germane. A pragmatic social science should represent the opportunity to reduce some of the conditions which make for the perpetuation of the failure to comprehend and for a reduction in the objective basis of disbelief in the ability of social science to generate practical knowledge.

But on what basis could such a claim possibly be made? It seems that most of the vigorous argument which surrounds the discussion of the social role of social science, the production of knowledge for practice and the ways in which such a purpose may be at odds with the ambition – often understood as the superior and more honorable goal – to achieve objective knowledge about phenomena which are socially constructed designs has been bugged and bogged down almost since the inception of social science by the perceived division of knowledge and action. The separation of knowledge and action is closely intertwined with the differentiation of the means and ends (effects) of conduct and the conviction that the proper role of all science can and should be to assist discussions about and selections of the means of human conduct. The model of instrumentality amounts to an ideal typical representation of this position. Science can only be successful and should confine its aspirations to instrumental reason. Both the support for, since it affirms the objectivity and neutrality of science, and the lament about such a role, because it reduces science to an apolitical agent, converge in the end and contribute to the persuasiveness of the same position.

The examination of the conditions for the possibility of social science knowledge and, by analogy, for scientific and technical knowledge, has shown that discussions of means, ends and effects are not superfluous. But the discussion also should have shown that concern with the **conditions** of action is equally, perhaps more important, both for the construction of useful social science knowledge and deliberations about the implementation of knowledge. Knowledge as a capacity for action can only be successfully translated into action in a particular context. Whether it will be possible to translate social science knowledge into action depends on the conditions, resources and structures found in a specific social context and the extent to which it can be modified to accommodate specific designs (cf. Radder, 1986).

Concern with a pragmatic social science shifts attention and discussion away from means and ends of action toward concerns with the social and material **conditions of action** and whether these conditions are desirable, can be maintained or can be changed over time, and what risks may be associated with a course of action. Such a shift in the terms of the discussion in which the social science community can participate in practical affairs is no longer merely a focus on the 'means' of social action but amounts to a 'political' discussion. Reflections involving the conditions of action which allow for the realization of (social science) knowledge cannot be reduced to a kind of socio-technical calculus but are a matter which extends to issues otherwise 'reserved' for political and moral discourse (see Stehr, 1981; Stehr and Meja, 1990).

Notes

1 Schelsky (1975:259) cautions that only a marginal insider is capable of executing a radical critique of the authority of sociology in modern society. The opponents of the domination of philosophical discourse were philosophers or employed the means of philosophical reasoning. Schelsky, therefore, compares himself to the aristocratic critics of feudalism or absolutism and likens his opposition to the radical critique of capitalism which issues from persons who switched sides in the class struggle (cf. Merton, 1972).

2 Keynes [1930] 1984a:332.

Conclusion

It has been argued that the realization of experimental scientific knowledge and social scientific knowledge is, for example in the form of a specific *Gedankenexperiment*, subject to the same contingencies of implementation. Any demarcation between natural and social science is, in this respect at least, meaningless. In the case of both sets of scientific disciplines, the transfer and implementation of knowledge is prompted and made possible by the availability (that is, their construction) of circumstances which allow for knowledge as a capacity for action to be translated into action. But as can easily be seen, the implementation is dependent on processes and conditions of action external to science which, once again, make a separation between natural science and social science knowledge obvious and relevant since their legitimacy in general in society varies considerably and the interests in outcomes made possible by each bundle of disciplines differs significantly. In the case of natural science knowledge explicit reference to the conditions of implementation external to science therefore rarely becomes a point of necessary reference in the construction of such knowledge claims. In social science, however, the incorporation of the conditions of implementation should often determine the response to knowledge claims generated by social scientists.

The problem of a pragmatic social science is not how to abolish politics in favor of science or how to substitute knowledge for politics, as utopian rationalists might attempt to achieve or as critics of technocratic aspirations would warn. On the contrary, the problem of a pragmatic social science is how to utilize and incorporate social science knowledge in practical action, including political decisions and what kind of social science knowledge may best be used in such a way. A pragmatic social science acknowledges the irreducibility of practical processes as political processes but also does not threaten the 'autonomy of inquiry'. The social science community remains the primary agent of cognitive and social control.[1] Both the identification of practical objectives or problems and their solutions or policies designed to cope with such issues are essentially contested political phenomena (cf. Ezrahi, 1980). The formulation and execution of policies always remains social action.

And social action is riddled with conflict, negotiation, compromises and cannot be insulated by knowledge against such contestability. The problem of a pragmatic social science is the situation-specific combination of social science knowledge and practical action, for example, political action.

The intellectual division of labor which has emerged within the social sciences in the past decades does not constitute a promising basis on which to build and develop social science knowledge that responds effectively to local conditions which, at times, can of course encompass many individuals and groups or a large territory for that matter. An analysis of research projects devoted to practical matters quickly confirms, on the whole, the disciplinary self-sufficiency (cf. Coleman, 1972a) of such research. The growing number and the growing tightness of cognitive boundaries of intellectual concerns and methodological practices of exclusion within social science are, for the most part, not a precondition, but a distinct barrier, as many have recognized, for the construction of social science knowledge which is practical knowledge. As long as the selection and incorporation of variables is driven by disciplinary or, even, subdisciplinary practices and traditions, then the probability is considerable that the outcomes of such cognitive efforts too are limited to the practitioners who inhabit and defend the territory within these boundaries. In principle, a broader integration of intellectual efforts for practical purposes is not impossible and may not even contradict further cognitive differentiation within the social science community. However, neither is work on the legitimation of labor directed toward practical knowledge in social science easy, nor is the optimistic conclusion justified that development in this direction will be without major difficulties. Entrenched intellectual and social forces within the social science community are very successful in operating in the opposite direction. Skepticism about the success of a program for practical knowledge is therefore in order.

One of the central questions perhaps which remains to be considered, after one has argued for and shown how a pragmatic social science might proceed, concerns the matter of the meaningful or responsible function of social science in society. But the details and the specific response to such a demand is a contingent one, as is practical knowledge. As long as one extrapolates from the extreme condition in which social scientists are not merely the producers of knowledge for action but are also able to determine the conditions of conduct and the purposes of social action, the germane and the critical question becomes whether social science can or should evolve into a kind of 'production-science' attempting to maximize its pragmatic implications to the fullest? Should the production of social science knowledge for practice remain tied closely to existing socio-political conditions or, should it perhaps invoke its own and possibly alternative criteria in judging a course of action and its consequences? These are matters each community of social scientists will have to answer in its own way, responding and confronting of course its local conditions of action.

From the perspective of social science, the conclusion is that the task of formulating practical social science knowledge requires that the moment of its use has to be built into, or at least explicitly taken into account in, the process of constructing knowledge from the beginning. This demands that particular features of the social realm in which such knowledge is expected to be employed ought to be taken into consideration as a mechanism of reducing the complexity of the usually broad spectrum of possible attributes which compete for attention. However, practical knowledge, it has to be stressed, does not displace knowledge in practice, namely the process of translating knowledge as a capacity for action into action. Practical social science may modify and moderate the tension between science and action but it does not eliminate the boundaries between the scientific community and society nor does it alter the need to produce further knowledge, namely knowledge which pertains to and results from the implementation of practical knowledge into action.

Note

1   Gunnar Myrdal (1944:1041), in his *An American Dilemma*, defends a similar view, when he argues that science becomes 'no better protected against biases by the entirely negative device of refusing to arrange its results for practical and political utilization'.

Bibliography

The bibliography contains a number of references in addition to those cited in the text; these items are of further relevance to the general topic of the relation between social science knowledge and practice.

Abrams, Philip (1985) 'The uses of British sociology, 1831–1932', pp. 181–205 in Martin Bulmer (ed.), *Essays on the History of British Sociological Research*. Cambridge: Cambridge University Press.

Abt, Clark W. (ed.) (n.d.) *Costs and Benefits of Applied Social Research*. Cambridge, Mass.: Abt Books.

Adams, Robert C., Neil J. Smelser and Donald J. Treiman (eds) (1982) *Behavioral and Social Science Research: A National Resource*. Washington, DC: National Academy Press.

Adams, Walter (1978) 'The contribution of economics to public policy formation', pp. 358–69 in J. Milton Yinger and Stephen J. Cutler (eds), *Major Social Issues. A Multidisciplinary View*. New York: Free Press.

Adorno, Theodor W. et al. (1969) *Der Positivismusstreit in der deutschen Soziologie*. Neuwied: Luchterhand.

Adorno, Theodor W. ([1957] 1972) 'Soziologie und empirische Forschung', pp. 196–216 in Theordor W. Adorno, *Gesammelte Schriften 8: Soziologische Schriften 1*. Frankfurt am Main: Suhrkamp.

Albert, Ethel M. (1954) 'Causality in the social sciences', *Journal of Philosophy*, 51:695–706.

Albert, Hans ([1971] 1972) 'Kritizismus und Naturalismus: Die Überwindung des klassischen Rationalitätsmodells und das Überbrückungsproblem', pp. 13–38 in Hans Albert (ed.), *Konstruktion und Kritik. Aufsätze zur Philosophie des kritischen Rationalismus*. Hamburg: Hoffmann and Campe.

Aldenhoff, Rita (1987) 'Max Weber and the Evangelical-Social Congress', pp. 193–201 in Wolfgang J. Mommsen and Jürgen Osterhammel (eds), *Max Weber and his Contemporaries*. London: Allen and Unwin.

Almond, Gabriel A. and Stephen J. Genco (1977) 'Clouds, clocks, and the study of politics', *World Politics*, 29:489–522.

Apel, Karl-Otto (1973a) 'Die Entfaltung der "sprachanalytischen" Philosophie und das Problem der Geisteswissenschaften', pp. 28–95 in Karl-Otto Apel, *Transformation der Philosophie*, band II: *Das Apriori der Kommunikationsgemeinschaft*. Frankfurt am Main: Suhrkamp.

Apel, Karl-Otto ([1973b] 1980) 'The communication community as the transcendental presupposition of the social sciences', pp. 136–79 in Karl-Otto Apel, *Transformation of Philosophy*. London: Routledge and Kegan Paul.

Aron, Raymond ([1960] 1985) 'Science and consciousness of society', pp. 199–226 in Raymond Aron, *History, Truth, Liberty. Selected Writings of Raymond Aron.* Chicago: University of Chicago Press.

Bacon, Francis ([1620] 1960) *Novum Organum.* New York: Liberal Arts Press.

Bailey, Kenneth D. (1990) *Social Entropy Theory.* Albany, New York: State University of New York Press.

Baldamus, W. (1972) 'The role of discoveries in science', pp. 276–302 in Teodor Shanin (ed.), *The Rules of the Game.* London: Tavistock.

Balogh, Thomas (1982) *The Irrelevance of Conventional Economics.* London: Weidenfeld and Nicolson.

Barber, Bernard (1987) *Effective Social Science. Eight Cases in Economics, Political Science, and Sociology.* New York: Russell Sage Foundation.

Barnes, J.A. (1980) *Who Should Know What? Social Science, Privacy and Ethics.* Cambridge: Cambridge University Press.

Barnes, Barry (1988) *The Nature of Power.* Urbana and Chicago: University of Illinois Press.

Bauman, Zygmunt (1978) *Hermeneutics and Social Science.* New York: Columbia University Press.

Bauman, Zygmunt (1990) *Thinking Sociologically.* Oxford: Basil Blackwell.

Beal, George M. et al. (eds) (1986) *Knowledge Generation, Exchange and Utilization.* Boulder, Co.: Westview.

Beck, Ulrich (1982) 'Folgeprobleme der Modernisierung und die Stellung der Soziologie in der Praxis', pp. 3–23 in Ulrich Beck (ed.), *Soziologie und Praxis. Erfahrungen, Konflikte, Perspektiven.* Sonderband 1, *Soziale Welt.* Göttingen: Otto Schwartz and Co.

Beck, Ulrich and Wolfgang Bonss (1984) 'Soziologie und Modernisierung: Zur Ortsbestimmung der Verwendungsforschung', *Soziale Welt,* 35:381–406.

Beck, Ulrich and Wolfgang Bonss (eds) (1989a) *Weder Sozialtechnologie noch Aufklärung? Analysen zur Verwendung sozialwissenschaftlichen Wissens.* Frankfurt am Main: Suhrkamp.

Beck, Ulrich and Wolfgang Bonss (1989b) 'Zum Strukturwandel von Sozialwissenschaft und Praxis', *Soziale Welt,* 40:196–214.

Beck, Ulrich and Christoph Lau (1982) 'Die "Verwendungstauglichkeit" sozialwissenschaftlicher Theorien: Das Beispiel der Bildungs- und Arbeitsmarktforschung', pp. 369–94 in Ulrich Beck (ed.), *Soziologie und Praxis. Erfahrungen, Konflikte, Perspektiven.* Sonderband 1, *Soziale Welt,* Göttingen: Otto Schwartz and Co.

Becker, George (1984) 'Pietism and science: A critique of Robert K. Merton's Hypothesis', *American Journal of Sociology,* 89:1065–90.

Beetham, David (1985) *Max Weber and the Theory of Modern Politics.* Cambridge: Polity Press.

Bell, Daniel (1973) *The Coming of Post-Industrial Society. A Venture in Social Forecasting.* New York: Basic Books.

Bell, Daniel (1987) 'The world and the United States in 2013', *Daedalus,* 116:1–31.

Bell, Daniel and Irving Kristol (eds) (1981) *The Crisis in Economic Theory.* New York: Basic Books.

Bennis, Warren G., Kenneth D. Benne and Robert Chin (eds) (1961) *The Planning of Change.* New York: Holt, Rinehart and Winston.

Berk, Richard A. (1987) 'How applied research can save sociologists from themselves', *The American Sociologist,* 18:119–24.

Beyer, Janice M. and Harrison M. Trice (1982) 'The utilization process: A conceptual framework and synthesis of empirical findings', *Administrative Science Quarterly*, 27:591–622.

Biddle, Bruce J. (1987) 'Social research and social policy', *The American Sociologist*, 18:158–66.

Bigler, Robert M. (1972) *The Politics of German Protestantism: The Rise of the Protestant Church Elite in Prussia*. Berkeley, Ca.: University of California Press.

Blalock, Hubert M. (1979) 'Dilemmas and strategies of theory construction', pp. 119–35 in William E. Snizek, Elsworth R. Fuhrman and Michael K. Miller (eds), *Contemporary Issues in Theory and Research. A Metasociological Perspective*. Westport, Conn.: Greenwood Press.

Bleaney, Michael (1985) *The Rise and Fall of Keynesian Economics. An Investigation of its Contribution to Capitalist Development*. New York: St Martin's Press.

Block, Fred and Larry Hirschhorn (1979) 'New productive forces and the contradictions of contemporary capitalism', *Theory and Society*, 7:363–95.

Blume, Stuart S. (1978) 'Policy as theory: A framework for understanding the contributions of social science to welfare policy', pp. 33–48 in H. Freeman (ed.), *Policies Studies: Review Annual*. Beverly Hills: Sage.

Boese, Franz (1939) *Geschichte des Vereins für Sozialpolitik, 1872–1932*. Berlin: Duncker and Humblot.

Böhme, Gernot and Nico Stehr (eds) (1986) *The Knowledge Society*. Dordrecht: Reidel.

Böhme, Gernot and Nico Stehr (1990) 'Wissensgesellschaften', *Universitas*, 45: 225–31.

Bombach, Gottfried (ed.) (1983) *Der Keynesianismus IV. Die beschäftigungspolitische Diskussion in der Wachstumsepoche der Bundesrepublik Deutschland. Dokumente und Analysen*. Berlin: Springer-Verlag.

Bös, Dieter and Hans-Dieter Stolper (eds) (1984) *Schumpeter oder Keynes? Zur Wirtschaftspolitik der neunziger Jahre*. Berlin: Springer-Verlag.

Boulding, Kenneth (1973) 'The shadow of the stationary state', *Daedalus*, 102: 89–101.

Bourdieu, Pierre (1980) *Le sans practique*. Paris: Les éditions de minuit.

Bressler, Marvin (1967) 'Sociology and collegiate education', pp. 45–77 in Paul F. Lazarsfeld et al. (eds), *The Uses of Sociology*. New York: Basic Books.

Brewer, Garry D. (1973) *Politicians, Bureaucrats, and the Consultant. A Critique of Urban Problem Solving*. New York: Basic Books.

Brothwell, John (1988) '*The General Theory* after fifty years – why are we not all Keynesians?', pp. 45–63 in John Hillard (ed.), *J.M. Keynes in Retrospect. The Legacy of the Keynesian Revolution*. Aldershot: Edward Elgar.

Brownlee, W. Elliot (1990) 'Economists and the formation of the modern tax system in the United States: the World War I crisis', pp. 401–35 in Mary O. Furner and Barry Supple (eds), *The State and Economic Knowledge. The American and British Experiences*. Cambridge: Cambridge University Press.

Brüning, Heinrich (1970) *Memoiren 1918–1934*. Stuttgart: Deutsche Verlags-Anstalt.

Brunner, Karl and Allan Meltzer (1977) 'The explanation of inflation: Some international evidence', *American Economic Review*, 67:148–54.

Bryant, Christopher G.A. and Henk A. Becker (eds) (1990) *What Has Sociology Achieved?* London: Macmillan.

Bulmer, Martin (1978) 'Social science research and policy-making in Great Britain', pp. 3–43 in Martin Bulmer (ed.), *Social Policy Research*. London: Macmillan.

Bulmer, Martin (ed) (1985) *Essays on the History of British Sociological Research*. Cambridge: Cambridge University Press.

Bulmer, Martin (ed) (1987) *Social Science Research and Government. Comparative Essays on Britain and the United States*. Cambridge: Cambridge University Press.

Bulmer, Martin (1990) 'Successful applications of sociology', pp. 117–42 in Christopher G.A. Bryant and Henk A. Becker (eds), *What Has Sociology Achieved?* London: Macmillan.

Carroll, James W. (1954) 'Merton's thesis on science', *American Journal of Economics and Sociology*, 13:427–32.

Cavell, S. (1969) *Must We Mean What We Say?*. New York: Charles Scribner.

Cherns, Albert (1979) *Using the Social Sciences*. London: Routledge and Kegan Paul.

Chick, Victoria (1987) 'Money matters', *Times Higher Educational Supplement*, 2 January:8.

Cicourel, Aaron V. (1986) 'The reproduction of objective knowledge: common sense reasoning in medical decision making', pp. 87–122 in Gernot Böhme and Nico Stehr (eds), *The Knowledge Society*. Dordrecht: Reidel.

Claessens, Dieter (1963) 'Soziologie als Beruf und das Problem möglicher Normativität angewandter Soziologie', *Soziale Welt*, 14:264–77.

Coddington, Alan (1974) 'What did Keynes really mean?', *Challenge* (November–December):13–19.

Coleman, James S. (1972a) 'Integration of sociology and other social sciences through policy analysis', pp. 162–74 in James C. Charlesworth (ed.), *Integration of the Social Sciences through Policy Analysis*. Monograph 14 of the American Academy of Political and Social Science. Philadelphia: The American Academy of Political and Social Science.

Coleman, James S. (1972b) *Methods of Policy Research in the Social Sciences*. Morristown, NJ: General Learning Press.

Coleman, James S. (1978) 'Sociological analysis and social policy', pp. 677–703 in Tom Bottomore and Robert Nisbet (eds), *A History of Sociological Analysis*. London: Heinemann.

Coleman, James S. (1987) 'The role of social policy research in society and in sociology', *The American Sociologist*, 18:127–33.

Collingridge, David and Colin Reeve (1986) *Science Speaks to Power. The Role of Experts in Policymaking*. London: Frances Pinter.

Comte, Auguste (1975) *Auguste Comte and Positivism. The Essential Writings*. New York: Harper and Row.

Converse, Phillip E. (1986) 'Generalization and the social psychology of "other worlds"', pp. 42–60 in Donald W. Fiske and Richard A. Shweder (eds), *Metatheory in Social Science. Pluralisms and Subjectivities*. Chicago: University of Chicago Press.

Cook, Thomas D. (1981) 'Dilemmas in evaluation of social programs', pp. 257–87 in Marilynn B. Brewer and Barry E. Collins (eds), *Scientific Inquiry and the Social Sciences*. San Francisco: Jossey-Bass.

Dahrendorf, Ralf (1963) *Die angewandte Aufklärung. Gesellschaft und Soziologie in Amerika*. Munich: Piper.

Dahrendorf, Ralf (1989) 'Einfuhrung in die Soziologie', *Soziale Welt*, 40:2–10.

Davidson, Paul (1978) *Money and the Real World.* New York: Wiley.

Davidson, Paul (1981) 'Post Keynesian economics', pp. 151–73 in Daniel Bell and Irving Kristol (eds), *The Crisis in Economic Theory.* New York: Basic Books.

Davidson, Paul ([1981] 1984) 'Die Postkeynesianische Wirtschaftswissenschaft: Die Lösung der Krise in der Wirtschaftstheorie', pp. 190-217 in Daniel Bell and Irving Kristol (eds), *Die Krise in der Wirtschaftstheorie.* Berlin: Springer-Verlag.

Davis, Howard R. (1973) 'Innovation and change', pp. 289–341 in Saul Feldman (ed.), *The Administration of Mental Health Services.* Springfield, Ill.: Charles C. Thomas.

Dewey, John (1970) 'The development of American pragmatism', pp. 23–40 in H.S. Thayer (ed.), *Pragmatism: The Classic Writings.* New York: New American Library.

Dibble, Vernon K. (1968) 'Social science and political commitment in the young Max Weber', *European Journal of Sociology,* 9:92–110.

Diesing, Paul (1982) *Science and Ideology in the Policy Sciences.* New York: Aldine.

Drucker, Peter F. (1971) 'The new markets and the new capitalism' pp. 44–79 in Daniel Bell and Irving Kristol (eds), *Capitalism Today.* New York: Basic Books.

Drucker, Peter F. ([1980] 1981a) 'Toward the next economics', pp. 1–21 in Peter F. Drucker, *Toward the Next Economics and Other Essays.* New York: Harper and Row.

Drucker, Peter F. (1981b) 'Toward the next economics'. pp. 4–18 In Daniel Bell and Irving Kristol (eds), *The Crisis of Economic Theory.* New York: Basic Books.

Drucker, Peter F. (1986) 'The changed world economy', *Foreign Affairs,* pp. 768–91.

Dubin, Robert (1976) 'Theory building in applied areas', pp. 17–39 in Marvin Dunnette (ed.), *Handbook of Industrial and Organizational Psychology.* Chicago: Rand-McNally.

Dunn, William N. and Burkart Holzner (1988) 'Knowledge in society: anatomy of an emergent field', *Knowledge in Society,* 1:3–26.

Dunn, William N., Burkart Holzner and Gerald Zaltman (1985) 'Knowledge utilization', pp. 2831–9 in Torsten Husen and T. Neville Postlewaite (eds), *International Encyclopedia of Education.* Vol. 5. Oxford: Pergamon Press.

Durkheim, Emile ([1895] 1964) *The Rules of Sociological Method.* New York: Free Press.

Durkheim, Emile ([1912] 1965) *The Elementary Forms of Religious Life.* New York: Free Press.

Durkheim, Emile ([1955] 1983) *Pragmatism and Sociology.* Cambridge: Cambridge University Press.

Eger, Hans (1931) *Der evangelisch-soziale Kongress. Ein Beitrag zu seiner Geschichte und Problemstellung.* Leipzig: M. Heinsius Nachf.

Elias, Norbert (1971) 'Sociology of knowledge: New perspectives', *Sociology,* 5:149–68, 335–70.

Elias, Norbert (1989) *Studien über die Deutschen. Machtkämpfe und Habitusentwicklung im 19. und 20. Jahrhundert.* Frankfurt am Main: Suhrkamp.

Ezrahi, Yaron (1980) 'Utopian and pragmatic rationalism: The political context of scientific advice', *Minerva,* 18:111–31.

Feuer, Lewis S. (1954) 'Causality in the social sciences', *Journal of Philosophy,* 51:681–95.

Feuer, Lewis S. (1963) *The Scientific Intellectual.* New York: Basic Books.

Feuer, Lewis S. (1979) 'Science and the ethic of protestant asceticism: A reply to Professor Robert K. Merton', *Research in Sociology of Knowledge, Sciences and Art,* II:1–23.

Fischer, Fritz (1951) 'Der deutsche Protestantismus und die Politik im 19. Jahrhundert'. *Historische Zeitschrift*, 171:473–518.

Fiske, Donald W. (1986) 'Specificity of method and knowledge in social science', pp. 61–82 in Donald W. Fiske and Richard A. Shweder (eds), *Metatheory in Social Science. Pluralisms and Subjectivities*. Chicago: University of Chicago Press.

Fitzgibbons, Athol (1988) *Keynes's Vision. A New Political Economy*. Oxford: Oxford University Press.

Freeman, C. (1977) 'Economics of research and development', pp. 223–75 in Ina Spiegel-Rösing and Derek de Solla Price (eds), *Science, Technology and Society: A Cross-Disciplinary Perspective*. Beverly Hills, Ca.: Sage.

Freeman, Howard S. (1963) 'The strategy of social policy research', pp. 143–56 in *Social Welfare Forum*. New York: Columbia University Press.

Fuller, Steve (1992) 'Will economics provide the solution to the modern problem of knowledge?', in Nico Stehr and Richard V. Ericsson (eds), *The Culture and Power of Knowledge*. London: de Gruyter (in press).

Furner, Mary O. and Barry Supple (eds) (1990a) *The State and Economic Knowledge. The American and British Experiences*. Cambridge: Cambridge University Press.

Furner, Mary O. and Barry Supple (eds) (1990b) 'Ideas, institutions, and the state in the United States and Britain: an introduction', pp. 3–39 in Mary O. Furner and Barry Supple (eds), *The State and Economic Knowledge. The American and British Experiences*. Cambridge: Cambridge University Press.

Galbraith, John K. (1971) *A Contemporary Guide to Economics, Peace and Laughter*. London: André Deutsch.

Gans, Herbert J. ([1971] 1975) 'Social science for social policy', pp. 3–23 in Irving L. Horowitz (ed.), *The Use and Abuse of Social Science*, 2nd edn. New Brunswick, NJ: Transaction Books.

Gehlen, Arnold ([1950] 1988) *Man. His Nature and Place in the World*. New York: Columbia University Press.

Gergen, Kenneth J. (1986) 'Correspondence versus autonomy in the language of understanding human action', pp. 136–62 in Donald W. Fiske and Richard A. Shweder (eds), *Metatheory in Social Science. Pluralisms and Subjectivities*. Chicago: University of Chicago Press.

Giddens, Anthony (1984) *The Constitution of Society. Outline of a Theory of Structuration*. Cambridge: Polity Press.

Giddens, Anthony (1987) 'Nine theses on the future of sociology', pp. 22–51 in Anthony Giddens, *Social Theory and Modern Sociology*. Cambridge: Polity Press.

Giddens, Anthony (1990) 'R.K. Merton on structural analysis', pp. 97–110 in Jon Clark, Celia Modgie and Sohan Modgie (eds), *Robert K. Merton: Consensus and Controversy*. London: Falmer Press.

Giersch, Herbert (1961) *Allgemeine Wirtschaftspolitik. Grundlagen*. Wiesbaden: Betriebswirtschaftlicher Verlag Gabler.

Giesen, Bernd (1983) 'Moralische Unternehmer und öffentliche Diskussion: Überlegungen zur gesellschaftlichen Thematisierung sozialer Probleme', *Kölner Zeitschrift für Soziologie und Sozialpsychologie*, 35:230–54.

Giesen, Bernd and Wolfgang L. Schneider (1984) 'Von Missionaren, Technokraten und Politikern, Deutungsmuster als Determinanten der Interaktion von Wissenschaftlern und Praktikern', *Soziale Welt*, 35:458–79.

Göhre, Paul (1891) *Drei Monate Fabrikarbeiter und Handwerksbursche*. Leipzig: Friedrich Wilhelm Grunow.

Göhre, Paul (1892) 'Zur Begrüssung unseres dritten Kongresses', *Mitteilungen des Evangelisch-sozialen Kongresses*, 4:1.

Göhre, Paul (1894) 'Die deutschen Landarbeiter', pp. 43–61 in *Bericht über die Verhandlungen des fünften Evangelisch-sozialen Kongresses*. Berlin: von Rehtwisch and Langewort.

Göhre, Paul (1896) *Die evangelisch-soziale Bewegung. Ihre Geschichte und ihre Ziele*. Leipzig: F.W. Grunow.

Goldschmidt, Salli (1899) *Die Landarbeiter in den evangelischen Gebieten Norddeutschlands in Einzeldarstellungen nach den Erhebungen des Evangelisch-Sozialen Kongresses*. Erstes Heft: *Die Landarbeiter in der Provinz Sachsen, sowie den älteren Herzogtümern Braunschweig und Anhalt. Mit einer Vorbemerkung von Max Weber*. Tübingen: Verlag der H. Laupp'schen Buchhandlung.

Gorz, André ([1980] 1982) *Farewell to the Working Class. An Essay on Post-Industrial Socialism*. London: Pluto Press.

Gouldner, Alvin W. (1956) 'Explorations in applied social science', *Social Problems*, 3:169–81.

Gouldner, Alvin W. (1957) 'Theoretical requirements of the applied social sciences', *American Sociological Review*, 22:92–102.

Gouldner, Alvin W. (1965) 'Explorations in applied social science', pp. 5–22 in Alvin W. Gouldner and S. M. Miller (eds), *Applied Sociology. Opportunities and Problems*. New York: Free Press.

Gouldner, Alvin W. (1970) 'Toward the radical reconstruction of sociology', *Social Policy*, 1:18–25.

Gouldner, Alvin W. (1976) *The Dialectic of Ideology and Technology. The Origins, Grammar, and Future of Ideology*. New York: Seabury Press.

Gouldner, Alvin W. (1979) *The Future of Intellectuals and the Rise of the New Class. A Frame of Reference, Theses, Conjectures, Arguments, and an Historical Perspectives on the Role of Intellectuals and Intelligentsia in the International Class Contest in the Modern Era*. New York: Continuum.

Greene, Wade (1974) 'Economists in recession', *New York Times Magazine*, 12 May:64.

Grice H.P. (1975) 'Logic and conversation', pp. 41–58 in P. Cole and Jerry L. Morgan (eds), *Syntax and Semantics*, vol. 3: *Speech Acts*. New York: Academic Press.

Groh, John E. (1982) *Nineteenth-Century German Protestantism: The Church as Social Model*. Washington, DC: University Press of America.

Habermas, Jürgen ([1964] 1974) 'Dogmatism, reason and decision: On theory and practice in our scientific civilization', pp. 253–82 in Jürgen Habermas, *Theory and Practice*. London: Heinemann.

Hall, A. Rupert (1963) 'Merton revisited or science and society in the seventeenth century', *History of Science*, 2:1–16.

Hammond, Kenneth P. et al. (1983) 'Fundamental obstacles to the use of scientific information in public policy making', *Technological Forecasting and Social Change*, 24:287–97.

Hansen, Alvin H. (1952) *A Guide to Keynes*. New York: McGraw-Hill.

Harnack, Adolf (1890) 'Der Evangelisch-soziale Congress zu Berlin' *Preussische Jahrbücher*, 65:566–76.

Harris, Jose (1990) 'Economic knowledge and British social policy' pp. 379–400 in Mary O. Furner and Barry Supple (eds), *The State and Economic Knowledge. The American and British Experiences*. Cambridge: Cambridge University Press.

Harrod, R.F. (1951) *The Life of John Maynard Keynes*. New York: Harcourt, Brace.

Havelock, Ronald G. and Kenneth D. Benne ([1966] 1969) 'An exploratory study of knowledge utilization', pp. 151–64 in Warren G. Bennis, Kenneth D. Benne and Robert Chin (eds) *The Planning of Change*, 2nd edn. New York: Holt, Rinehart and Winston.

Hayek, Friedrich A. von (1952) *The Counter-Revolution of Science. Studies on the Abuse of Reason*. Glencoe, Ill: Free Press.

Hayek, Friedrich A. von (1959) *Missbrauch und Verfall der Vernunft. Ein Fragment*. Frankfurt am Main: F. Knapp.

Hayek, Friedrich A. von (1967) *Studies in Philosophy, Politics and Economics*. Chicago: University of Chicago Press.

Hayek, Friedrich A. von ([1945] 1969) 'The use of knowledge in society', pp. 77–91 in Friedrich A. von Hayek, *Individualism and Economic Order*. Chicago: University of Chicago Press.

Hayek, Friedrich A. von ([1974] 1975a) 'The pretence of knowledge', (Nobel lecture), pp. 30–42 in Friedrich A. von Hayek, *Full Employment at Any Price?* London: Institute of Economic Affairs.

Hayek, Friedich A. von (1975b) 'Inflation, the misdirection of labour and unemployment', pp. 15–29 in Friedrich A. von Hayek, *Full Employment at Any Price?* London: Institute of Economic Affairs.

Helmer, Olaf ([1966] 1970) 'Sozialtechnik', pp. 293–329 in Claus Koch and Dieter Senghaas (eds), *Texte zur Technokratiediskussion*. Frankfurt am Main: Europäische Verlagsanstalt.

Henderson, David (1986) *Innocence and Design. The Influence of Economic Ideas on Policy*. Oxford: Basil Blackwell.

Hennis, Wilhelm ([1987] 1988) *Max Weber. Essays in Reconstruction*. London: Allen and Unwin.

Herz, Johannes (ed.) (1940) *Evangelisches Ringen um Gemeinschaft*. Leipzig: Hinrichs and Klotz.

Hicks, John R. (1937) 'Mr. Keynes and the classics: A suggested interpretation', *Econometrica*, 5:147–59.

Hicks, John R. (1974) *The Crisis of Keynesian Economics*. Oxford: Basil Blackwell.

Hicks, John R. (1985) 'Keynes and the world economy', pp. 21–7 in Fausto Vicarelli (ed.), *Keynes's Relevance Today*. London: Macmillan.

Hirschman, Albert O. (1989) 'How Keynes was spread from America', *States and Social Structures Newsletter*, No. 10:1–5.

Homans, Peter (1989) *The Ability to Mourn. Disillusionment and the Social Origins of Psychoanalysis*. Chicago: University of Chicago Press.

Honigsheim, Paul (1926) 'Der Max-Weber-Kreis in Heidelberg', *Kölner Vierteljahrshefte für Soziologie*, 5:270–87.

Hoos, Ida R. (1969) *Systems Analysis in Social Policy*. London: The Institute of Economic Affairs.

Horowitz, Irving L. (1965) 'The life and death of Project Camelot', *Transaction*, 3: 3–7, 44–7.

Horowitz, Irving L. (1970) 'Social science mandarins: Policymaking as a political formula', *Policy Sciences*, 1:339–60.

Horowitz, Irving L. (ed.) (1971) *The Use and Abuse of Social Science*. New Brunswick, NJ: Transaction Books.

Hotz-Hart, Beat (1983) 'Regierbarkeit im wirtschaftlichen Strukturwandel. Der weltwirtschaftliche Umbruch als Herausforderung wirtschaftspolitischer Institutionen', *Schweizerisches Jahrbuch für politische Wissenschaft*, 23:293–314.

Howard, Ronald L. (1981) *A Social History of American Family Sociology: 1865–1940*. Westport, Conn.: Greenwood Press.

Hunt, Morton (1985) *Profiles of Social Research. The Scientific Study of Human Interactions*. New York: Russell Sage Foundation.

Inciardi, James A. (1987) 'Sociology and American drug policy', *American Sociologist*, 18:179–88.

Jänicke, Martin (1986) *Staatsversagen. Die Ohnmacht der Politik in der Industriegesellschaft*. Munich: Piper.

Janowitz, Morris (1971) *Sociological Models and Social Policy*. Morristown, NJ: General Learning Systems.

Janowitz, Morris (1972) 'Professionalization of sociology', *American Journal of Sociology*, 78:105–35.

Janowitz, Morris (1978) *The Last Half-Century. Societal Change and Politics in America*. Chicago: University of Chicago Press.

Johnson, Elizabeth S. and Harry G. Johnson (1978) *The Shadow of Keynes. Understanding Keynes, Cambridge and Keynesian Economics*. Oxford: Basil Blackwell.

Kaldor, Nicholas (1983) *Grenzen der 'General Theory'*. Berlin: Springer-Verlag.

Katona, George (1978) 'Behavioral economics', *Challenge*, 21:17–18.

Katz, James E. (1987) 'Telecommunications and computers: Whither privacy policy?', *Society*, 25:81–6.

Kaufmann, Franz-Xaver (1969) 'Soziologie und praktische Wirksamkeit', pp. 68–79 in Bernhard Schäfers (ed.), *Thesen zur Kritik der Soziologie*. Frankfurt am Main: Suhrkamp.

Kaufmann, Franz-Xaver (1977) 'Sozialpolitisches Erkenntnisinteresse und Soziologie', pp. 35–75 in Christian von Ferber and Franz-Xaver Kaufmann (eds), *Soziologie und Sozialpolitik*. Sonderheft 19, *Kölner Zeitschift für Soziologie und Sozialpolitik*. Opladen: Westdeutscher Verlag.

Keane, John (1988) *Democracy and Civil Society*. London: Verso.

Keane, John and John Owens (1986) *After Full Employment*. London: Verso.

Kettler, David, Volker Meja and Nico Stehr (1984) *Karl Mannheim*. London: Tavistock.

Keynes, John M. (1932) 'Die wirtschaftlichen Aussichten für 1932', *Wirtschaftsdienst*, Heft 5, 15 January.

Keynes, John Maynard (1936) *The General Theory of Employment, Interest and Money*. London: Macmillan.

Keynes, John M. (1956) *Politik und Wirtschaft. Männer und Probleme. Ausgewählte Abhandlungen*. Tübingen: J.B.C. Mohr (Paul Siebeck).

Keynes, John M. ([1930] 1971) *Treatise on Money*, in *Collected Writings*, vol. V. London: Macmillan.

Keynes, John M. ([1933] 1972a) *The Means to Prosperity*, in *Collected Writings*, vol. IX: *Essays in Persuasion*. London: Macmillan.

Keynes, John M. ([1933] 1972b) *Collected Writings*, vol. X: *Essays in Biography*. London: Macmillan.

Keynes, John M. (1973) *Collected Writings*, vol. XIV: *The General Theory and After. Part II: Defence and Development* (ed. Donald Moggridge). London: Macmillan.

Keynes, John M. (1978) *Collected Writings*, Vol. XVIII: *Activities 1922–1932* (ed. Elizabeth Johnson). London: Macmillan.

Keynes, John M. (1980) *Collected Writings*, vol. XXVII: *Activities 1940–1946* (ed. Donald Moggridge). London: Macmillan.

Keynes, John M. (1982) *Collected Writings*, vol. XXI: *Activities 1931–1939* (ed. Donald Moggridge). London: Macmillan.

Keynes, John M. ([1931] 1982) 'The currency question', pp. 1–111 in *Collected Writings*, vol. XXI: *Activities 1931–1939* (ed. Donald Moggridge). Cambridge: Cambridge University Press.

Keynes, John M. ([1932] 1982a) 'The economic prospects 1932', pp. 39–48 in *Collected Writings*, vol. XXI: *Activities 1931–1939: World Crises and Policies in Britain and America* (ed. Donald Moggridge). London: Macmillan.

Keynes, John M. ([1932] 1982b) 'The world's economic crisis and the way of escape' (Halley-Stewart Lecture), pp. 50–62 in *Collected Writings*, vol. XXI: *Activities 1931–1939: World Crises and Policies in Britain and America* (ed. Donald Moggridge). London: Macmillan.

Keynes, John M. ([1926] 1984) 'The end of lassez-faire', pp. 253–71 in *Collected Writings*, vol. IX: *Essays in Persuasion*. Cambridge: Cambridge University Press.

Keynes, John M. ([1929] 1984) 'Can Lloyd George do it?', pp. 86–125 in *Collected Writings*, vol. IX: *Essays in Persuasion*. Cambridge: Cambridge University Press.

Keynes, John M. ([1930] 1984a) 'Economic possibilities for our grandchildren', pp. 321–32 in *Collected Writings*, vol. IX: *Essays in Persuasion*. Cambridge: Cambridge University Press.

Keynes, John M. ([1930] 1984b) 'The great slump of 1930', pp. 126–34 in *Collected Writings* vol. IX: *Essays in Persuasion*. Cambridge: Cambridge University Press.

Keynes, John M. ([1931] 1984a) 'Economy', pp. 135–49 in *Collected Writings*, vol. IX: *Essays in Persuasion*. Cambridge: Cambridge University Press.

Keynes, John M. ([1931] 1984b) 'Proposals for a revenue tariff', pp. 231–44 in *Collected Writings*, vol. IX: *Essays in Persuasion*. Cambridge: Cambridge University Press.

Keynes, John M. ([1973] 1987) *Collected Writings*, vol. XIII: *The General Theory and After. Part I: Preparation* (ed. Donald Moggridge). London: Macmillan.

King, Lauriston R. and Philip H. Melanson (1972) 'Knowledge and politics: Some experiences from the 1960s', *Public Policy*, 20:83–101.

Kneen, Peter (1984) *Soviet Scientists and the State*. Albany, NY: State University of New York Press.

Knorr, Karin D. (1977) 'Policymakers' use of social science knowledge: symbolic or instrumental?', pp. 165–82 in Carol Weiss (ed.), *Using Social Science Research in Public Policy Making*. Lexington, Mass.: Lexington-Heath.

Knorr-Cetina, Karin D. (1981) 'Time and context in practical action: underdetermination and knowledge use', *Knowledge*, 3:143–65.

König, René (ed.) (1952) *Praktische Sozialforschung. Das Interview; Formen, Technik, Auswertung*. Zürich: Regio.

König, René (1961) 'Einleitung', pp. 21–82 in Emile Durkheim, *Regeln der soziologischen Methode*. Neuwied: Luchterhand.

König, René ([1958] 1967) 'Einleitung', pp. 8–14 in René König (ed.), *Soziologie*. Frankfurt am Main: Fischer.

König, René (1979) 'Gesellschaftliches Bewusstsein und Soziologie: Eine spekulative Überlegung', pp. 358–70 in Günther Lüschen (ed.), *Deutsche Soziologie seit 1945*. Sonderheft 21, *Kölner Zeitschrift für Soziologie und Sozialpsychologie*. Opladen: Westdeutscher Verlag.

König, René (1987) 'Vorwort: In eigener Sache', pp. 9–20 in *Soziologie in Deutschland. Begründer, Verfechter, Verächter*. Munich: Hanser.

Konrád, George and Ivan Szelényi (1979) *The Intellectuals on the Road to Class Power*. Brighton, Sussex: Harvester.

Kouri, E.I. (1984) *Der deutsche Prostestantismus und die soziale Frage 1890-1919. Zur Sozialpolitik im Bildungsbürgertum*. Berlin: Walter de Gruyter.

Kretschmar, Gottfried (1972) *Der Evangelisch-soziale Kongress*. Stuttgart: Evangelisches Verlagwerk.

Krohn, Claus-Dieter (1981) *Wirtschaftstheorien als politische Interessen. Die akademische Nationalökonomie in Deutschland 1918–1933*. Frankfurt am Main: Campus.

Krohn, Claus-Dieter (1987) *Wissenschaft im Exil. Deutsche Wirtschafts- und Sozialwissenschaftler in den USA und die New School of Social Research*. Frankfurt am Main: Campus.

Krohn, Wolfgang (1981) '"Wissen ist Macht": Zur Soziogenese eines neuzeitlichen wissenschaftliches Geltungsanspruchs', pp. 29–57 in K. Bayertz (ed.), *Wissenschaftsgeschichte und wissenschaftliche Revolution*. Köln: Pahl-Rugenstein.

Krohn, Wolfgang (1987) *Francis Bacon*. Munich: C.H. Beck.

Krohn, Wolfgang (1988) 'Zur Entwicklung der Wissenschaft', pp. 175–99 in H.H. Holz (ed.), *Die Dialektik und die Wissenschaften. Philosophische Fragen moderner Entwicklungskonzeptionen*. Köln: Pahl-Rugenstein.

Krohn, Wolfgang and Werner Rammert (1985) 'Technologieentwicklung: Autonomer Prozess und Industrialisierung', pp. 411–33 in Burkart Lutz (ed.), *Soziologie und gesellschaftliche Entwicklung. Verhandlungen des 22. Deutschen Soziologentages*. Frankfurt am Main: Campus.

Krohn, Wolfgang and Johannes Weyer (1989) 'Gesellschafts als Labor. Die Erzeugung sozialer Risiken durch experimentelle Forschung', *Soziale Welt*, 40:349–73.

Kroll, Gerhard (1958) *Von der Weltwirtschaftskrise zur Staatskonjunktur*. Berlin: Duncker and Humblot.

Kuhn, Thomas S. (1970) *The Structure of Scientific Revolution*, 2nd edn. Chicago: University of Chicago Press.

Kuttner, Robert (1985) 'The poverty of economics', *Atlantic Monthly* (February): 74–84.

Kuznets, Simon (1971) *Qualitative Economic Research: Trends and Problems*. New York: Columbia University Press.

Lammers, Cornelius J. (1974) 'Mono- and polyparadigmatic developments in natural and social sciences', pp. 123–47 in Richard Whitley (ed.), *Social Processes of Scientific Development*. London: Routledge and Kegan Paul.

Landfried, Christine (1976) 'Wissenschaft und Politik in der Krise um 1930 in Deutschland', pp. 151–83 in Bernard Badura (ed.), *Seminar: Angewandte Sozialforschung. Studien über die Voraussetzungen und Bedingungen der Produktion, Diffusion und Verwertung sozialwissenschaftlichen Wissens*. Frankfurt am Main: Suhrkamp.

Landmann, Oliver (1981) 'Theoretische Grundlagen für eine aktive Krisenbekämpfung in Deutschland 1930-1933', pp. 215–420 in Gottfried Bombach (ed.), *Der Keynesianismus III. Die geld- und beschäftigungstheoretische Diskussion in Deutschland zur Zeit Keynes. Dokumente und Analysen*. Berlin: Springer-Verlag.

Latour, Bruno (1983) 'Give me a laboratory and I will raise the world', pp. 141–70 in Karin D. Knorr-Cetina and Michael Mulkay (eds), *Science Observed. Perspectives on the Social Study of Science*. London: Sage.

Lau, Christoph (1984) 'Soziologie im öffentlichen Diskurs: Voraussetzungen und Grenzen der sozialwissenschaftlichen Rationalisierung', *Soziale Welt*, 35:407–28.

Lau, Christoph and Ulrich Beck (1989) *Definitionsmacht und Grenzen angewandter Sozialwissenschaft. Eine Untersuchung am Beispiel der Bildungs- und Arbeitsmarksforschung*. Opladen: Westdeutscher Verlag.

Lazarsfeld, Paul F. and Jeffry G. Reitz (1975) *An Introduction to Applied Sociology*. New York: Elsevier.

Lazarsfeld, Paul F., William H. Sewell and Harold L. Wilensky (eds) (1967) *The Uses of Sociology*. New York: Basic Books.

Leff, Nathaniel H. (1988) 'Disjunction between policy research and practice: Social benefit-cost analysis and investment policy at the World Bank', *Studies in Comparative International Research*, pp. 77–87.

Leijonhufvud, Axel (1968) *On Keynesian Economics and the Economics of Keynes. A Study in Monetary Theory*. New York: Oxford University Press.

Lekachman, Robert (1968) *The Age of Keynes*. New York: Random House.

Leontief, Wassily ([1971] 1985) 'Theoretical assumptions and nonobserved facts,' pp. 272–82 in Wassily Leontief, *Esssays in Economics*. New Brunswick, NJ: Transaction Books.

Leontief, Wassily (1985) 'Introduction to the Transaction Edition: Academic Economics', pp. 1–18 in Wassily Leontief, *Essays in Economics*. New Brunswick, NJ: Transaction Books.

Liebersohn, Harry (1986) *Religion and Industrial Society: The Protestant Social Congress in Wilhelmine Germany*. Transactions of the American Philosophical Society, vol. 76, Part 6. Philadelphia: The American Philosophical Society.

Lieberson, Stanley (1985) *Making it Count. The Improvement of Social Research and Theory*. Berkeley: University of California Press.

Liesner, Thelma (1985) *Economic Statistics 1900-1983. United Kingdom, United States of America, France, Germany, Italy, Japan*. New York: Facts on File Publications.

Lindblom, Charles E. (1972) 'Integration of economics and other social sciences through policy analysis', pp. 1–14 in James C. Charlesworth (ed.), *Integration of the Social Sciences through Policy Analysis*. Philadelphia: AAPSS.

Lindblom, Charles E. and David K. Cohen (1979) *Usable Knowledge: Social Science and Social Problem Solving*. New Haven, Conn.: Yale University Press.

Lindenlaub, Dieter (1967) *Richtungskämpfe im Verein für Sozialpolitik (1890–1914)*. Two volumes: *Vierteljahresschrift für Sozial- und Wirtschaftsgeschichte*. Wiesbaden: Steiner.

Lingwood, David A. (1979) 'Producing usable research', *American Behavioral Scientist*, 22:339–62.

Lippitt, Ronald (1968) 'Kurt Lewin', pp. 266–71 in David Sills (ed.), *International Encyclopedia of the Social Sciences*, vol. 9. New York: Macmillan and Free Press.

Lipset, Seymour M. (1979) 'Predicting the future of post-industrial society', pp. 1–35 in Seymour M. Lipset (ed.), *The Third Century. America as a Post-Industrial Society*. Chicago: University of Chicago Press.

Lipset, Seymour M. ([1979] 1985) 'Predicting the future: The limits of social science', pp. 329–60 in Seymour M. Lipset, *Consensus and Conflict. Essays in Political Sociology*. New Brunswick, NJ: Transaction Books.

Lipsey, Richard G. (1992) 'Global change and economic growth', in Nico Stehr and Richard V. Ericson (eds), *The Culture and Power of Knowledge: Inquiries into Contemporary Society*. Berlin and New York: de Gruyter (in press).

Lowe, Adolph (1965) *On Economic Knowledge. Toward a Science of Political Economics.* London: Harper and Row.

Lowe, Adolph (1977) *On Economic Knowledge. Toward a Science of Political Economics*, enlarged edn. White Plains, NY: M.E. Sharpe.

Lubasz, Heinz (1981) 'Popper in utopia', *Times Higher Educational Supplement*, 477:10.

Luckmann, Thomas (1981) 'Vorüberlegungen zum Verhältnis von Alltagswissen und Wissenschaft', pp. 39–51 in Peter Janich (ed.), *Wissenschaftstheorie und Wissenschaftsforschung.* Munich: C.H. Beck.

Luhmann, Niklas (1970) 'Soziologische Aufklärung', pp. 66–92 in Niklas Luhmann, *Soziologische Aufklärung, Aufsätze zur Theorie sozialer Systeme.* Opladen: Westdeutscher Verlag.

Luhmann, Niklas (1977) 'Theoretische und praktische Probleme der anwendungsbezogenen Sozialwissenschaften', pp. 16–39 in Wissensschaftszentrum (ed.), *Interaktion von Wissenschaft und Politik. Theoretische und praktische Probleme der anwendungsorientierten Sozialwissenschaften.* Frankfurt am Main: Campus.

Luhmann, Niklas (1981) 'Gesellschaftsstrukturelle Bedingungen und Folgerungen des naturwissenschaftlich-technischen Fortschritts', pp. 113–34 in Reinhard Löw (ed.), *Fortschritt ohne Mass?* Munich: Piper.

Luhmann, Niklas (1987) 'Die gesellschaftliche Verantwortung der Soziologie', pp. 109–21 in Helmut de Rudder und Heinz Sahner (eds), *Wissenschaft und gesellschaftliche Verantwortung.* Berlin: Arno Spitz.

Lundberg, George A. ([1947] 1967) *Can Science Save Us?*, 2nd edn. New York: David McKay.

Lynd, Robert (1940) *Knowledge for What? The Place of Social Science in American Culture.* Princeton, NJ: Princeton University Press.

MacIntyre, Alasdair (1983) 'The indispensability of political theory', pp. 17–33 in David Miller and Lary Siedentop (eds), *The Nature of Political Theory.* Oxford: Oxford University Press.

MacKenzie, Donald (1987) 'Missile accuracy: A case study in the social processes of technological change', pp. 195–222 in Wiebe E. Bijker, Thomas P. Hughes and Trevor J. Pinch (eds), *The Social Constructions of Technological Systems.* Cambridge, Mass.: MIT Press.

MacRae, Duncan Jr (1976) *The Social Function of Social Science.* New Haven: Yale University Press.

Mannheim, Karl (1932) *Die Gegenwartsaufgaben der Soziologie. Ihre Lehrgestalt.* Tübingen: J.C.B. Mohr (Paul Siebeck).

Mannheim, Karl ([1929] 1936) *Ideology and Utopia. An Introduction to the Sociology of Knowledge.* London: Routledge and Kegan Paul.

Mannheim, Karl (1940) *Man and Society in an Age of Reconstruction.* London: Routledge and Kegan Paul.

Mannheim, Karl ([1928] 1952) 'Competition as a cultural phenonemon', pp. 191–229 in Karl Mannheim, *Essays on the Sociology of Knowledge.* London: Routledge and Kegan Paul.

Marcuse, Herbert (1964) *One-Dimensional Man. Studies in the Ideology of Advanced Industrial Society.* Boston, Mass.: Beacon Press.

Marshall, Alfred ([1890] 1948) *Principles of Economics.* New York: Macmillan.

Meehan, Eugene J. (1982) *Economics and Policymaking. The Tragic Illusion.* Westport, Conn.: Greenwood Press.

Meja, Volker and Nico Stehr (1985) 'Sozialwissenschaftlicher und erkenntnis-theoretischer Diskurs', *Soziale Welt*, 36:361–80.

Meja, Volker und Nico Stehr (1988) 'Social science, epistemology, and the problem of relativism', *Social Epistemology*, 2:263–71.

Merton, Robert K. (1949) 'The role of applied social science in the formation of policy: a research memorandum', *Philosophy of Science*, 16:161–81.

Merton, Robert K. ([1949] 1957) *Social Theory and Social Structure*, rev. and enlarged edn. New York: Free Press.

Merton, Robert K. (1963) 'Basic research and the potentials of relevance', *The American Behavioral Scientist*, 6:86–90.

Merton, Robert K. (1972) 'Insiders and outsiders: A chapter in the sociology of knowledge', *American Journal of Sociology*, 77:9–47.

Merton, Robert K. ([1970] 1973) 'Social and cultural contexts of science', pp. 173–90 in Robert K. Merton, *The Sociology of Science. Theoretical and Empirical Investigations*. Chicago Ill.: University of Chicago Press.

Merton, Robert K. (1973) *The Sociology of Science*. Chicago: University of Chicago Press.

Merton, Robert K. (1975) 'Social knowledge and public policy. Sociological perspectives on four presidential commissions', pp. 153–77 in Mirra Komarovsky (ed.), *Sociology and Public Policy. The Case of Presidential Commissions*. New York: Elsevier.

Merton, Robert K. (1977) 'The sociology of science: An episodic memoir', pp. 3–141 in Robert K. Merton and Jerry Gaston (eds), *The Sociology of Science in Europe*. Carbondale and Edwardsville Ill.: Southern Illinois University Press.

Merton, Robert K. (1984) 'The fallacy of the latest word: The case of "Pietism and Science"', *American Journal of Sociology*, 89:1091–121.

Mies, Thomas (1986) *Der Praxisbezug der Sozialwissenschaften. Am Beispiel der angewandten Sozialforschung in den USA 1960–1980*. Frankfurt am Main: Campus.

Mill, John Stuart (1950) *Philosophy of Scientific Method*. New York: Hafner.

Mills, C. Wright ([1959] 1970) *The Sociological Imagination*. Harmondsworth: Penguin.

Mitzman, Arthur ([1969] 1985) *The Iron Cage. An Historical Interpretation of Max Weber*. New Brunswick, NJ: Transaction.

Mommsen, Wolfgang ([1959] 1984) *Max Weber and German Politics, 1890–1920*. Chicago Ill.: University of Chicago Press.

Moynihan, Daniel P. (1969) *Maximum Feasible Misunderstanding. Community Action in the War on Poverty*. New York: Free Press.

Moynihan, Daniel P. (1970) 'The role of social scientists in action research', *SSRC Newsletter*.

Mulligan. Lotte (1973) 'Civil war politics, religion and the Royal Society', *Past and Present*, 59:92–116.

Myrdal, Gunnar (1944) *An American Dilemma*. New York: Harper.

Myrdal, Gunnar (1972) 'The social sciences and their impact on society', pp. 347–59 in Teodor Shanin (ed.), *The Rules of the Game. Cross-disciplinary Essays on Models in Scholarly Thought*. London: Tavistock.

Naumann, Friedrich (1893) 'Der Evangelisch-soziale Kursus in Berlin', *Die christliche Welt. Evangelisch-Lutherisches Gemeindeblatt für Gebildete aller Stände*, 7:Col. 1083–8.

Needham, Joseph (1986) 'Science, technology, progress and the break-through: China as a case study in human history', pp. 5–22 in Tord Ganelius (ed.), *Progress in Science and Its Social Conditions*. Nobel Symposium 58. Oxford: Pergamon Press.

Neurath, Otto ([1931] 1973) *Empiricism and Sociology*. Dordrecht: D. Reidel.

Niskanen, William A. (1986) 'Economists and politicians', *Journal of Policy Analysis and Management*, 5:234–44.

Nobbe, Moritz August (1897) *Der Evangelisch-soziale Kongress und seine Gegner*. Göttingen: Vandenhoeck and Ruprecht.

Noble, David (1984) *Forces of Production. A Social History of Industrial Automation*. New York: Knopf.

Nowotny, Helga (1975) 'Die gesellschaftliche Irrelevanz der Sozialwissenschaften', pp. 445–56 in Nico Stehr and René König (eds), *Wissenschaftssoziologie. Studien und Materialien*. Sonderheft 18, *Kölner Zeitschrift für Soziologie und Sozialpsychologie*. Opladen: Westdeutscher Verlag.

Nowotny, Helga and Jane Lambiri-Dimaki (eds) (1985) *The Difficult Dialogue between Producers and Users of Social Science Research*. Vienna: European Centre for Social Welfare Training and Research.

Oberschall, Anthony (1965) *Empirical Social Research in Germany, 1848–1914*. New York: Basic Books.

O'Connor, James (1984) *Accumulation Crisis*. Oxford: Basil Blackwell.

Offe, Claus (1977) 'Die kritische Funktion der Sozialwissenschaften', pp. 321–9 Wissenschaftszentrum (ed.), *Interaktion von Wissenschaft und Politik. Theoretische und praktische Probleme der anwendungsorientierten Sozialwissenschaften*. Frankfurt am Main: Campus Verlag.

Offe, Claus (1981) 'Sozialwissenschaften zwischen Auftragsforschung und sozialer Bewegung', pp. 98–108 in Bodo von Greiff (ed.), *Das Orwellsche Jahrzehnt und die Zukunft der Wissenschaft*. Hochschultage der Freien Universität Berlin 1980. Opladen: Westdeutscher Verlag.

Orlans, Harold (1968) 'Making social research more useful to government', *Social Science Information*, 7:151–8.

Orlans, Harold (1976) 'The advocacy of social science in Europe and North America', *Minerva*, 14:6–32.

Parkin, Michael and Robin Bade (1986) *Modern Macroeconomics*, 2nd edn. Scarborough, Ontario: Prentice-Hall.

Parsons, Talcott (1959) 'Some problems confronting sociology as a profession', *American Sociological Review*, 24:547–59.

Patinkin, Don (1982) *Anticipations of the General Theory? And Other Essays on Keynes*. Chicago Ill.: University of Chicago Press.

Payne, G., Robert Dingwall, Judy Payne and Mick Carter (1980) 'Sociology and policy research', pp. 142–59 in G. Payne *Sociology and Social Research*. London: Routledge and Kegan Paul.

Pigou, Arthur C. (1950) *Keynes' General Theory. A Retrospective View*. London: Macmillan.

Pilling, Geoffrey (1986) *The Crisis of Keynesian Economics. A Marxist View*. London: Croom Helm.

Platt, Jennifer (1976) *Realities of Social Research: An Empirical Study of British Sociologists*. London: Sussex University Press.

Plessner, Helmut ([1928] 1981) *Die Sufen des Organischen und der Mensch. Einleitung in the philosophische Anthropologie.* Gesammelte Schriften IV. Frankfurt am Main: Suhrkamp.

Poincaré, Henri (1914) *Science and Method.* London: T. Nelson and Sons.

Popper, Karl R. ([1957] 1972) *The Poverty of Historicism.* London: Routledge and Kegan Paul.

Popper, Karl R. (1972a) 'Epistemology without a knowing subject', pp. 106–52 in Karl R. Popper, *Objective Knowledge. An Evolutionary Approach.* Oxford: Clarendon Press.

Popper, Karl R. (1972b) 'Of cloud and clocks. An approach to the problem of rationality and the freedom of man', pp. 206–55 in Karl R. Popper, *Objective Knowledge. An Evolutionary Approach.* Oxford: Clarendon Press.

Radder, Hans (1986) 'Experiment, technology and the intrinsic connection between knowledge and power', Social Studies of Science, 16:663–83.

Ravetz, Jerome R. (1971) *Scientific Knowledge and Its Social Problems.* Oxford: Oxford University Press.

Ravetz, Jerome R. (1985) 'Usable knowledge, usable ignorance: incomplete science with policy implications', in D. Clark and C. Mum (eds), *Sustainable Development of the Biosphere.* Cambridge: Cambridge University Press.

Rehberg, Karl-Siegbert (1986) 'Deutungswissen der Moderne oder "administrative Hilfswissenschaft"? Konservative Schwierigkeiten mit der Soziologie', pp. 7–47 in Sven Papcke (ed.), *Ordnung und Theorie. Beiträge zur Geschichte der Soziologie in Deutschland.* Darmstadt: Wissenschaftliche Buchgesellschaft.

Rich, Georg (1983) 'Weltwirtschaftliche Verpflechtung und geldpolitische Handlungsfähigkeit der Schweiz', *Schweizerisches Jahrbuch für Politische Wissenschaft,* 23:271–91.

Rich, Robert F. (1977) 'Uses of social science information by federal bureaucrats: knowledge for action vs. knowledge for understanding', pp. 199–212 in Carol H. Weiss (ed.), *Using Social Research in Public Policy Making.* Lexington: D.C. Heath.

Riecken, Henry W. (1969) 'Social sciences and social problems', *Social Science Information,* 8:101–29.

Riesebrodt, Martin (1984a) 'Einleitung', pp. 1–17 in Max Weber, *Die Lage der Landarbeiter im ostelbischen Deutschland.* Tübingen: J.B.C. Mohr (Paul Siebeck).

Riesebrodt, Martin (1984b) 'Editorischer Bericht', pp. 18–33 in Max Weber, *Die Lage der Landarbeiter im ostelbischen Deutschland.* Tübingen: J.B.C. Mohr (Paul Siebeck).

Riesebrodt, Martin (1985) 'Vom Patriarchalismus zum Kapitalismus', *Kölner Zeitschrift für Soziologie und Sozialpsychologie,* 37:546–67.

Robinson, E.A.G. (1956) 'John Maynard Keynes 1883–1946', pp.1–69 in John Maynard Keynes, *Politik und Wirtschaft. Männer und Probleme. Ausgewählte Abhandlungen.* Tübingen: J.C.B. Mohr (Paul Siebeck).

Röpke, Wilhelm (1932) *Krise und Konjunktur.* Leipzig: Quelle and Meyer.

Rosecrance, Richard (1987) *Der neue Handelsstaat. Herausforderungen für Politik und Wirtschaft.* Frankfurt am Main: Campus.

Ross, H. Laurence (1987) 'Reflections on doing policy-relevant sociology: How to cope with MADD mothers', *American Sociologist,* 18:173–8.

Rossi, Peter H. (1987) 'No good applied social research goes unpunished', *Society,* 24:73–9.

Rossi, Peter H., James D. Wright and Sonia R. Wright (1978) 'The theory and practice of applied social research', *Evaluation Journal*, 2:171–91.

Rothschild, Kurt W. (1971) *Power in Economics*. London: Penguin.

Rouse, Joseph (1987) *Knowledge and Power. Toward a Political Philosophy of Science*. Ithaca, NY: Cornell University Press.

Salant, Walter (1989) 'The spread of Keynesian doctrine and practice in the United States', pp. 27–51 in Peter A. Hall (ed.), *The Political Power of Economic Ideas*. Princeton, NJ: Princeton University Press.

Sanmann, Horst (1965) 'Daten und Alternativen der deutschen Wirtschafts- und Finanzpolitik in der Aera Brüning', *Hamburger Jahrbuch für Wirtschafts- und Gesellschaftspolitik*, 10:109–40.

Scaff, Lawrence A. (1984) 'Weber before Weberian sociology', *British Journal of Sociology*, 35:190–215.

Scharpf, Fritz (1973) *Planung als poltischer Prozess. Aufsätze zur Theorie der planenden Demokratie*. Frankfurt am Main: Surhkamp.

Schelsky, Helmut (1961) *Der Mensch in der wissenschaftlichen Zivilisation*. Köln/ Opladen: Westdeutscher Verlag.

Schelsky, Helmut (1975) *Die Arbeit tun die anderen. Klassenkampf und Priesterherr- schaft der Intellektuellen*. 2. *Auflage*. Opladen: Westdeutscher Verlag.

Schelsky, Helmut (1976) 'Die metawissenschaftlichen Wirkungen der Soziologie', pp. 171–82 in Werner Becker and Kurt Hübner (eds), *Objektivität in den Natur- und Geisteswissenschaften*. Hamburg: Hoffmann und Campe.

Scherf, Harald (1986) *Marx und Keynes*. Frankfurt am Main: Suhrkamp.

Schick, Manfred (1970) *Kulturprotestantismus und soziale Frage*. Tübingen: J.C.B. Mohr (Paul Siebeck).

Schiller, Karl (1987) 'Wir sollten jetzt ein Zeichen setzen' (*Spiegel* Gespräch mit Karl Schiller), *Der Spiegel*, 45:40–55.

Schmölders, Günter (1962) *Geschichte der Volkswirtschaftslehre*. Reinbek bei Ham- burg: Rowohlt.

Schmölders, Günter, Rudolf Schröder and Hellmut Seidenfuss (1956) *John Maynard Keynes als Psychologe*. Berlin: Duncker and Humblot.

Schon, Donald A. (1963) *The Displacement of Concepts*. London: Tavistock.

Schumpeter, Joseph A. (1946) 'Science and ideology', *American Economic Review*, 34:345–59.

Schumpeter, Joseph A. ([1912] 1951) *Theory of Economic Development*. New York: Oxford University Press.

Schumpeter, Joseph A. (1952) *Ten Great Economists*. London: Allen and Unwin.

Schumpeter, Joseph A. (1954) *History of Ecomomic Analysis*. New York: Oxford University Press.

Scott, Robert A. and Arnold R. Shore (1974) 'Sociology and policy analysis', *American Sociologist*, 9:51–9.

Scott, Robert A. and Arnold R. Shore (1979) *Why Sociology Does Not Apply: A Study of the Use of Sociology in Public Policy*. New York: Elsevier.

Searle, John (1969) *Speech Acts. An Essay in the Philosophy of Language*. London: Cambridge University Press.

Sieber, Sam D. (1981) *Fatal Remedies. The Ironies of Social Intervention*. New York: Plenum Press.

Simmel, Georg (1890) *Über sociale Differenzierung. Sociologische und psycholo- gische Untersuchungen*. Leipzig: Duncker and Humblot.

Simmel, Georg (1919) *Philosophische Kultur. Gesammelte Essais. Zweite um einige Zusätze vermehrte Auflage.* Leipzig: Alfred Kröner.

Simmel, Georg ([1907] 1978) *The Philosophy of Money.* London: Routledge and Kegan Paul.

Sjoberg, Gideon (1967) 'Project Camelot: Selected reactions and personal reflections', pp. 141–61 in Gideon Sjoberg (ed.), *Ethics, Politics, and Social Research.* Cambridge, Mass.: Schenkman.

Skidelsky, Robert (1979) 'The decline of Keynesian politics', pp. 55–87 in Colin Crouch (ed.), *State and Economy in Contemporary Capitalism.* London: Croom Helm.

Skocpol, Theda (1987) 'Governmental structures, social science, and the development of economic and social policies', pp. 40–50 in Martin Bulmer (ed.), *Social Science Research and Government. Comparative Essays on Britain and the United States.* Cambridge: Cambridge University Press.

Smith, Cyril S. (1987) 'Networks of influence: The social sciences in Britain since the war', pp. 61–76 in Martin Bulmer (ed.), *Social Science Research and Government. Comparative Essays on Britain and the United States.* Cambridge: Cambridge University Press.

Spahn, Heinz-Peter (1976) 'Keynes in der heutigen Wirtschaftspolitik', pp. 213–92 in Gottfried Bombach (ed.), *Der Keynesianismus I: Theorie und Praxis keynesianischer Wirtschaftspolitik.* Berlin: Springer-Verlag.

Spencer, Herbert (1961) *The Study of Sociology.* Ann Arbor: University of Michigan Press.

Stanfield, John H. (1985) *Philanthrophy and Jim Crow in American Social Science.* Westport, Conn.: Greenwood Press.

Stehr, Nico (1981) 'The magic triangle: In defense of a general sociology of knowledge', *Philosophy of the Social Sciences,* 11:225–9.

Stehr, Nico (1992) *Arbeit, Eigentum und Wissen: Zur Theorie von Wissensgesellschaften.* Frankfurt am Main: Suhrkamp.

Stehr, Nico and W. Baldamus (1983) 'Accounts and action: The logic(s) of social science and pragmatic knowledge', pp. 73–8 in Burkart Holzner, Karin D. Knorr and Hermann Strasser (eds), *Realizing Social Science Knowledge.* Würzburg: Physica.

Stehr, Nico and Volker Meja (1990) 'Relativism and the sociology of knowledge', pp. 285–306 in Volker Meja and Nico Stehr (eds), *Knowledge and Politics. The Sociology of Knowledge Dispute.* London: Routledge.

Stehr, Nico and Anthony Simmons (1979) 'The diversity of discourse', *Society,* 16:45–9.

Steindl, Josef (1985) 'J.M. Keynes: Society and the Economist', pp. 99–125 in Fausto Vicarelli (ed.), *Keynes's Relvance Today.* London: Macmillan.

Taylor, Charles (1983) 'Political theory and practice', pp. 61–85 in Christopher Lloyd (ed.), *Theory and Political Practice.* Oxford: Oxford University Press.

Tenbruck, Friedrich H. ([1967] 1971) 'Zu einer Theorie der Planung', pp. 91–117 in Volker Ronge and Günter Schmieg (eds.), *Politische Planung in Theorie und Praxis.* Munich: R. Piper.

Tenbruck, Friedrich H. (1984) *Die unbewältigten Sozialwissenschaften.* Graz: Styria.

Tenbruck, Friedrich H. (1986) *Geschichte und Gesellschaft.* Berlin: Duncker and Humblot.

Thomas, Kenneth W. and Walter G. Tymon Jr. (1982) 'Necessary properties of

relevant research: Lessons from recent criticisms of the organizational sciences',
Academy of Management Review, 7:345–52.

Thompson, John B. (1987) 'Language and ideology: A framework for analysis',
Sociological Review, 35:516–36.

Tichy, Noel M. (1974) 'Agents of planned social change: Congruences of values,
cognitions and actions', *Administrative Science Quarterly*, 19:164–82.

Tobin, James (1986) 'Keynes's policies in theory and practice', pp. 13–21 in Harold
L. Wattel (ed.), *The Policy Consequences of John Maynard Keynes*. London:
Macmillan.

Tribe, Keith (1983) 'Prussian agriculture – German politics: Max Weber 1892–1897',
Economy and Society, 12:181–226.

Ulrich, Peter (1987) *Transformation der ökonomischen Vernunft. Fortschritts-
perspektiven der modernen Industriegesellschaft*. Bern und Stuttgart: Paul Haupt.

van de Vall, Mark and Cheryl A. Bolas (1981) 'External vs. internal social policy
researchers', *Knowledge: Creation, Diffusion, Utilization*, 2:461–81.

van de Vall, Mark and Cheryl A. Bolas (1982) 'Using social policy research for
reducing social problems: An empirical analysis of structure and functions', *The
Journal of Applied Behavioral Science*, 18:49–67.

Verhandlungen (1891) *Bericht über die Verhandlungen des Zweiten Evangelisch-
sozialen Kongresses*. Berlin: von Rehtwisch and Seeler.

Verhandlungen (1892) *Bericht über die Verhandlungen des Dritten Evangelisch-
sozialen Kongresses*. Berlin, 20 and 21 April 1892. Berlin: von Rehtwisch and
Seeler.

Verhandlungen (1893) *Bericht über die Verhandlungen des Vierten Evangelisch-
sozialen Kongresses*. Berlin, 1 and 2 June 1893. Berlin: von Rehtwisch and
Langewort.

Verhandlungen (1894) *Bericht über die Verhandlungen des Fünften Evangelisch-
sozialen Kongresses*. Frankfurt am Main, 16 and 17 May 1894. Berlin: von
Rehtwisch and Langewort.

Verhandlungen (1896) *Bericht über die Verhandlungen des Siebenten Evangelisch-
sozialen Kongresses*. Stuttgart, 28 and 29 May 1896. Berlin: Karl Georg Wiegandt.

Verhandlungen (1897) *Die Verhandlungen des Achten Evangelisch-sozialen Kongresses*. Leipzig, 10 and 11 June 1897. Göttingen: Vandenhoeck und Ruprecht.

Verhandlungen (1898) *Die Verhandlungen des Neunten Evangelisch-sozialen Kongresses*. Berlin, 2 and 3 June 1898. Göttingen: Vandenhoeck und Ruprecht.

Verhandlungen (1899) *Die Verhandlungen des Zehnten Evangelisch-sozialen Kongresses*. Kiel, 25 and 26 May 1899. Göttingen: Vandenhoeck und Ruprecht.

Verhandlungen (1900) *Die Verhandlungen des Elften Evangelisch-sozialen Kongresses*. Karlsruhe, 7 and 8 June 1900. Göttingen: Vandenhoeck und Ruprecht.

vom Bruch, Rüdiger (1980) *Wissenschaft, Politik und öffentliche Meinung:
Gelehrtenpolitik im Wilhelminischen Deutschland (1890–1914)*. Historische
Studien Heft 435. Husum: Matthiesen.

von Mises, Ludwig (1931) *Die Ursachen der Wirtschaftskrise*. Tübingen: Siebeck
(Mohr).

von Schelting, Alexander (1934) *Max Webers Wissenschaftslehre*. Tübingen: J.C.B.
Mohr (Paul Siebeck).

Wagner, Adolf (1892) 'Das neue sozialdemokratische Programm', pp. 57–99 in
Bericht über die Verhandlungen des Dritten Evangelisch-sozialen Kongresses.
Berlin: von Rehtwisch and Seeler.

Wagner, Peter (1990) *Sozialwissenschaften und Staat. Frankreich, Italien und Deutschland 1870–1980*. Frankfurt am Main: Campus.

Ward, W.R. (1979) *Theology, Sociology and Politics. The German Protestant Conscience 1890–1933*. Berne: Peter Lang.

Wattel, Harold L. (1985) 'Introduction', pp. 3–12 in Harold L. Wattel (ed.), *The Policy Consequences of John Maynard Keynes*. London: Macmillan.

Weaver, Warren (1948) 'Science and complexity', *American Scientist*, 36:536–44.

Weber, Alfred (1931) 'Grundlagen und Grenzen der Sozialpolitik', *Schriften des Vereins für Sozialpolitik*, 182: 23–58.

Weber, Alfred (1932) *Volkswirtschaftslehre. Eine Einführung*, vol. 2. Munich and Leipzig.

Weber, Alfred ([1935] 1956) *Kurzgefasste Volkswirtschaftslehre.* Siebente, neubearbeitete Auflage. Berlin: Duncker and Humblot.

Weber, Marianne ([1926] 1975) *Max Weber: A Biography*. New York: Wiley.

Weber, Max (1892a) 'Zur Rechtfertigung Göres', *Die Christliche Welt. Evangelisch-Lutherisches Gemeindeblatt für Gebildete aller Stände*, 6: col.1104–9.

Weber, Max (1892b) 'Privatenqueten über die Lage der Landarbeiter', *Mitteilungen des Evangelisch-sozialen Kongresses*, No. 4, pp. 3–5: No. 5, pp. 3–6; No. 6, pp. 1–5.

Weber, Max (1893a) 'Die Evangelisch-sozialen Kurse in Berlin im Herbst dieses Jahres', *Die Christliche Welt. Evangelisch-Lutherisches Gemeindeblatt für Gebildete aller Stände*, 7: col.766–8.

Weber, Max (1893b) 'Die Erhebung des *Vereins für Socialpolitik* über die Lage der Landarbeiter', *Das Land*, 1: 8–9, 24–6, 43–5, 58–9, 129–30, 147–8.

Weber, Max (1893c) 'Die Erhebung des Evangelisch-sozialen Kongresses über die Verhältnisse der Landarbeiter Deutschlands', *Die Christliche Welt. Evangelisch-Lutherisches Gemeindeblatt für Gebildete aller Stände*, 7: col.535–40.

Weber, Max (1893d) Review of von der Goltz (1893), *Jahrbücher für National-ökonomie und Statistik*, 3, vol. 6, pp. 289–96.

Weber, Max ([1892] 1984) 'Die Verhältnisse der Landarbeiter im ostelbischen Deutschland', in Max Weber, *Die Lage der Landarbeiter im ostelbischen Deutschland. Max Weber Gesamtausgabe*, vol. 3. Tübingen: J.B.C. Mohr (Paul Siebeck).

Weber, Max (1894a) 'Koreferat', pp. 61–82 in *Bericht über die Verhandlungen des fünften Evangelisch-sozialen Kongresses*. Berlin: von Rehwisch and Langewort.

Weber, Max (1894b) 'Entwicklungstendenzen in der Lage der ostelbischen Landarbeiter', *Archiv für soziale Gesetzgebung und Statistik*, Bd. 7, pp. 1–41.

Weber, Max (1894c) 'Zum Pressestreit über den Evangelisch-sozialen Kongress', *Die Christliche Welt*, 8: col.668–73.

Weber, Max (1894d) 'Was heisst Christlich-Sozial? Gesammelte Aufsätze von Fr. Naumann', *Die Christliche Welt. Evangelisch-Lutherisches Gemeindeblatt*, 8: col.472–7.

Weber, Max (1896) 'Diskussionsbeitrag', pp. 122–3 in *Bericht über die Verhandlungen des Siebenten Evangelisch-sozialen Kongresses*. Berlin: Karl Georg Wiegandt.

Weber, Max (1897) 'Diskussionsbeitrag', pp. 105–13 in *Die Verhandlungen des Achten evangelisch-sozialen Kongresses*. Göttingen: Vandenhoeck and Ruprecht.

Weber, Max ([1895] 1921) 'Der Nationalstaat und die Volkswirtschaftspolitik', pp. 8–30 in Max Weber, *Gesammelte politische Schriften*. Munich: Drei Masken Verlag.

Weber, Max ([1919] 1922) 'Wissenschaft als Beruf', pp. 524–55 in Max Weber, *Gesammelte Aufsätze zur Wissenschaftslehre*. Tübingen: J.C.B. Mohr (Paul Siebeck).

Weber, Max (1936) *Jugendbriefe*. Tübingen: J.C.B. Mohr (Paul Siebeck).

Weber, Max ([1904] 1949) ' "Objectivity" in social science and social social policy', pp. 49–112 in Max Weber, *The Methodology of the Social Sciences*. New York: The Free Press.

Weber, Max ([1921] 1958) *Gesammelte politische Schriften*. Zweite Auflage. Tübingen: J.C.B. Mohr (Paul Siebeck).

Weber, Max ([1925] 1964) *Wirtschaft und Gesellschaft. Studienausgabe*. Köln: Kiepenheuer and Witsch.

Weber, Max ([1922] 1968) *Economy and Society*. New York: Bedminster Press.

Weber, Max ([1922] 1972) *Gesammelte Aufsätze zur Religionssoziologie*. Tübingen: J.C.B. Mohr (Paul Siebeck).

Weber, Max ([1910] 1978a) 'Antikritisches Schlusswort zum "Geist des Kapitalismus" ' pp. 283–344 in Johannes Winkelmann (ed.), *Die Protestantische Ethik II: Kritiken und Anti-Kritiken*. Hamburg: Siebenstern.

Weber, Max ([1910] 1978b) 'Antikritisches Schlusswort zum "Geist des Kapitalismus" ', pp. 149–87 in Johannes Winkelmann (ed.), *Die Protestantische Ethik II: Kritiken und Anti-Kritiken*. Hamburg: Siebenstern.

Weber, Max ([1910] 1978c) 'Anticritical Last Word on The Spirit of Capitalism', *American Journal of Sociology*, 83: 1105–31.

Weir, Margaret and Theda Skocpol (1985) 'State structures and the possibilities for "Keynesian" responses to the Great Depression in Sweden, Britain, and the United States', pp. 107–63 in Peter B. Evans, Dietrich Rueschemeyer and Theda Skocpol (eds), *Bringing the State Back In*. Cambridge: Cambridge University Press.

Weiss, Carol H. (1978) 'Broadening the concept of research utilization', *Sociological Symposium*, 21:20–31.

Weiss Carol H. (with Michael J. Bucuvalas) (1980) *Social Science Research and Decision-Making*. New York: Columbia University Press.

Weiss, Carol H. (1983) 'Three terms in search of reconceptualization: Knowledge, utilization, and decision-making', pp. 201–19 in Burkart Holzner, Karin D. Knorr and Hermann Strasser (eds), *Realizing Social Science Knowledge*. Würzburg: Physica.

Weiss, Janet A. and Carol H. Weiss (1981) 'Social scientists and decision-makers look at the usefulness of mental health research', *American Psychologist*, 36:837–47.

Wenger, G. Clare (ed.) (1987) *The Research Relationship. Practice and Politics in Social Research*. London: Allen and Unwin.

Whyte, William Foote (1982) 'Social inventions for solving human problems', *American Sociological Review*, 47:1–13.

Whyte, William Foote (1984) *Learning from the Field*. Beverly Hills: Sage.

Whyte, William Foote (1986) 'On the uses of social science research', *American Sociological Review*, 51:555–63.

Wilensky, Harold L. (1971) *Organizational Intelligence. Knowledge and Policy in Government and Industry*. New York: Basic Books.

Winch, Donald (1972) *Economics and Policy. A Historical Study*. London: Hodder and Stoughton.

Wingens, Matthias (1988) *Soziologisches Wissen und politische Praxis. Neuere theoretische Entwicklungen der Verwendungsforschung*. Frankfurt am Main: Campus.

Wollmann, Hellmut (1980) 'Implementationsforschung – eine Chance für kritische Verwaltungsforschung?' pp. 9–48 in Hellmut Wollmann (ed.), *Politik im Dickicht der Bürokratie. Beiträge zur Implementationsforschung.* Opladen: Westdeutscher Verlag.

Zaltman, Gerald (1979) 'Knowledge utilization as planned social change', *Knowledge*, 1:82–105.

Zetterberg, Hans L. (1962) *Social Theory and Social Practice.* New York: Bedminster Press.

Appendix

Selected Macro-economic Trends for Canada, USA, (West) Germany and Great Britain, 1920–1987

1 Canada

Year	CPI	Unemploy-ment	Long-term interest		Export	GDP
1920	15.7	na	na	6.10	na	na
1921	−11.8	5.8	na	6.00	na	na
1922	−8.4	4.4	na	5.40	na	na
1923	0.0	3.2	na	5.10	na	na
1924	0.0	4.5	na	5.50	na	na
1925	0.5	4.4	na	4.90	na	na
1926	1.1	3.0	na	4.90	1.63	5.14
1927	−1.6	1.8	9.5	4.60	1.60	5.56
1928	0.0	1.7	9.1	4.50	1.75	6.05
1929	1.6	2.9	0.4	4.90	1.61	6.13
1930	1.1	9.1	−4.3	4.70	1.27	5.72
1931	−9.8	11.6	−12.7	4.60	0.95	4.69
1932	−9.0	17.6	−10.4	5.10	0.79	3.81
1933	−4.6	19.3	−6.7	4.60	0.81	3.49
1934	1.4	14.5	12.1	4.00	1.00	3.96
1935	0.7	14.2	7.8	4.60	1.12	4.30
1936	2.0	12.8	4.4	3.30	1.41	4.63
1937	2.7	9.1	10.0	3.20	1.57	5.24
1938	1.3	11.4	8.2	3.10	1.34	5.27
1939	−0.6	11.4	7.4	3.20	1.43	5.62
1940	3.9	9.2	13.8	3.30	1.74	6.71
1941	5.6	4.4	14.6	3.10	2.44	8.28
1942	5.3	3.0	18.6	3.10	3.66	10.26
1943	1.7	1.7	4.0	3.00	4.04	11.05
1944	0.5	1.4	4.0	3.00	4.53	11.84
1945	0.5	1.6	−2.2	2.90	4.40	11.86
1946	3.3	2.6	−2.7	2.60	3.27	11.88
1947	9.5	1.9	4.3	2.60	3.66	13.47
1948	13.9	1.6	2.5	2.90	4.04	15.50
1949	3.4	2.0	3.8	2.80	4.00	16.80
1950	2.9	2.0	7.6	2.80	4.15	18.49
1951	10.7	1.5	5.0	3.20	5.05	21.64
1952	2.2	2.0	8.9	3.60	5.55	24.58
1953	−0.7	3.0	5.1	3.70	5.36	25.83
1954	0.7	4.6	−1.2	3.10	5.12	25.91
1955	0.0	4.4	9.4	3.10	5.73	28.52
1956	1.4	3.4	8.4	3.60	6.33	32.05
1957	3.1	4.6	2.4	4.20	6.36	33.51

Year	CPI	Unemploy-ment	Long-term interest		Export	GDP
1958	2.7	7.0	2.3	4.50	6.31	34.77
1959	1.3	6.0	3.8	5.00	6.65	36.84
1960	1.3	7.0	2.9	5.10	6.98	38.35
1961	0.6	7.1	2.8	5.00	7.62	39.64
1962	1.2	5.9	6.8	5.10	8.23	42.92
1963	1.5	0.5	5.2	5.10	9.06	50.28
1964	1.8	4.7	6.7	5.10	10.50	55.36
1965	2.4	3.6	9.7	5.30	11.18	61.82
1966	3.5	3.4	6.9	5.70	13.04	66.40
1967	3.7	3.8	3.3	6.00	14.66	72.58
1968	4.1	4.5	5.8	6.70	16.79	79.81
1969	4.5	4.4	5.3	7.60	18.73	85.68
1970	3.3	5.7	2.5	8.00	21.16	94.45
1971	2.4	6.2	6.9	7.00	22.18	105.23
1972	5.2	6.2	6.1	7.20	24.58	123.56
1973	7.6	5.5	7.5	7.60	30.72	147.52
1974	10.5	9.3	3.6	8.90	38.90	165.34
1975	10.8	6.1	9.2	9.00	40.03	191.03
1976	7.5	7.1	5.8	9.20	40.01	271.31
1977	8.0	8.1	2.0	8.70	46.33	281.12
1978	8.8	8.4	3.6	9.20	55.31	293.98
1979	9.2	7.5	3.2	10.20	68.27	305.36
1980	10.2	7.5	1.1	12.30	79.21	309.89
1981	12.5	7.5	3.3	15.00	87.16	321.27
1982	10.8	11.1	−4.4	14.40	87.91	310.52
1983	5.8	11.3	9.3	11.80	94.60	320.18
1984	4.4	11.3	5.0	12.70	116.97	337.94
1985	4.0	10.5	na	11.04	124.25	351.35
1986	4.2	9.6	na	9.52	125.31	362.37
1987	4.4	8.9	na	10.34	130.09	381.38

2   Great Britain

Year	CPI	Unemploy-ment	Long-term interest		Export	GDP
1920	10.8	2.0		5.3	13.6	67.9
1921	9.7	11.3		5.2	11.3	61.3
1922	7.9	9.8		4.4	14.3	63.5
1923	7.7	8.1		4.3	15.6	65.4
1924	7.7	7.2		4.4	16.1	67.4
1925	7.7	7.9		4.4	16.1	70.7
1926	7.5	8.8		4.6	14.7	67.5
1927	7.2	6.8		4.6	16.6	72.2
1928	7.2	7.5		4.5	16.7	73.4
1929	7.2	7.3		4.6	17.2	75.1
1930	6.8	11.2		4.5	14.8	75.1
1931	6.4	15.1		4.4	11.9	71.2
1932	6.2	15.6		3.7	11.7	71.4
1933	6.2	14.1		3.4	11.8	72.3
1934	6.2	11.9		3.1	12.3	77.1
1935	6.2	11.0		2.9	13.9	80.0
1936	6.4	9.4		2.9	13.5	82.5
1937	6.6	7.8		3.3	14.2	86.0

Year	CPI	Unemploy-ment	Long-term interest	Export	GDP
1938	6.8	9.3	3.4	13.2	88.6
1939	7.0	5.8	3.7	12.2	92.1
1940	7.9	3.3	3.4	8.4	105.3
1941	8.7	1.2	3.1	7.2	111.7
1942	9.3	0.5	3.0	6.5	112.8
1943	9.7	0.4	3.1	7.2	114.9
1944	9.7	0.4	3.1	9.1	109.7
1945	10.1	0.5	2.9	7.3	102.9
1946	10.6	1.9	2.6	12.4	102.3
1947	11.2	1.4	2.8	12.4	99.8
1948	11.8	1.5	3.2	15.1	102.4
1949	2.2	1.6	3.3	16.8	105.5
1950	12.5	1.6	3.5	19.2	109.4
1951	13.6	1.3	3.8	19.0	111.8
1952	14.9	2.2	4.2	18.6	113.0
1953	15.4	1.8	4.1	19.4	118.1
1954	15.6	1.5	3.8	20.5	122.8
1955	16.4	1.2	4.2	21.7	127.0
1956	17.2	1.3	4.7	22.7	129.1
1957	17.8	1.6	5.0	23.2	131.6
1958	18.4	2.2	5.0	22.9	131.9
1959	18.5	2.3	4.8	23.5	137.2
1960	18.7	1.7	5.4	24.9	143.9
1961	19.3	1.6	6.2	25.7	148.3
1962	20.1	2.1	6.0	26.1	149.9
1963	20.5	2.6	5.6	27.4	156.2
1964	21.2	1.7	6.0	28.4	164.4
1965	22.2	1.5	6.4	29.8	168.1
1966	23.1	1.6	6.8	31.2	171.4
1967	23.6	2.5	6.7	31.4	176.2
1968	24.7	2.5	7.4	35.4	183.6
1969	26.1	2.4	8.9	38.9	186.0
1970	27.7	2.6	9.2	41.0	190.2
1971	30.3	3.5	9.1	43.8	195.3
1972	32.5	3.3	9.1	44.3	199.8
1973	35.5	3.7	10.7	49.5	215.6
1974	41.2	2.6	15.0	53.1	213.3
1975	51.1	2.6	14.7	51.7	211.8
1976	59.5	4.0	14.3	56.3	220.1
1977	69.0	5.5	12.3	59.9	222.2
1978	74.7	5.8	11.9	61.1	230.3
1979	84.8	5.7	11.4	63.4	235.2
1980	100.0	5.3	11.7	63.3	230.2
1981	111.9	6.8	13.0	62.1	227.6
1982	121.5	10.5	11.89	62.7	231.9
1983	127.1	12.1	na	63.3	239.6
1984	133.5	11.1	na	70.4	244.1
1985	141.6	11.3	na	78.3	253.7
1986	146.4	11.4	na	72.8	261.1
1987	152.5	10.2	na	79.8	270.7

3　(West) Germany

Year	CPI	Unemploy-ment	Long-term interest	Export	GDP
1920	201.7	3.8	na	na	na
1921	265.5	2.8	na	na	na
1922	na	1.5	na	na	na
1923	na	9.6	na	6.10	na
1924	25.3	13.5	12.00	6.67	na
1925	27.8	6.7	11.15	9.28	308.7
1926	28.1	18.0	7.90	10.42	296.2
1927	29.3	8.8	7.24	10.80	351.4
1928	30.2	8.4	8.00	12.06	359.5
1929	30.5	9.3	8.11	13.49	363.5
1930	29.4	15.3	5.93	12.04	341.0
1931	27.0	23.3	8.58	9.59	306.7
1932	23.9	30.1	6.21	5.74	278.0
1933	23.4	26.3	5.00	4.87	305.8
1934	24.0	14.9	5.00	4.18	334.9
1935	24.4	11.6	5.00	4.27	365.6
1936	24.7	8.3	5.00	4.78	403.5
1937	24.8	4.6	5.00	5.92	428.1
1938	24.9	2.1	4.00	5.26	461.2
1939	25.0	na	5.65	5.65	na
1940	25.8	na	4.89	4.89	na
1941	26.4	na	6.84	6.84	na
1942	27.1	na	7.56	7.56	na
1943	27.4	na	8.59	8.59	na
1944	28.0	na	na	na	na
1945	29.1	na	na	na	na
1946	32.1	na	na	na	na
1947	34.2	na	na	na	na
1948	39.3	4.2	5.0	1.82	104.8
1949	41.8	8.3	4.0	3.81	236.1
1950	39.3	10.2	6.0	8.36	274.7
1951	42.2	9.0	6.0	14.58	303.5
1952	43.0	8.4	4.5	16.91	330.2
1953	42.2	7.5	4.0	18.53	357.6
1954	42.2	7.0	4.0	22.04	384.9
1955	43.1	5.1	4.5	25.72	431.3
1956	43.6	4.0	7.3	30.86	462.3
1957	44.9	3.4	7.7	35.97	488.3
1958	45.9	3.5	5.9	37.00	505.5
1959	46.3	2.4	6.2	41.18	543.0
1960	46.8	1.2	6.2	47.95	591.4
1961	48.1	0.8	6.0	50.98	612.5
1962	49.4	0.7	6.1	52.98	649.1
1963	50.0	0.8	6.0	58.31	669.3
1964	51.0	0.7	6.4	64.92	714.4
1965	53.0	0.6	7.7	71.65	754.1
1966	56.0	0.7	7.7	80.63	773.7
1967	56.6	2.1	6.8	87.05	773.0
1968	57.8	1.5	6.3	99.55	818.8

Year	CPI	Unemploy-ment	Long-term interest		Export	GDP
1969	59.0	0.9		7.6	133.56	879.9
1970	60.0	0.7		8.2	125.28	925.1
1971	63.0	0.8		7.1	36.01	953.7
1972	67.6	1.1		8.6	149.02	993.3
1973	72.4	1.2		9.6	178.40	1038.6
1974	77.3	2.6		9.8	230.58	1044.2
1975	82.2	4.7		8.3	221.59	1026.5
1976	85.2	4.6		7.3	256.64	1082.9
1977	88.4	4.5		5.7	273.61	1116.0
1978	91.3	4.3		6.3	284.91	1150.4
1979	94.3	3.8		7.3	314.47	1198.4
1980	100.0	3.8		8.3	350.33	1220.5
1981	105.5	5.5		9.7	396.90	1219.5
1982	111.6	7.7		7.4	427.74	1206.8
1983	114.9	9.2		8.2	432.28	1218.6
1984	117.3	9.1		7.8	590.80	1467.9
1985	119.5	9.3		6.6	647.00	1541.6
1986	119.7	9.0		5.6	636.40	1616.2
1987	120.0	8.9		5.8	636.50	1709.6

4 USA

Year	CPI	Unemploy-ment	Long-term interest		Export	GDP
1920	14.6	5.2	−4.5	6.12	na	221.7
1921	−11.4	11.7	−9.1	5.97	na	216.5
1922	−6.5	6.7	14.7	5.10	na	229.2
1923	1.7	2.4	11.4	5.12	na	259.5
1924	0.3	5.0	−0.2	5.00	na	267.3
1925	2.5	3.2	8.0	4.88	na	273.7
1926	0.8	1.8	5.8	4.73	na	291.5
1927	−1.8	3.3	−0.1	4.57	na	294.2
1928	−1.3	4.2	0.6	4.55	na	297.9
1929	0.0	3.2	6.5	4.73	16.7	315.7
1930	−2.5	8.9	−10.0	4.55	14.2	285.6
1931	−9.4	16.3	−8.1	4.58	11.7	263.5
1932	−10.7	24.1	−14.9	5.01	9.3	227.1
1933	−5.4	25.2	−2.2	4.49	9.1	222.1
1934	3.3	22.0	7.4	4.00	9.7	239.1
1935	2.5	20.3	8.4	3.60	10.5	260.0
1936	1.0	17.0	12.8	3.24	11.2	295.5
1937	3.5	14.3	4.9	3.26	14.0	310.2
1938	−1.8	19.1	−4.4	3.19	13.5	296.7
1939	−1.4	17.2	7.5	3.01	14.3	319.8
1940	1.0	14.6	7.3	2.84	15.5	344.1
1941	4.9	9.9	15.2	2.77	16.4	400.4
1942	10.1	4.7	14.2	2.83	11.4	461.7
1943	6.0	1.9	14.1	2.73	9.8	531.6
1944	1.7	1.2	6.8	2.72	10.5	569.1
1945	2.3	1.9	−1.5	2.62	13.8	560.4
1946	8.2	3.9	−15.8	2.53	27.3	478.3
1947	13.4	3.9	−1.7	2.61	32.2	470.3
1948	7.5	3.8	4.1	2.82	26.3	489.8

Year	CPI	Unemployment	Long-term interest		Export	GDP
1949	−1.0	5.0	0.5	2.66	25.8	492.2
1950	1.0	5.3	8.3	2.62	23.6	534.8
1951	7.6	3.3	8.0	2.86	28.6	579.4
1952	2.2	3.0	3.6	2.96	27.9	600.8
1953	0.8	2.9	3.7	3.20	26.6	623.6
1954	0.5	5.5	−1.2	2.90	27.8	616.1
1955	−0.4	4.4	6.5	3.06	30.7	657.5
1956	1.5	4.1	2.1	3.36	35.3	671.6
1957	3.5	4.3	1.8	3.83	8.0	683.8
1958	2.7	6.8	−0.4	3.73	3.2	680.9
1959	0.8	5.5	5.8	4.38	33.8	721.7
1960	1.6	5.5	2.1	4.41	38.4	737.2
1961	1.0	6.7	2.6	4.35	39.3	756.6
1962	1.1	5.5	5.6	4.33	41.8	800.3
1963	1.2	5.7	3.9	4.26	44.8	832.5
1964	1.3	5.2	5.1	4.40	50.3	876.4
1965	1.7	4.5	5.9	4.45	1.7	929.3
1966	2.8	3.8	5.8	5.13	54.4	984.8
1967	2.8	3.8	2.7	5.51	56.7	1011.4
1968	4.1	3.6	4.5	6.18	61.2	1058.1
1969	5.2	3.5	2.7	7.03	65.0	1087.6
1970	5.8	4.9	−0.2	8.04	70.5	1085.6
1971	4.2	5.0	3.3	7.37	1.0	1122.4
1972	3.2	5.6	5.5	7.21	77.5	1185.9
1973	6.0	4.5	5.7	7.44	7.3	1254.3
1974	10.4	5.6	−0.6	8.57	108.5	1246.3
1975	8.7	8.5	−1.1	8.83	103.5	1231.6
1976	5.6	7.7	5.2	8.43	110.1	1298.2
1977	6.3	7.0	5.3	8.02	112.9	1369.7
1978	7.4	6.0	4.6	8.73	126.7	1438.6
1979	10.7	5.8	3.2	9.63	146.2	1479.4
1980	12.7	7.1	−0.2	11.94	159.1	1475.0
1981	9.7	9.6	2.0	14.17	160.2	1512.2
1982	6.2	9.7	na	11.07	147.6	1480.0
1983	3.2	9.6	na	8.95	139.5	1534.7
1984	4.3	7.5	na	9.89	217.9	na
1985	3.6	7.2	na	7.73	213.1	na
1986	1.9	7.0	na	6.13	217.3	na
1987	3.7	6.2	na	6.01	250.4	na
					1983	3355.9
					1984	3724.8
					1985	3970.5
					1986	4194.5
					1987	4461.2

Sources: The data for the USA, Great Britain and (West) Germany for the years 1920−83 are taken from Liesner (1985). The data for Canada for the years 1920−83 can be found in Parkin and Bade (1986) while the most recent figures are extracted from the 1988 *Yearbook of International Financial Statistics* published by the International Monetary Fund.

Index